ACCA

FINANCIAL MANAGEMENT (FM)

PRACTICE & REVISION KIT

BPP Learning Media is an **ACCA Approved Content Provider** for the ACCA qualification. This means we work closely with ACCA to ensure our products fully prepare you for your ACCA exams.

In this Practice & Revision Kit, which has been reviewed by the **ACCA examining team,** we:

- Discuss the **best strategies** for revising and taking your ACCA exams

- Ensure you are well **prepared** for your exam

- Provide you with **lots of great guidance** on tackling questions

- Provide you with **three** mock exams

- Provide **ACCA exam answers** as well as our own for selected questions

Our **Passcards** also support the Financial Management syllabus.

FOR EXAMS IN SEPTEMBER 2018, DECEMBER 2018, MARCH 2019 AND JUNE 2019

First edition 2008

Eleventh edition February 2018

ISBN 9781 5097 1670 8
(previous ISBN) 9781 5097 0860 4

e-ISBN 9781 5097 1700 2

Cataloguing-in-Publication Data
A catalogue record for this book
is available from the British Library

Published by

BPP Learning Media Ltd
BPP House, Aldine Place
London W12 8AA

www.bpp.com/learningmedia

Printed in the United Kingdom

Your learning materials, published by BPP Learning Media Ltd, are printed on paper obtained from traceable sustainable sources.

We are grateful to the Association of Chartered Certified Accountants for permission to reproduce past examination questions. The suggested solutions in the Practice & Revision Kit have been prepared by BPP Learning Media Ltd, except where otherwise stated.

BPP Learning Media is grateful to the IASB for permission to reproduce extracts from the International Financial Reporting Standards including all International Accounting Standards, SIC and IFRIC Interpretations (the Standards). The Standards together with their accompanying documents are issued by:

The International Accounting Standards Board (IASB) 30 Cannon Street, London, EC4M 6XH, United Kingdom. Email: info@ifrs.org Web: www.ifrs.org

Disclaimer: The IASB, the International Financial Reporting Standards (IFRS) Foundation, the authors and the publishers do not accept responsibility for any loss caused by acting or refraining from acting in reliance on the material in this publication, whether such loss is caused by negligence or otherwise to the maximum extent permitted by law.

About this Practice & Revision Kit

ACCA have commenced the transition of this exam to becoming a computer-based examination (CBE), beginning with a pilot in limited markets in September 2016.

This Practice & Revision Kit is valid for paper-based and CBE exams from the September 2018 sitting through to the June 2019 sitting and in this Practice & Revision Kit you will find questions in both multiple choice question (MCQ) and objective testing question (OTQ) format. OTQs include a wider variety of questions types including MCQ as well as number entry, multiple response and drag and drop. More information on these question types will be available on the ACCA website.

OTQ's will only appear in computer-based exams but these questions will still provide valuable practice for all students whichever version of the exam is taken. These are clearly marked on the contents page as either CBE style OTQ bank or CBE style OTQ case.

More information on the exam formats can be found on page xviii.

All timings given throughout this Practice & Revision Kit are based on the computer-based exam which is 3 hours and 20 minutes long. Within session CBEs there will be additional questions used for quality assurance purposes, to ensure that all students now and in the future receive fair and equal exams. These extra questions are referred to by the technical term 'seeded questions' and do not contribute to a student's result. As a result, sessions CBEs will contain 110 marks of exam content, 100 marks contributing to the student result. Exam timings are allocated on the basis of 110 marks across the 3 hours and 20 minutes. Time management is a key skill for success in this exam and so we recommend you use these indicative timings when attempting questions to time.

ACCA are recommending that all students consult the ACCA website on a regular basis for updates on the launch of the new CBEs.

These materials are reviewed by the ACCA examining team. The objective of the review is to ensure that the material properly covers the syllabus and study guide outcomes, used by the examining team in setting the exams, in the appropriate breadth and depth. The review does not ensure that every eventuality, combination or application of examinable topics is addressed by the ACCA Approved Content. Nor does the review comprise a detailed technical check of the content as the Approved Content Provider has its own quality assurance processes in place in this respect.

Contents

Question index

The headings in this checklist/index indicate the main topics of questions, but questions often cover several different topics.

Questions set under the old F9 (UK) exam format are included in this kit because their style and content are similar to those which may appear in the exam. The questions have been amended to reflect the current exam format.

	Marks	Time allocation Mins	Page number Question	Answer

Part G: Risk management

Section A Questions				
267–276 MCQ bank – Foreign currency risk	20	36	92	223
277–281 MCQ bank – Interest rate risk	10	18	95	224
Section B Questions				
282–286 Rose Co (6/15, amended)	10	18	96	226
287–291 Edwen (pilot, amended)	10	18	98	226
292–296 CBE style OT case Zigto Co (6/12, amended)	10	18	100	227
297–301 CBE style OT case PGT Co	10	18	101	228
302–306 CBE style OT case TGA Co	10	18	103	228

Mock exam 1 (September 2016 CBE)

Mock exam 2 (Specimen exam CBE)

Mock exam 3 (December 2016 PBE)

Topic index

Listed below are the key syllabus topics and the numbers of the questions in this Kit covering those topics.

If you need to concentrate your practice and revision on certain topics or if you want to attempt all available questions that refer to a particular subject, you will find this index useful.

Syllabus topic	Question numbers
Asset replacement decisions	125, 132–133, 142–143, 155, 164
Business valuation	186, 223–231, 237–240, 242–244, 246–249, 252–260, 264
Capital rationing	128–130, 134, 140–141, 155–156, 158–159
Capital structure	196–205, 262
Cash management	56–58, 82, 86, 88
Cash operating cycle	41–43, 84, 87
Cost of capital	187–195, 206, 208–210, 212–217, 219–220, 250–251
Dividend policy	171–175, 213, 217, 220, 261
Economics	21–23, 25, 31–40, 161
Financial intermediaries and markets	24, 26–30
Financial management	2, 6, 15
Foreign currency risk	267–276, 282–285, 287–306
Gearing	176–181, 211–212
Interest rate risk	265–266, 277–281, 286
Inventory management	46–48, 53, 55, 62–63, 66–67, 76–77, 83
IRR	97, 103-106, 108, 139, 149, 154, 160, 164-165
Leasing	107, 126–127, 131, 157
Market efficiency	222, 232–236, 241, 245, 263
NPV	93–95, 99–102, 109–119, 147, 150–153, 156, 161–162, 164–165
Objectives	5, 7, 9, 10–13, 19–20, 207
Overtrading	70, 74, 85
Payables management	54, 86
Payback	91, 96, 148, 164
Ratio analysis	1, 3, 4, 8, 14, 16–18, 71
Receivables management	44, 49–52, 64–65, 68, 78, 82–84, 86, 89
ROCE	90, 92, 98, 145–146
Risk and uncertainty	120–124, 135–138, 144, 157, 159–160, 162–163
Sources of finance	166–176, 182–185, 211–212, 215, 217–219, 221
Working capital financing	59–60, 80–81, 85, 87
Working capital management	45, 61, 69, 72–73, 75, 79, 83, 85

Helping you with your revision

BPP Learning Media – ACCA Approved Content Provider

As an ACCA **Approved Content Provider**, BPP Learning Media gives you the **opportunity** to use revision materials reviewed by the ACCA examining team. By incorporating the ACCA examining team's comments and suggestions regarding the depth and breadth of syllabus coverage, the BPP Learning Media Practice & Revision Kit provides excellent, **ACCA approved** support for your revision.

Tackling revision and the exam

Using feedback obtained from the ACCA examining team review:

- We look at the dos and don'ts of revising for, and taking, ACCA exams
- We focus on revising the syllabus, what to do (and what not to do) in the exam, how to approach different types of question and ways of obtaining easy marks

Selecting questions

We provide signposts to help you plan your revision.

- A full **question index**
- A **topic index** listing all the questions that cover key topics, so that you can locate the questions that provide practice on these topics, and see the different ways in which they might be examined

Making the most of question practice

At BPP Learning Media we realise that you need more than just questions and model answers to get the most from your question practice.

- Our **top tips** included for certain questions provide essential advice on tackling questions, presenting answers and the key points that answers need to include.
- We show you how you can pick up **easy marks** on some questions, as we know that picking up all readily available marks often can make the difference between passing and failing.
- We include **marking guides** to show you what the examining team rewards.
- We include **comments from the examining team** to show you where students struggled or performed well in the actual exam.
- We refer to the **Study Text** (for exams in September 2018, December 2018, March 2019 and June 2019) for detailed coverage of the topics covered in questions.

Attempting mock exams

There are three mock exams that provide practice at coping with the pressures of the exam day. We strongly recommend that you attempt them under exam conditions. **Mock exam 1** is the September 2016 CBE. **Mock exam 2** is the Specimen CBE. **Mock exam 3** is the December 2016 PBE.

Revising Financial Management

The exam consists of 15 objective test questions, 3 objective test cases and 2 longer form questions, all of which are compulsory. No one section in the syllabus is more important than another so there are no short-cuts. You will have to be able to answer questions on the entire syllabus.

Question practice

Practising as many exam-style questions as possible will be the key to passing this exam. You must do questions under **timed conditions** and ensure you write full answers to the discussion parts as well as doing the calculations.

Make sure you practise written sections as well as the calculations.

Passing the FM exam

Displaying the right qualities

The aim of the Financial Management exam is to develop the knowledge and skills expected of a finance manager in relation to investment, financing and dividend decisions.

You need to be able to communicate your understanding clearly in an exam context. Calculations and discussions are equally important so do not concentrate on the numbers and ignore the written parts.

You need to be able to:

- Understand the role and purpose of the financial management function
- Assess and understand the impact of the economic environment on financial management
- Discuss and apply working capital management techniques
- Carry out effective investment appraisal
- Identify and evaluate alternative sources of business finance
- Explain and calculate cost of capital and the factors that affect it
- Understand and apply risk management techniques in business

Avoiding weaknesses

- There is no choice in this exam, all questions have to be answered. You must therefore study the entire syllabus, there are no short-cuts.

- Ability to answer objective test questions and cases improves with practice. Try to get as much practice with these questions as you can.

- The longer questions will be based on simple scenarios and answers must be focused and specific to the organisation.

- Answer plans for the longer questions will help you to focus on the requirements of the question and enable you to manage your time effectively – but there will not be much time.

- Answer all parts of the constructed response questions. Even if you cannot do all the calculation elements, you will still be able to gain marks in the descriptive parts.

Gaining the easy marks

Multiple choice questions

Some MCQs are easier than others. Answer those that you feel fairly confident about as quickly as you can. Come back later to those you find more difficult. This could be a way of making use of the time in the examination most efficiently and effectively.

Many MCQs will not involve calculations. Make sure that you understand the wording of 'written' MCQs before selecting your answer.

Calculations in Section C questions

The calculations within a question will get progressively harder and easy marks will be available in the early stages. Set our your calculations clearly and show all your workings in a clear format. Use a proforma, for example in complex NPV questions and slot the simpler figures into the proforma straight away before you concentrate on the figures that need a lot of adjustment.

Discussions in Section C questions

A Section C question may separate discussion requirements from calculations, so that you do not need to do the calculations first in order to answer the discussion part. This means that you should be able to gain marks from making sensible, practical comments without having to complete the calculations.

Discussions that are focused on the specific organisation in the question will gain more marks than regurgitation of knowledge. Read the question carefully and more than once, to ensure you are actually answering the specific requirements.

Pick out key words such as 'describe', 'evaluate' and 'discuss'. These all mean something specific.

* 'Describe' means to communicate the key features of
* 'Evaluate' means to assess the value of
* 'Discuss' means to examine in detail by argument

Clearly label the points you make in discussions so that the marker can identify them all rather than getting lost in the detail.

Provide answers in the form requested. Use a report format if asked for and give recommendations if required.

Tackling objective test case questions (OTQs)

First, read the whole case scenario. Make a note of any specific instructions or assumptions, such as 'ignore inflation' in a net present value question.

Then skim through the requirements of the five questions. The questions are independent of each other and can be answered in any order.

Some of the OTQs will be easier than others. For example, you may be asked to identify the advantages of the internal rate of return in investment appraisal. Answer these OTQs quickly.

Other OTQs will be more difficult and/or complex. There are two types of OTQs that may take you longer to answer.

The first more time-consuming OTQ will involve doing a computation. For example, you may be asked to calculate the net present value of a project. You will probably need to jot down a quick proforma to answer a computational question like this. If the OTQ is a multiple choice question, remember that the wrong answers will usually involve common errors so don't assume that because you have the same answer as one of the options that your answer is necessarily correct! Double check to make sure you haven't made any silly mistakes. If you haven't got the same answer as any of the options, rework your computation, thinking carefully about what errors you could have made. If you still haven't got one of the options, choose the one which is nearest to your answer.

The second more time-consuming OTQ is one where you are asked to consider a number of statements and identify which one (or more) of them is correct. Make sure that you read each statement at least twice before making your selection. Be careful to follow the requirements of the OTQ exactly, for example if you are asked to identify **TWO** correct statements.

BPP
LEARNING MEDIA

Exam formulae

Set out below are the formulae which you will be given in the exam, and formulae which you should learn. If you are not sure what the symbols mean, or how the formulae are used, you should refer to the appropriate chapter in this Study Text

Exam formulae	Chapter in Study Text

Economic Order Quantity

5

$$= \sqrt{\frac{2C_0D}{C_h}}$$

Miller-Orr Model

6

Return point = Lower limit + $(1/3 \times \text{spread})$

$$\text{Spread} = 3 \left[\frac{\frac{3}{4} \times \text{transaction cost} \times \text{variance of cash flows}}{\text{interest rate}} \right]^{\frac{1}{3}}$$

The Capital Asset Pricing Model

14

$$E(r_i) = R_f + \beta_i (E(r_m) - R_f)$$

The Asset Beta Formula

16

$$\beta_a = \left[\frac{V_e}{(V_e + V_d(1-T))} \beta_e \right] + \left[\frac{V_d(1-T)}{(V_e + V_d(1-T))} \beta_d \right]$$

The Growth Model

17

$$P_0 = \frac{D_0(1+g)}{(r_e - g)} \qquad r_e = \frac{D_0(1+g)}{P_0} + g$$

Gordon's Growth Approximation

17

$$g = br_e$$

The weighted average cost of capital

14

$$\text{WACC} = \left[\frac{V_e}{V_e + V_d} \right] k_e + \left[\frac{V_d}{V_e + V_d} \right] k_d (1-T)$$

The Fisher formula

19

$$(1 + i) = (1 + r)(1 + h)$$

Purchasing Power Parity and Interest Rate Parity

$$S_1 = S_0 \times \frac{(1+h_c)}{(1+h_b)}$$

19

$$F_0 = S_0 \times \frac{(1+i_c)}{(1+i_b)}$$

19

Formulae to learn

Profitability ratios include:

$$\text{ROCE} = \frac{\text{Profit before interest and tax (PBIT)}}{\text{Capital employed}}$$

$$\text{ROCE} = \frac{\text{PBIT}}{\text{Revenue}} \times \frac{\text{Revenue}}{\text{Capital employed}}$$

Debt ratios include:

$$\text{Gearing} = \frac{\text{Debt}}{\text{Equity}} \text{ or } \frac{\text{Debt}}{\text{Debt} + \text{Equity}} \text{ (and either book values or market values can be used)}$$

$$\text{Interest coverage} = \frac{\text{PBIT}}{\text{Interest}}$$

Liquidity ratios include:

Current ratio = Current assets : Current liabilities

Acid Test ratio = Current assets less inventory : Current liabilities

Shareholder investor ratios include:

$$\text{Dividend yield} = \frac{\text{Dividend per share}}{\text{Market price per share}} \times 100$$

$$\text{Earnings per share} = \frac{\text{Profits distributable to ordinary shareholders}}{\text{Number of ordinary shares issued}}$$

$$\text{Price earnings (P/E) ratio} = \frac{\text{Market price per share}}{\text{EPS}}$$

Accounts receivable days $= \dfrac{\text{Receivables}}{\text{(credit) sales}} \times 365 \text{ days}$

Inventory days

(a) Finished goods $= \dfrac{\text{Finished goods}}{\text{Cost of sales}} \times 365 \text{ days}$

(b) WIP $= \dfrac{\text{Average WIP}}{\text{Cost of sales}} \times 365 \text{ days}$

(c) Raw material: $\dfrac{\text{Average raw material inventory}}{\text{Annual raw material purchases}} \times 365 \text{ days}$

Accounts payable period $\dfrac{\text{Payables}}{\text{Credit purchases (or cost of sales if purchases unavailable)}} \times 365 \text{ days}$

IRR $= a + \dfrac{\text{NPV}_a}{\text{NPV}_a - \text{NPV}_b} (b - a)$

Equivalent annual cost $= \dfrac{\text{PV of cost over one replacement cycle}}{\text{Annuity factor for the number of years in the cycle}}$

Cost of debt $= K_d = \dfrac{i(1 - T)}{P_0}$

Cost of preference shares $= K_{pref} = \dfrac{\text{Preference Dividend}}{\text{Market Value}_{(\text{ex div})}} = \dfrac{d}{P_0}$

Profitability index $= \dfrac{\text{PV of cash flows (or NPV of project)}}{\text{Capital investment}}$

Exam information

Computer-based exams

ACCA have commenced the launch of computer-based exams (CBEs) for this exam. They have been piloting computer-based exams in limited markets since September 2016 with the aim of rolling out into all markets internationally over a five-year period. Paper-based examinations will be run in parallel while the CBE's are phased in and BPP materials have been designed to support you, whichever exam option you choose.

Format of the exam

The exam format is the same irrespective of the mode of delivery and will comprise three exam sections.

Section	Style of question type	Description	Proportion of exam, %
A	Objective test (OT)	15 questions × 2 marks	30
B	Objective test (OT) case	3 questions × 10 marks Each question will contain 5 subparts each worth 2 marks	30
C	Constructed Response (Long questions)	2 questions × 20 marks	40
Total			100

Section A and B questions will be selected from the entire syllabus. The paper version of these objective test questions contain multiple choice only and the computer based versions will contain a variety. The responses to each question or subpart in OT cases are marked automatically as either correct or incorrect by computer.

Section C questions will mainly focus on the following syllabus areas but a minority of marks can be drawn from any other area of the syllabus

- Working capital management (syllabus area C)
- Investment appraisal (syllabus area D)
- Business finance (syllabus area E)

The responses to these questions are human marked.

Additional information

The study guide provides more detailed guidance on the syllabus and can be found by visiting the exam resource finder on the ACCA website: www.accaglobal.com/uk/en/student/exam-support-resources.html

Useful websites

The websites below provide additional sources of information of relevance to your studies for *Financial Management*.

- www.accaglobal.com

  ACCA's website. The students' section of the website is invaluable for detailed information about the qualification, past issues of Student Accountant (including technical articles) and a free downloadable Student Planner App.

- www.bpp.com

  Our website provides information about BPP products and services, with a link to the ACCA website.

- www.reuters.com

  This website provides information about current international business. You can search for information and articles on specific industry groups as well as individual companies.

Questions

PART A: FINANCIAL MANAGEMENT FUNCTION

Questions 1 to 20 cover Financial management function, the subject of Part A of the BPP Financial Management Study Text.

MCQ bank – Financial management and financial objectives

18 mins

1   Last year ABC Co made profits before tax of $2,628,000. Tax amounted to $788,000.

ABC Co's share capital was $2,000,000 (2,000,000 shares of $1) and $4,000,000 6% preference shares.

What was the earnings per share (EPS) for the year?

A   31c
B   80c
C   92c
D   119c

(2 marks)

2   Sep/Dec 15

Which of the following statements describes the main objective of financial management?

A   Efficient acquisition and deployment of financial resources to ensure achievement of objectives
B   Providing information to management for day to day functions of control and decision making
C   Providing information to external users about the historical results of the organisation
D   Maximisation of shareholder wealth

(2 marks)

3   A company has recently declared a dividend of 12c per share. The share price is $3.72 cum div and earnings for the most recent year were 60c per share.

What is the P/E ratio?

A   0.17
B   6.00
C   6.20
D   6.60

(2 marks)

4   6/15

The following information relates to a company:

Year	0	1	2	3
Earnings per share (cents)	30.0	31.8	33.9	35.7
Dividends per share (cents)	13.0	13.2	13.3	15.0
Share price at start of year ($)	1.95	1.98	2.01	2.25

Which of the following statements is correct?

A   The dividend payout ratio is greater than 40% in every year in the period
B   Mean growth in dividends per share over the period is 4%
C   Total shareholder return for the third year is 26%
D   Mean growth in earnings per share over the period is 6% per year

(2 marks)

5   12/14

Which of the following is **LEAST** likely to fall within financial management?

A   The dividend payment to shareholders is increased.
B   Funds are raised to finance an investment project.
C   Surplus assets are sold off.
D   Non-executive directors are appointed to the remuneration committee.

(2 marks)

(Total = 10 marks)

CBE style OTQ bank – Financial management and financial objectives

6   PT Co has just paid a dividend of 15 cents per share and its share price one year ago was $3.00 per share. The total shareholder return for the year was 25%.

What is the current share price? (to 2 decimal places)

$ [   ]

(2 marks)

7   Which of the following does **NOT** form part of the objectives of a corporate governance best practice framework?

[ ] Separation of chairperson and CEO roles

[ ] Establishment of audit, nomination and remuneration committees

[ ] Minimisation of risk

[ ] Employment of non-executive directors

(2 marks)

8

Are the following statements true or false?

		True	False
1	Maximising market share is an example of a financial objective.	[ ]	[ ]
2	Shareholder wealth maximisation is the primary financial objective for a company listed on a stock exchange.	[ ]	[ ]
3	Financial objectives should be quantitative so that their achievement can be measured.	[ ]	[ ]

(2 marks)

9   A school decides to have larger classes, and examination results suffer as a result. In terms of the 'value for money' framework, which of the following statements is true?

[ ] Economy has increased but efficiency has decreased.

[ ] Efficiency has increased but effectiveness has decreased.

[ ] Economy has increased but effectiveness has decreased.

[ ] Economy has increased but efficiency and effectiveness have decreased.   **(2 marks)**

10   H Co's share price is $3.50 at the end of 20X1 and this includes a capital gain of $0.75 since the beginning of the period. A dividend of $0.25 has been paid for 20X1.

What is the shareholder return (to 1 dp)?

[   ]%

(2 marks)

11

Are the following statements true or false?

		True	False
1	Accounting profit is not the same as economic profit.	[ ]	[ ]
2	Profit takes account of risk.	[ ]	[ ]
3	Accounting profit can be manipulated by managers.	[ ]	[ ]

(2 marks)

12   A government body uses measures based upon the 'three Es' to measure value for money generated by a publicly funded hospital.

Which of the following relates to efficiency?

☐   Cost per successfully treated patient
☐   Cost per operation
☐   Proportion of patients readmitted after unsuccessful treatment
☐   Percentage change in doctors' salaries compared with previous year

(2 marks)

13

6/15

Which of the following statements is NOT correct?

☐   Return on capital employed can be defined as profit before interest and tax divided by the sum of shareholders' funds and prior charge capital.

☐   Return on capital employed is the product of net profit margin and net asset turnover.

☐   Dividend yield can be defined as dividend per share divided by the ex dividend share price.

☐   Return on equity can be defined as profit before interest and tax divided by shareholders' funds.

(2 marks)

14

Sep/Dec 17

Geeh Co paid an interim dividend of $0.06 per ordinary share on 31 October 20X6 and declared a final dividend of $0.08 on 31 December 20X6. The ordinary shares in Geeh Co are trading at a cum-div price of $1.83.

What is the dividend yield (to one decimal place)?

☐ %

(2 marks)

15   Are the following statements true or false?

		True	False
1	Cash flow forecasting is primarily the responsibility of financial reporting.	☐	☐
2	Whether to undertake a particular new project is a financial management decision.	☐	☐

(2 marks)

(Total = 20 marks)

ABC Co

The following scenario relates to questions 16–20.

Summary financial information for ABC Co is given below, covering the last two years.

STATEMENT OF PROFIT OR LOSS (EXTRACT)

	20X8	20X7
	$'000	$'000
Revenue	74,521	68,000
Cost of sales	28,256	25,772
Salaries and wages	20,027	19,562
Other costs	11,489	9,160
Profit before interest and tax	14,749	13,506
Interest	1,553	1,863
Tax	4,347	3,726
Profit after interest and tax	8,849	7,917
Dividends payable	4,800	3,100

	20X8	20X7
STATEMENT OF FINANCIAL POSITION (EXTRACT)	$'000	$'000
Shareholders' funds	39,900	35,087
Long-term debt	14,000	17,500
	53,900	52,587
Other information		
Number of shares in issue ('000)	14,000	14,000
P/E ratio (average for year)		
ABC Co	14.0	13.0
Industry	15.2	15.0
Shareholders' investment		
EPS	$0.63	$0.57
Share price	$8.82	$7.41
Dividend per share	$0.34	$0.22

16 What is the percentage increase in return on capital (ROCE) for ABC Co between 20X7 and 20X8?

- A 6.2%
- B 6.6%
- C 7.9%
- D 8.6%

(2 marks)

17 What is the operating profit margin for 20X8?

- A 5.05%
- B 8.42%
- C 11.9%
- D 19.8%

(2 marks)

18 What is the shareholder return?

- A 14.4%
- B 19.0%
- C 19.8%
- D 23.6%

(2 marks)

19   As well as the information above, the following extra data is available:

	20X8	20X7
Gearing (debt/equity)	35.1%	49.9%
Interest cover (PBIT/interest)	9.5	7.2
Inflation	3%	3%

Based on all of the information available, are the following statements true or false?

1   Employees may be unhappy with their wages in 20X8.
2   Financial risk for shareholders appears to be a problem area.

A   Statement 1 is true and statement 2 is false.
B   Both statements are true.
C   Statement 1 is false and statement 2 is true.
D   Both statements are false.   **(2 marks)**

20   Accounting profits may not be the best measure of a company's performance.

Which of the following statements support this theory?

1   Profits are affected by accounting policies.
2   Profits take no account of risk.
3   Profits take no account of the level of investment made during the year.
4   Profits are measures of short-term historic performance.

A   2 and 4 only
B   1, 2, 3 and 4
C   2 and 3 only
D   1 only   **(2 marks)**

(Total = 10 marks)

PART B: FINANCIAL MANAGEMENT ENVIRONMENT

Questions 21 to 40 cover Financial management environment, the subject of Part B of the BPP Financial Management Study Text.

MCQ bank – Financial management environment   18 mins

21   A government has adopted a contractionary fiscal policy.

How would this typically affect businesses?

A   Higher interest rates and higher inflation
B   Lower taxes and higher government subsidies
C   Higher taxes and lower government subsidies
D   Lower inflation and lower interest rates   **(2 marks)**

22   A government follows an expansionary monetary policy.

How would this typically affect businesses?

A   Higher demand from customers, lower interest rates on loans and increased availability of credit
B   A contraction in demand from customers, higher interest rates and less available credit
C   Lower taxes, higher demand from customers but less government subsidies/available contracts
D   Lower interest rates, lower exchange rates and higher tax rates   **(2 marks)**

23   As the economy booms and approaches the limits of productivity at a point in time, a manufacturing business would typically feel which of the following effects?

A   Increased inflation (higher sales prices and higher costs), difficulty in finding suitable candidates to fill roles and higher interest rates

B   High export demand, increasing growth rates, high inflation and high interest rates

C   Reducing inflation, falling demand, reducing investment, increasing unemployment

D   Higher government spending, lower tax rates, high inflation and low unemployment   **(2 marks)**

24   6/17

Which of the following statements relating to money markets is/are true?

1   Lending is for periods greater than one year.
2   Lending is securitised.
3   Borrowers are mainly small companies.

A   1 and 2
B   2 and 3
C   1 and 3
D   2 only   **(2 marks)**

25   Which of the following organisations is most likely to benefit from a period of high price inflation?

A   An organisation which has a large number of long-term payables

B   An exporter of goods to a country with relatively low inflation

C   A supplier of goods in a market where consumers are highly price sensitive and substitute imported goods are available

D   A large retailer with a high level of inventory on display and low rate of inventory turnover

(2 marks)

(Total = 10 marks)

26 Which of the following is **NOT** a function that financial intermediaries fulfil for customers and borrowers?

    A   Maturity transformation
    B   Fund aggregation
    C   Dividend creation
    D   Pooling of losses

(2 marks)

27 Which of the following are money market instruments?

    1   Certificate of deposit
    2   Corporate bond
    3   Commercial paper
    4   Treasury bill

    A   1, 2 and 4 only
    B   1 and 3 only
    C   1, 3 and 4 only
    D   1, 2, 3 and 4

(2 marks)

28 What role would the money market have in a letter of credit arrangement?   Sept/Dec 17

    A   Initial arrangement of the letter of credit.
    B   Acceptance of the letter of credit.
    C   Issuing of a banker's acceptance.
    D   Discounting the banker's acceptance.

(2 marks)

29 AB plc, a company listed in the UK and Australia, decides to issue unsecured US dollar bonds in Australia.

Which of the following is the correct definition for these bonds?

    A   Junk bonds
    B   Commercial paper
    C   Eurobonds
    D   Intercontinental bills

(2 marks)

30 Rank the following from highest risk to lowest risk from the investor's perspective.

    1   Preference share
    2   Treasury bill
    3   Corporate bond
    4   Ordinary share

    A   1, 4, 3, 2
    B   1, 4, 2, 3
    C   4, 2, 1, 3
    D   4, 1, 3, 2

(2 marks)

(Total = 10 marks)

31

Are the following statements true or false?

		True	False
1	Securitisation is the conversion of illiquid assets into marketable securities.	☐	☐
2	The reverse yield gap refers to equity yields being higher than debt yields.	☐	☐
3	Disintermediation arises where borrowers deal directly with lending individuals.	☐	☐

(2 marks)

32

Governments have a number of economic targets as part of their fiscal policy.

Which of the following government actions relate predominantly to fiscal policy?

1   Decreasing interest rates in order to stimulate consumer spending
2   Reducing taxation while maintaining public spending
3   Using official foreign currency reserves to buy the domestic currency
4   Borrowing money from the capital markets and spending it on public works

☐   1 only
☐   1 and 3
☐   2 and 4 only
☐   2, 3 and 4

(2 marks)

33

Which of the following statements are correct?

(1)   A certificate of deposit is an example of a money market instrument
(2)   Money market deposits are short-term loans between organisations such as banks
(3)   Treasury bills are bought and sold on a discount basis

☐   1 and 2 only

☐   1 and 3 only

☐   2 and 3 only

☐   1, 2 and 3

(2 marks)

34

Are the following statements true or false?

		True	False
(1)	Capital market securities are assets for the seller but liabilities for the buyer	☐	☐
(2)	Financial markets can be classified into exchange and over-the-counter markets	☐	☐
(3)	A secondary market is where securities are bought and sold by investors	☐	☐

(2 marks)

Are the following statements true or false?

		True	False
(1)	Monetary policy seeks to influence aggregate demand by increasing or decreasing the money raised through taxation	☐	☐
(2)	When governments adopt a floating exchange rate system, the exchange rate is an equilibrium between demand and supply in the foreign exchange market.	☐	☐
(3)	Fiscal policy seeks to influence the economy and economic growth by increasing or decreasing interest rates.	☐	☐

(2 marks)
(Total = 10 marks)

CBE style OTQ bank – Financial management environment

36   The following statements relate to fiscal policy and demand management.

Are the statements true or false?

		True	False
1	If a government spends more by borrowing more, it will raise demand in the economy.	☐	☐
2	If demand in the economy is high then government borrowing will fall.	☐	☐

(2 marks)

37   If the US dollar weakens against the pound sterling, will UK exporters and importers suffer or benefit?

	Benefit	Suffer
UK exporters to US	☐	☐
UK importers from US	☐	☐

(2 marks)

38   Which of the following represent forms of market failure where regulation may be a solution?

1   Imperfect competition
2   Social costs or externalities
3   Imperfect information

☐   1 only
☐   1 and 2 only
☐   2 and 3 only
☐   1, 2 and 3

(2 marks)

39   Which TWO of the following are among the main goals of macroeconomic policy?

☐   Encouraging waste recyling
☐   Low and stable inflation
☐   Achievement of a balance between exports and imports
☐   Encouraging an equitable distribution of income

(2 marks)

40   If a government has a macroeconomic policy objective of expanding the overall level of economic activity, which TWO of the following measures would be consistent with such an objective?

☐   Increasing public expenditure
☐   Increasing interest rates
☐   Increasing the exchange rate
☐   Decreasing taxation

(2 marks)

(Total = 10 marks)

PART C: WORKING CAPITAL MANAGEMENT

Questions 41 to 89 cover Working capital management, the subject of Part C of the BPP Financial Management Study Text.

MCQ bank – Working capital

18 mins

41

3/17

A company's typical inventory holding period at any time is:

Raw materials : 15 days
Work in progress: 35 days
Finished goods: 40 days

Annual cost of goods sold as per the financial statements is $100m of which the raw materials purchases account for 50% of the total.

The company has implemented plans to reduce the level of inventory held, the effects of which are expected to be as follows:

(1) Raw material holding time to be reduced by 5 days
(2) Production time to be reduced by 4 days
(3) Finished goods holding time to be reduced by 5 days.

Assuming a 365-day year, what will be the reduction in inventory held?

A $2.603m
B $3.836m
C $1.918m
D $3.151m

(2 marks)

42   D Co decides to offer a 2% early settlement discount that half of all customers take up. They pay in one month instead of the usual two. D Co pays 10% per annum for its overdraft facility.

What impact will this have?

	Cash operating cycle	Reported profits
A	Reduce	Increase
B	Unaffected	Increase
C	Reduce	Reduce
D	Unaffected	Reduce

(2 marks)

43   WW Co has a current ratio of 2. Receivables are $3m and current liabilities are $2m.

What are inventory days if cost of sales is $10m per annum and WW Co has a zero cash balance? Assume a 365-day year.

A   36.5 days
B   91.25 days
C   14.6 days
D   243.3 days

(2 marks)

44

Wallace Co has annual credit sales of $4,500,000 and on average customers take 60 days to pay, assuming a 360 day year. As a result, Wallace Co has a trade receivables balance of $750,000. The company relies on an overdraft to finance this at an annual interest rate of 10%.

Wallace Co is considering offering an early settlement discount of 1% for payment in 30 days. It expected that 25% of its customers (representing 35% of the annual credit sales figure) will pay in 30 days in order to obtain the discount.

If Wallace Co introduces the proposed discount, what will be the **NET** impact?

A $1,875 saving
B $1,875 cost
C $2,625 saving
D $2,625 cost

(2 marks)

45

A company has annual credit sales of $27m and related cost of sales of $15m. The company has the following targets for the next year:

Trade receivables days   50 days
Inventory days   60 days
Trade payables   45 days

Assume there are 360 days in the year.

What is the net investment in working capital required for the next year?

A $8,125,000
B $4,375,000
C $2,875,000
D $6,375,000

(2 marks)
(Total = 10 marks)

46   TS Co has daily demand for ball bearings of 40 a day for each of the 250 working days (50 weeks) of the year. The ball bearings are purchased from a local supplier for $2 each. The cost of placing an order is $64 per order, regardless of the size of the order. The inventory holding costs, expressed as a percentage of inventory purchase price, is 25% per annum.

What is the economic order quantity (EOQ)?

☐ ball bearings

(2 marks)

47   EE Co has calculated the following in relation to its inventories.

Buffer inventory level	50 units
Reorder size	250 items
Fixed order costs	$50 per order
Cost of holding onto one item pa	$1.25 per year
Annual demand	10,000 items
Purchase price	$2 per item

What are the total inventory related costs for a year (to the nearest whole $)?

$ ☐

(2 marks)

48   **12/14**

Which of the following statements concerning working capital management are correct?

1   Working capital should increase as sales increase.
2   An increase in the cash operating cycle will decrease profitability.
3   Overtrading is also known as undercapitalisation.

☐ 1 and 2 only
☐ 1 and 3 only
☐ 2 and 3 only
☐ 1, 2 and 3

(2 marks)

49   XYZ Co has annual credit sales of $20m and accounts receivable of $4m. Working capital is financed by an overdraft at 12% interest per year. Assume 365 days in a year.

What is the annual financial effect if management reduces the collection period to 60 days by offering an early settlement discount of 1% that all customers adopt?

☐ $85,479 benefit
☐ $114,521 cost
☐ $85,479 cost
☐ $285,479 benefit

(2 marks)

50   **6/15**

Which of the following statements is/are correct?

(1)   Factoring with recourse provides insurance against bad debts
(2)   The expertise of a factor can increase the efficiency of trade receivables management for a company

☐ 2 only
☐ 1 only
☐ Neither 1 nor 2
☐ 1 and 2

51   Which of the following is **LEAST** likely to be used in the management of foreign accounts receivable?

☐   Letters of credit
☐   Bills of exchange
☐   Invoice discounting
☐   Commercial paper   **(2 marks)**

52   L Co is considering whether to factor its sales invoices. A factor has offered L Co a non-recourse package at a cost of 1.5% of sales and an admin fee of $6,000 per annum. Bad debts are currently 2% of sales per annum and sales are $1.5m per annum.

What is the cost of the package of L Co?

$ ☐   **(2 marks)**

53   Which of the following is **NOT** a drawback of the EOQ model?

☐   Assumes certain or zero lead times
☐   Assumes certainty in demand
☐   Assumes a small number of close suppliers
☐   Ignores hidden costs such as the risk of obsolescence   **(2 marks)**

54   Which of the following is **NOT** a potential hidden cost of increasing credit taken from suppliers?

☐   Damage to goodwill
☐   Early settlement discounts lost
☐   Business disruption
☐   Increased risk of bad debts   **(2 marks)**

55   Which **TWO** of the following would be most likely to arise from the introduction of a just-in-time inventory ordering system?

☐   Lower inventory holding costs
☐   Less risk of inventory shortages
☐   More frequent deliveries
☐   Lower ordering costs   **(2 marks)**

(Total = 20 marks)

CBE style OTQ bank – Working capital finance

56   JP Co has budgeted that sales will be $300,100 in January 20X2, $501,500 in February, $150,000 in March and $320,500 in April. Half of sales will be credit sales. 80% of receivables are expected to pay in the month after sale, 15% in the second month after sale, while the remaining 5% are expected to be bad debts. Receivables who pay in the month after sale can claim a 4% early settlement discount.

What level of sales receipts should be shown in the cash budget for March 20X2 (to the nearest $)?

$ [   ]

(2 marks)

57   6/15

A company needs $150,000 each year for regular payments. Converting the company's short-term investments into cash to meet these regular payments incurs a fixed cost of $400 per transaction. These short-term investments pay interest of 5% per year, while the company earns interest of only 1% per year on cash deposits.

According to the Baumol Model, what is the optimum amount of short-term investments to convert into cash in each transaction? (to the nearest $'000)

$ [   ]

58   The treasury department in TB Co has calculated, using the Miller-Orr model, that the lowest cash balance they should have is $1m, and the highest is $10m. If the cash balance goes above $10m they transfer the cash into money market securities.

Are the following true or false?

		True	False
1	When the balance reaches $10m they would buy $6m of securities.	☐	☐
2	When the cash balance falls to $1m they will sell $3m of securities.	☐	☐
3	If the variance of daily cash flows increases the spread between upper and lower limit will be increased.	☐	☐

(2 marks)

59   Which statement best reflects an aggressive working capital finance policy?

☐ More short-term finance is used because it is cheaper although it is risky.
☐ Investors are forced to accept lower rates of return.
☐ More long-term finance is used as it is less risky.
☐ Inventory levels are reduced.

(2 marks)

60   What are the **TWO** key risks for the borrower associated with short-term working capital finance?

☐ Rate risk
☐ Renewal risk
☐ Inflexibility
☐ Maturity mismatch

(2 marks)

(Total = 10 marks)

Section B questions

PKA Co (12/07, amended)

18 mins

The following scenario relates to questions 61–65.

PKA Co is a European company that sells goods solely within Europe. The recently appointed financial manager of PKA Co has been investigating working capital management objectives and the working capital management of the company, and has gathered the following information about the inventory policy and accounts receivable.

Inventory management

The current policy is to order 100,000 units when the inventory level falls to 35,000 units. Forecast demand to meet production requirements during the next year is 625,000 units. The cost of placing and processing an order is $250, while the cost of holding a unit in stores is $0.50 per unit per year. Both costs are expected to be constant during the next year. Orders are received two weeks after being placed with the supplier. You should assume a 50-week year and that demand is constant throughout the year.

Accounts receivable management

Customers are allowed 30 days' credit, but the financial statements of PKA Co show that the average accounts receivable period in the last financial year was 75 days. This is in line with the industry average. The financial manager also noted that bad debts as a percentage of sales, which are all on credit, increased in the last financial year from 5% to 8%. The accounts receivables department is currently short staffed.

61 What are the main objectives of working capital management at PKA?

    1   To ensure that PKA Co has sufficient liquid resources
    2   To increase PKA Co's profitability
    3   To ensure that PKA Co's assets give the highest possible returns

    A   1 only
    B   1 and 2 only
    C   2 and 3 only
    D   1, 2 and 3   **(2 marks)**

62 What is the current minimum inventory level at PKA Co?

    A   10,000
    B   12,500
    C   22,500
    D   35,000   **(2 marks)**

63 What is the economic order quantity?

    A   250
    B   3,536
    C   17,678
    D   25,000   **(2 marks)**

64 What are the best ways for PKA Co to improve the management of accounts receivable?

    1   Assess the creditworthiness of new customers
    2   Introduce early settlement discounts
    3   Take legal action against the slow payers and non-payers

    A   1 and 2 only
    B   2 only
    C   1 and 3 only
    D   1, 2 and 3   **(2 marks)**

65   In order to improve the management of receivables, PKA Co is considering using a debt factor on a 'with-recourse' basis.

Which of the following are benefits of 'with-recourse' factoring for PKA Co?

1   A fall in bad debts
2   A reduction in accounts receivable staffing costs
3   An improvement in short-term liquidity

A   2 only
B   1, 2 and 3
C   2 and 3 only
D   1 and 3 only

(2 marks)

(Total = 10 marks)

Plot Co

18 mins

The following scenario relates to questions 66–70.

Plot Co sells Product P with sales occurring evenly throughout the year.

Product P

The annual demand for Product P is 300,000 units and an order for new inventory is placed each month. Each order costs $267 to place. The cost of holding Product P in inventory is 10 cents per unit per year. Buffer inventory equal to 40% of one month's sales is maintained.

Other information

Plot Co finances working capital with short-term finance costing 5% per year. Assume that there are 365 days in each year.

66 What is the total cost of the current ordering policy (to the nearest whole number)?

    A $2,250
    B $2,517
    C $3,204
    D $5,454

    (2 marks)

67 What is the total cost of an ordering policy using the economic order quantity (EOQ) (to the nearest whole number)?

    A $3,001
    B $5,004
    C $28,302
    D $40,025

    (2 marks)

68 Plot Co is considering offering a 2% early settlement discount to its customers. Currently sales are $10m and customers take 60 days to pay. Plot Co estimates half the customers will take up the discount and pay cash. Plot is currently financing working capital using an overdraft on which it pays a 10% charge. Assume 365 days in a year.

What will be the effect of implementing the policy?

    A   Benefit of $17,808
    B   Cost of $17,808
    C   Benefit of $82,192
    D   Benefit of $182,192

    (2 marks)

69 Plot Co managers are considering the cost of working capital management.

Are the following statements about working capital management true or false?

    1   A conservative working capital finance approach is low risk but expensive.
    2   Good working capital management adds to the wealth of shareholders.

    A   Statement 1 is true and statement 2 is false.
    B   Statement 2 is true and statement 1 is false.
    C   Both statements are true.
    D   Both statements are false.

    (2 marks)

70   If Plot Co were overtrading, which **TWO** of the following could be symptoms?

    1   Decreasing levels of trade receivables
    2   Increasing levels of inventory
    3   Increasing levels of long-term borrowings
    4   Increasing levels of current liabilities

    A   1 and 3
    B   1 and 4
    C   2 and 3
    D   2 and 4

(2 marks)

(Total = 10 marks)

CBE style OT case Gorwa Co (12/08, amended)   18 mins

The following scenario relates to questions 71–75.

The financial manager of Gorwa Co is worried about the level of working capital and that the company may be overtrading.

The following extract financial information relates to the last two years:

	20X7	20X6
	$'000	$'000
Sales (all on credit)	37,400	26,720
Cost of sales	34,408	23,781
Operating profit	2,992	2,939

	20X7		20X6	
	$'000	$'000	$'000	$'000
Current assets				
Inventory	4,600		2,400	
Trade receivables	4,600		2,200	
		9,200		4,600
Current liabilities		7,975		3,600

71   What is the sales/net working capital ratio for 20X7 (to 2 dp)?

[   ] times   (2 marks)

72   What is the increase in inventory days between 20X6 and 20X7? (to the nearest whole day)

[   ] days   (2 marks)

73   Are the following statements true or false for Gorwa Co?

	True	False
Accounts receivable days have increased	☐	☐
Inventory turnover has slowed down	☐	☐

                                                                                         (2 marks)

74   Gorwa Co is concerned about overtrading.

Which **TWO** of the following are symptoms of overtrading?

☐ Rapid reduction in sales revenue
☐ Slowdown in inventory turnover
☐ Shortening of payment period to accounts payables
☐ A fall in the current ratio

                                                                                         (2 marks)

75   Gorwa Co's net working capital (ie current assets less current liabilities) is most likely to increase in which of the following situations?

☐ Payments to suppliers are delayed
☐ The period of credit extended to customers is reduced
☐ Non-current assets are sold
☐ Inventory levels are increased

                                                                                         (2 marks)

                                                                                (Total = 10 marks)

CBE style OT case Cat Co

18 mins

The following scenario relates to questions 76–80.

Cat Co places monthly orders with a supplier for 10,000 components which are used in its manufacturing processes. Annual demand is 120,000 components. The current terms are payment in full within 90 days, which Cat Co meets, and the cost per component is $7.50. The cost of ordering is $200 per order, while the cost of holding components in inventory is $1.00 per component per year.

The supplier has offered a discount of 3.6% on orders of 30,000 or more components. If the bulk purchase discount is taken, the cost of holding components in inventory would increase to $2.20 per component per year due to the need for a larger storage facility.

76 What is the current total annual cost of inventory?

$\boxed{}$

(2 marks)

77 What is the total annual inventory cost if Cat Co orders 30,000 components at a time?

$\boxed{}$

(2 marks)

78 Cat Co has annual credit sales of $25m and accounts receivable of $5m. Working capital is financed by an overdraft at 10% interest per year. Assume 365 days in a year.

What is the annual finance cost saving if Cat Co reduces the collection period to 60 days (to the nearest whole number)?

$\boxed{}$

(2 marks)

79 Cat Co is reviewing its working capital management.

Which **TWO** of the following statements concerning working capital management are correct?

- [ ] The twin objectives of working capital management are profitability and liquidity.
- [ ] A conservative approach to working capital investment will increase profitability.
- [ ] Working capital management is a key factor in a company's long-term success.
- [ ] Liquid assets give the highest returns leading to conflicts of objectives.

(2 marks)

80 Management at Cat Co are considering an aggressive approach to financing working capital.

Which of the following statements relate to an aggressive approach to financing working capital management?

1 All non-current assets, permanent current assets and part of fluctuating current assets are financed by long-term funding.

2 There is an increased risk of liquidity and cash flow problems.

- [ ] Both statements
- [ ] Neither statement
- [ ] Statement 1 only
- [ ] Statement 2 only

(2 marks)

(Total = 10 marks)

Section C questions

81 APX Co (12/09, amended)

36 mins

APX Co achieved a revenue of $16m in the year that has just ended and expects revenue growth of 8.4% in the next year.

The financial statements of APX Co for the year that has just ended contain the following statement of financial position:

	$m	$m
Non-current assets		22.0
Current assets		
Inventory	2.4	
Trade receivables	2.2	
		4.6
Total assets		26.6
Equity finance:		
Ordinary shares	5.0	
Reserves	7.5	
		12.5
Long-term bank loan		10.0
		22.5
Current liabilities		
Trade payables	1.9	
Overdraft	2.2	
		4.1
Total equity and liabilities		26.6

The long-term bank loan has a fixed annual interest rate of 8% per year. APX Co pays taxation at an annual rate of 30% per year.

The following accounting ratios have been forecast for the next year:

Gross profit margin:	30%
Operating profit margin:	20%
Dividend payout ratio:	50%
Inventory turnover period:	110 days
Trade receivables period:	65 days
Trade payables period:	75 days

Overdraft interest in the next year is forecast to be $140,000. No change is expected in the level of non-current assets and depreciation should be ignored.

Required

(a) Prepare the following forecast financial statements for APX Co using the information provided:

    (i) A statement of profit or loss for the next year

    (ii) A statement of financial position at the end of the next year   **(9 marks)**

(b) Analyse and discuss the working capital financing policy of APX Co.   **(6 marks)**

(c) Discuss the role of financial intermediaries in providing short-term finance for use by business organisations.   **(5 marks)**

    (Total = 20 marks)

82 Pangli Co Mar/Jun 17

It is is the middle of December 20X6 and Pangli Co is looking at working capital management for January 20X7.

Forecast financial information at the start of January 20X7 is as follows:

Inventory	$455,000
Trade receivables	$408,350
Trade payables	$186,700
Overdraft	$240,250

All sales are on credit and they are expected to be $3.5m for 20X6. Monthly sales are as follows:

November 20X6 (actual)	$270,875
December 20X6 (forecast)	$300,000
January 20X7 (forecast)	$350,000

Pangli Co has a gross profit margin of 40%. Although Pangli Co offers 30 days credit, only 60% of customers pay in the month following purchase, while remaining customers take an additional month of credit.

Invetoey is expected to increase by $52,250 during January 20X7.

Pangli Co plans to pay 70% of trade payables in January 20X7 and defer paying the remaining 30% until the end of February 20X7. All suppliers of the company require payment within 30 days. Credit purchases from suppliers during January 20X7 are expected to be $250,000.

Interest of $70,000 is due to be paid in January 20X7 on fixed rate bank debt. Operating cash outflows are expected to be $146,500 in January 20X7. Pangli Co has no cash and relies on its overdraft to finance daily operations. The company has no plans to raise long-term finance during January 20X7.

Assume that each year has 360 days.

Requried

(a)	(i)	Calculate the cash operating cycle of Pangli Co at the start of January 20X7.	**(2 marks)**
	(ii)	Calculate the overdraft expected at the end of January 20X7.	**(4 marks)**
	(iii)	Calcualate the current ratios at the start and end of January 20X7.	**(4 marks)**
(b)		Discuss FIVE techniques that Pangli Co could use in managing trade receivables.	**(10 marks)**

(Total = 20 marks)

83 WQZ Co (12/10, amended)

WQZ Co is considering making the following changes in the area of working capital management:

Inventory management

It has been suggested that the order size for Product KN5 should be determined using the economic order quantity (EOQ) model.

WQZ Co forecasts that demand for Product KN5 will be 160,000 units in the coming year and it has traditionally ordered 10% of annual demand per order. The ordering cost is expected to be $400 per order while the holding cost is expected to be $5.12 per unit per year. A buffer inventory of 5,000 units of Product KN5 will be maintained, whether orders are made by the traditional method or using the EOQ model.

Receivables management

WQZ Co could introduce an early settlement discount of 1% for customers who pay within 30 days and, at the same time, through improved operational procedures, maintain a maximum average payment period of 60 days for credit customers who do not take the discount. It is expected that 25% of credit customers will take the discount if it were offered.

It is expected that administration and operating cost savings of $753,000 per year will be made after improving operational procedures and introducing the early settlement discount.

Credit sales of WQZ Co are currently $87.6m per year and trade receivables are currently $18m. Credit sales are not expected to change as a result of the changes in receivables management. The company has a cost of short-term finance of 5.5% per year.

Required

(a) Calculate the cost of the current ordering policy and the change in the costs of inventory management that will arise if the EOQ is used to determine the optimum order size for Product KN5. **(5 marks)**

(b) Calculate and comment on whether the proposed changes in receivables management will be acceptable. Assuming that only 25% of customers take the early settlement discount, what is the maximum early settlement discount that could be offered? **(7 marks)**

(c) Discuss the factors that should be considered in formulating working capital policy on the management of trade receivables. **(8 marks)**

(Total = 20 marks)

84 Bold Co (12/11, amended)

36 mins

Extracts from the recent financial statements of Bold Co are given below.

		$'000
Revenue		21,300
Cost of sales		16,400
Gross profit		4,900

	$'000	$'000
Non-current assets		3,000
Current assets		
Inventory	4,500	
Trade receivables	3,500	
		8,000
Total assets		11,000
Equity		
Ordinary shares	1,000	
Reserves	1,000	
		2,000
Non-current liabilities		
Bonds		3,000
Current liabilities		
Trade payables	3,000	
Overdraft	3,000	
		6,000
Total equity and liabilities		11,000

A factor has offered to manage the trade receivables of Bold Co in a servicing and factor-financing agreement. The factor expects to reduce the average trade receivables period of Bold Co from its current level to 35 days; to reduce bad debts from 0.9% of revenue to 0.6% of revenue; and to save Bold Co $40,000 per year in administration costs. The factor would also make an advance to Bold Co of 80% of the revised book value of trade receivables. The interest rate on the advance would be 2% higher than the 7% that Bold Co currently pays on its overdraft. The factor would charge a fee of 0.75% of revenue on a with-recourse basis, or a fee of 1.25% of revenue on a non-recourse basis. Assume that there are 365 working days in each year and that all sales and supplies are on credit.

Required

(a) Explain the meaning of the term 'cash operating cycle' and discuss the relationship between the cash operating cycle and the level of investment in working capital. Your answer should include a discussion of relevant working capital policy and the nature of business operations.　**(8 marks)**

(b) Calculate the cash operating cycle of Bold Co (ignore the factor's offer in this part of the question).
　(4 marks)

(c) Calculate the value of the factor's offer:

(i) On a with-recourse basis
(ii) On a non-recourse basis　**(8 marks)**

(Total = 20 marks)

85 Wobnig Co (6/12, amended)

The following financial information relates to Wobnig Co.

	20X1	20X0
	$'000	$'000
Revenue	14,525	10,375
Cost of sales	10,458	6,640
Profit before interest and tax	4,067	3,735
Interest	355	292
Profit before tax	3,712	3,443
Taxation	1,485	1,278
Distributable profit	2,227	2,165

	20X1		20X0	
	$'000	$'000	$'000	$'000
Non-current assets		15,284		14,602
Current assets				
Inventory	2,149		1,092	
Trade receivables	3,200		1,734	
		5,349		2,826
Total assets		20,633		17,428
Equity				
Ordinary shares	8,000		8,000	
Reserves	4,268		3,541	
		12,268		11,541
Non-current liabilities				
7% bonds		4,000		4,000
Current liabilities				
Trade payables	2,865		1,637	
Overdraft	1,500		250	
		4,365		1,887
Total equity and liabilities		20,633		17,428

Average ratios for the last two years for companies with similar business operations to Wobnig Co are as follows:

Current ratio	1.7 times
Quick ratio	1.1 times
Inventory days	55 days
Trade receivables days	60 days
Trade payables days	85 days
Sales revenue/net working capital	10 times

Required

(a) Using suitable working capital ratios and analysis of the financial information provided, evaluate whether Wobnig Co can be described as overtrading (undercapitalised). **(12 marks)**

(b) Critically discuss the similarities and differences between working capital policies in the following areas:

   (i)   Working capital investment
   (ii) Working capital financing   **(8 marks)**

(Total = 20 marks)

86 KXP Co (12/12, amended)

KXP Co is an e-business which trades solely over the internet. In the last year the company had sales of $15m. All sales were on 30 days' credit to commercial customers.

Extracts from the company's most recent statement of financial position relating to working capital are as follows:

	$'000
Trade receivables	2,466
Trade payables	2,220
Overdraft	3,000

In order to encourage customers to pay on time, KXP Co proposes introducing an early settlement discount of 1% for payment within 30 days, while increasing its normal credit period to 45 days. It is expected that, on average, 50% of customers will take the discount and pay within 30 days, 30% of customers will pay after 45 days, and 20% of customers will not change their current paying behaviour.

KXP Co currently orders 15,000 units per month of Product Z, demand for which is constant. There is only one supplier of Product Z and the cost of Product Z purchases over the last year was $540,000. The supplier has offered a 2% discount for orders of Product Z of 30,000 units or more. Each order costs KXP Co $150 to place and the holding cost is 24 cents per unit per year. KXP Co has an overdraft facility charging interest of 6% per year.

Required

(a) Calculate the net benefit or cost of the proposed changes in trade receivables policy and comment on your findings. **(5 marks)**

(b) Calculate whether the bulk purchase discount offered by the supplier is financially acceptable and comment on the assumptions made by your calculation. **(5 marks)**

(c) Identify and discuss the factors to be considered in determining the optimum level of cash to be held by a company. **(5 marks)**

(d) Discuss the factors to be considered in formulating a trade receivables management policy. **(5 marks)**

(Total = 20 marks)

87 CSZ Co (6/14, amended)   36 mins

The current assets and liabilities of CSZ Co at the end of March 20X4 are as follows:

	$'000	$'000
Inventory	5,700	
Trade receivables	6,575	12,275
Trade payables	2,137	
Overdraft	4,682	6,819
Net current assets		5,456

For the year to end of March 20X4, CSZ Co had sales of $40m, all on credit, while cost of sales was $26m.

For the year to end of March 20X5, CSZ Co has forecast that credit sales will remain at $40m while cost of sales will fall to 60% of sales. The company expects current assets to consist of inventory and trade receivables, and current liabilities to consist of trade payables and the company's overdraft.

CSZ Co also plans to achieve the following target working capital ratio values for the year to the end of March 20X5:

Inventory days:	60 days
Trade receivables days:	75 days
Trade payables days:	55 days
Current ratio:	1.4 times

Required

(a)   Calculate the working capital cycle (cash collection cycle) of CSZ Co at the end of March 20X4 and discuss whether a working capital cycle should be positive or negative.   **(6 marks)**

(b)   Calculate the target quick ratio (acid test ratio) and the target ratio of sales to net working capital of CSZ Co at the end of March 20X5.   **(5 marks)**

(c)   Analyse and compare the current asset and current liability positions for March 20X4 and March 20X5, and discuss how the working capital financing policy of CSZ Co would have changed.   **(9 marks)**

(Total = 20 marks)

88 Flit Co (12/14, amended)

36 mins

Flit Co is preparing a cash flow forecast for the three-month period from January to the end of March. The following sales volumes have been forecast:

	December	January	February	March	April
Sales (units)	1,200	1,250	1,300	1,400	1,500

Notes

1   The selling price per unit is $800 and a selling price increase of 5% will occur in February. Sales are all on one month's credit.

2   Production of goods for sale takes place one month before sales.

3   Each unit produced requires two units of raw materials, costing $200 per unit. No raw materials inventory is held. Raw material purchases are on one month's credit.

4   Variable overheads and wages equal to $100 per unit are incurred during production, and paid in the month of production.

5   The opening cash balance at 1 January is expected to be $40,000.

6   A long-term loan of $300,000 will be received at the beginning of March.

7   A machine costing $400,000 will be purchased for cash in March.

Required

(a)   Calculate the cash balance at the end of each month in the three-month period.   **(5 marks)**

(b)   Calculate the forecast current ratio at the end of the three-month period.   **(2 marks)**

(c)   Assuming that Flit Co expects to have a short-term cash surplus during the three-month period, discuss whether this should be invested in shares listed on a large stock market.   **(3 marks)**

(d)   Explain how the Baumol model can be employed to reduce the costs of cash management.   **(5 marks)**

(e)   Renpec Co, a subsidiary of Flit Co, has set a minimum cash account balance of $7,500. The average cost to the company of making deposits or selling investments is $18 per transaction and the standard deviation of its cash flows was $1,000 per day during the last year. The average interest rate on investments is 5.11%.

Determine the spread, the upper limit and the return point for the cash account of Renpec Co using the Miller-Orr model and explain the relevance of these values for the cash management of the company.

(5 marks)

(Total = 20 marks)

89 Widnor Co (6/15, amended)

The finance director of Widnor Co has been looking to improve the company's working capital management. Widnor Co has revenue from credit sales of $26,750,000 per year and, although its terms of trade require all credit customers to settle outstanding invoices within 40 days, on average customers have been taking longer. Approximately 1% of credit sales turn into bad debts which are not recovered.

Trade receivables currently stand at $4,458,000 and Widnor Co has a cost of short-term finance of 5% per year.

The finance director is considering a proposal from a factoring company, Nokfe Co, which was invited to tender to manage the sales ledger of Widnor Co on a with-recourse basis. Nokfe Co believes that it can use its expertise to reduce average trade receivables days to 35 days, while cutting bad debts by 70% and reducing administration costs by $50,000 per year. A condition of the factoring agreement is that the company would also advance Widnor Co 80% of the value of invoices raised at an interest rate of 7% per year. Nokfe Co would charge an annual fee of 0.75% of credit sales.

Assume that there are 360 days in each year.

Required

(a) Advise whether the factor's offer is financially acceptable to Widnor Co.   **(7 marks)**

(b) Briefly discuss how the creditworthiness of potential customers can be assessed.   **(3 marks)**

(c) Discuss how risks arising from granting credit to foreign customers can be managed and reduced.

(10 marks)

(Total = 20 marks)

PART D: INVESTMENT APPRAISAL

Questions 90 to 165 cover Investment appraisal, the subject of Part D of the BPP Financial Management Study Text.

MCQ bank – Investment decisions

36 mins

The following information relates to questions 90 and 91.

NW Co is considering investing $46,000 in a new delivery lorry that will last for 4 years, after which time it will be sold for $7,000. Depreciation is charged on a straight-line basis. Forecast operating profits/(losses) to be generated by the machine are as follows.

Year	$
1	16,500
2	23,500
3	13,500
4	(1,500)

90   What is the return on capital employed (ROCE) for the lorry (using the average investment method)?

A   70%
B   28%
C   49%
D   36%

(2 marks)

91   Assuming operational cash flows arise evenly over the year, what is the payback period for this investment (to the nearest month)?

A   1 year 7 months
B   2 years 7 months
C   1 year 5 months
D   3 years 2 months

(2 marks)

92   Which of the following are benefits of the ROCE method of investment appraisal?

1   It considers the whole project.

2   It is cash flow based.

3   It is a percentage which, being meaningful to non-finance professionals, helps communicate the benefits of investment decisions.

A   1, 2 and 3
B   1 and 3 only
C   1 and 2 only
D   2 and 3 only

(2 marks)

93   SW Co has a barrel of chemicals in its warehouse that it purchased for a project a while ago at a cost of $1,000. It would cost $400 for a professional disposal company to collect the barrel and dispose of it safely. However, the chemicals could be used in a potential project which is currently being assessed.

What is the relevant cost of using the chemicals in a new project proposal?

A $1,000 cost
B $400 benefit
C $400 cost
D   Zero

(2 marks)

94   A new project being considered by BLW Co would require 1,000 hours of skilled labour. The current workforce is already fully employed but more workers can be hired in at a cost of $20 per hour. The current workers are paid $15 per hour on a project that earns a contribution of $10 per hour.

What is the relevant cost of labour to be included in the project appraisal?

A $10,000
B $15,000
C $20,000
D $25,000   **(2 marks)**

95   LW Co has a half empty factory on which it pays $5,000 pa rent. If it takes on a new project, it will have to move to a new bigger factory costing $17,000 pa and it could rent the old factory out for $3,000 pa until the end of the current lease.

What is the rental cost to be included in the project appraisal?

A $14,000
B $17,000
C $9,000
D $19,000   **(2 marks)**

96   Which of the following is a drawback of the payback period method of investment appraisal?

A   It is cash flow based.
B   It considers the time value of money.
C   It doesn't measure the potential impact on shareholder wealth.
D   It is profit based.   **(2 marks)**

97   A company is evaluating an investment project with the following forecast cash flows:

Time	0	1	2	3	4
Cash flow ($m)	(6.5)	2.4	3.1	2.1	1.8

Using discount rates of 15% and 20%, what is the internal rate of return of the investment project?

A   15.8%
B   17.2%
C   17.8%
D   19.4%   **(2 marks)**

98   EE Co is considering investing in a new 40-year project which will require an initial investment of $50,000 (with zero scrap value) and has a payback period of 20 years. The 40-year project has consistent cash flows each year.

What is the ROCE (using the average investment method)?

A   2.5%
B   10%
C   7.5%
D   5%   **(2 marks)**

99   An accountant is paid $30,000 per annum and spends 2 weeks working on appraising project Alpha.

Why should the accountant **NOT** charge half of his month's salary to the project?

A   Because his salary cannot be apportioned
B   Because his salary is not incremental
C   Because his salary is not a cash flow
D   Because his salary is an opportunity cost   **(2 marks)**

(Total = 20 marks)

MCQ bank – Investment appraisal using DCF

100   An investor has a cost of capital of 10%. She is due to receive a 5-year annuity starting in 3 years' time of $7,000 per annum.

What lump sum amount would you need to offer today to make her indifferent between the annuity and your offer?

A $26,537
B $19,936
C $16,667
D $21,924

(2 marks)

101   A newspaper reader has won first prize in a national competition and they have a choice as to how they take the prize:

Option 1   Take $90,000 per annum indefinitely starting in 3 years' time (and bequeath this right to their children and so on); or

Option 2   Take a lump sum of $910,000 in 1 year's time.

Assuming a cost of capital of 10%, which would you advise and why?

A   Option 1 because $90,000 pa indefinitely is an infinite amount of money compared to a one-off payment

B   Option 1 because it is worth more in present value terms

C   Option 2 because it is worth more in present value terms

D   Option 2 because the lump sum has the flexibility to be invested and earn a larger return than $90,000 pa

(2 marks)

The following information relates to questions 102 and 103.

JCW Co is appraising an opportunity to invest in some new machinery that has the following cash flows.

Initial investment	$40,000
Net cash inflows for 5 years in advance	$12,000 per annum
Decommissioning costs after 5 years	$15,000

102   At a cost of capital of 10% what is the net present value of this project (to the nearest $100)?

A   Negative $3,800
B   Positive $14,800
C   Positive $700
D   Negative $11,275

(2 marks)

103   What is the internal rate of return of the project (to the nearest whole %)?

A   12
B   10
C   14
D   9

(2 marks)

104 Four mutually exclusive projects have been appraised using net present value (NPV), internal rate of return (IRR), return on capital employed (ROCE) and payback period (PP). The company objective is to maximise shareholder wealth.

Which should be chosen?

	NPV	IRR	ROCE	PP
A Project A	$1m	40%	34%	4 years
B Project B	$1.1m	24%	35%	2.5 years
C Project C	$0.9m	18%	25%	3 years
D Project D	$1.5m	12%	18%	7 years

(2 marks)

105 Which of the following are advantages of the IRR approach to investment appraisal?

1   Clear decision rule
2   Takes into account the time value of money
3   Assumes funds are reinvested at the IRR
4   Considers the whole project

A   1, 2 and 4 only
B   2, 3 and 4 only
C   2 and 4 only
D   1, 2 and 3 only

(2 marks)

106 A project has an initial outflow followed by years of inflows.

What would be the effect on NPV and the IRR of an increase in the cost of capital?

	NPV	IRR
A	Decrease	Decrease
B	Increase	Decrease
C	Decrease	No change
D	Increase	No change

(2 marks)

107 A lease agreement has an NPV of ($26,496) at a rate of 8%. The lease involves an immediate down payment of $10,000 followed by 4 equal annual payments.

What is the amount of the annual payment?

A $11,020
B $4,981
C $11,513
D $14,039

(2 marks)

108 Which of the following statements about NPV and IRR is accurate?

A   Two NPV calculations are needed to estimate the IRR using linear interpolation.

B   The graphical approach to IRR is only an estimate; linear interpolation using the formula is required for a precise answer.

C   The IRR is unique.

D   An IRR graph with NPV on the 'Y' axis and discount rate on the 'X' axis will have a negative slope.

(2 marks)

109 Paulo plans to buy a holiday villa in five years' time for cash. He estimates the cost will be $1.5m. He plans to set aside the same amount of funds each year for five years, starting immediately and earning a rate of 10% interest per annum compound.

To the nearest $100, how much does he need to set aside each year?

A $223,400
B $245,600
C $359,800
D $395,600

(2 marks)

(Total = 20 marks)

MCQ bank – Allowing for tax and inflation

110   SW Co has a 31 December year end and pays corporation tax at a rate of 30%, 12 months after the end of
the year to which the cash flows relate. It can claim tax-allowable depreciation at a rate of 25% reducing
balance. It pays $1m for a machine on 31 December 20X4. SW Co's cost of capital is 10%.

What is the present value on 31 December 20X4 of the benefit of the first portion of tax-allowable
depreciation?

A $250,000
B $227,250
C $68,175
D $75,000

(2 marks)

111   A company receives a perpetuity of $20,000 per annum in arrears, and pays 30% corporation tax 12 months
after the end of the year to which the cash flows relate.

At a cost of capital of 10%, what is the after-tax present value of the perpetuity?

A $140,000
B $145,454
C $144,000
D $127,274

(2 marks)

112   A project has the following projected cash inflows.

Year 1   100,000
Year 2   125,000
Year 3   105,000

Working capital is required to be in place at the start of each year equal to 10% of the cash inflow for that
year. The cost of capital is 10%.

What is the present value of the working capital?

A $Nil
B $(30,036)
C $(2,735)
D $33,000

(2 marks)

113   AW Co needs to have $100,000 working capital in place immediately for the start of a 2-year project. The
amount will stay constant in real terms. Inflation is running at 10% per annum, and AW Co's money cost of
capital is 12%.

What is the present value of the cash flows relating to working capital?

A $(21,260)
B $(20,300)
C $(108,730)
D $(4,090)

(2 marks)

114   NCW Co is considering investing $10,000 immediately in a 1-year project with the following cash flows.

Income $100,000
Expenses $35,000

The cash flows will arise at the end of the year. The above are stated in current terms. Income is subject to
10% inflation; expenses will not vary. The real cost of capital is 8% and general inflation is 2%.

Using the money cost of capital to the nearest whole percentage, what is the net present value of the
project?

A $68,175
B $60,190
C $58,175
D $78,175

(2 marks)

115 AM Co will receive a perpetuity starting in 2 years' time of $10,000 per annum, increasing by the rate of inflation (which is 2%).

What is the present value of this perpetuity assuming a money cost of capital of 10.2%?

A $90,910
B $125,000
C $115,740
D $74,403

(2 marks)

116 FW Co is expecting a net of tax receipt of $10,000 (in real terms) in 1 year's time.

If FW Co expects inflation to increase, what impact will this have on the present value of that receipt?

A   Nil
B   Reduce
C   Increase
D   Cannot say

(2 marks)

117 Shadowline Co has a money cost of capital of 10%. If inflation is 4%, what is Shadowline Co's real cost of capital?

A   6%
B   5.8%
C   14%
D   14.4%

(2 marks)

118 Juicy Co is considering investing in a new industrial juicer for use on a new contract. It will cost $150,000 and will last 2 years. Juicy Co pays corporation tax at 30% (as the cash flows occur) and, due to the health benefits of juicing, the machine attracts 100% tax-allowable depreciation immediately.

Given a cost of capital of 10%, what is the minimum value of the pre-tax contract revenue receivable in two years which would be required to recover the net cost of the juicer?

A $150,000
B $105,000
C $127,050
D $181,500

(2 marks)

119 Which of the following is true about the 'inflation' figure that is included in the money cost of capital?

A   It is historic and specific to the business.
B   It is historic general inflation suffered by the investors.
C   It is expected and specific to the business.
D   It is expected general inflation suffered by the investors.

(2 marks)

(Total = 20 marks)

CBE style OTQ bank – Project appraisal and risk

120

Are the following statements true or false?

		True	False
(1)	The sensitivity of a project variable can be calculated by dividing the project net present value by the present value of the cash flows relating to that project variable.	☐	☐
(2)	The expected net present value is the value expected to occur if an investment project with several possible outcomes is undertaken once.	☐	☐
(3)	The discounted payback period is the time taken for the cumulative net present value to change from negative to positive.	☐	☐

121

An investment project has a cost of $12,000, payable at the start of the first year of operation. The possible future cash flows arising from the investment project have the following present values and associated probabilities:

PV of Year 1 cash flow $	Probability	PV of Year 2 cash flow $	Probability
16,000	0.15	20,000	0.75
12,000	0.60	(2,000)	0.25
(4,000)	0.25		

What is the expected value of the net present value of the investment project? (to the nearest $100)

$ ☐

(2 marks)

122 SAC Co has a cost of capital of 8% and is appraising project Gamma. It has the following cash flows.

T0	Investment	100,000
T1–5	Net cash inflow	40,000

What is the adjusted payback period for this project?

☐ 2.5 years
☐ Just under 3 years
☐ 2 years
☐ Just over 4 years

(2 marks)

123 A project has the following cash flows.

T0	Outflow	$110,000
T1–4	Inflow	$40,000

At the company's cost of capital of 10% the NPV of the project is $16,800.

Applying sensitivity analysis to the cost of capital, what percentage change in the cost of capital would cause the project NPV to fall to zero?

☐ 70%
☐ 17%
☐ 5%
☐ 41%

(2 marks)

A company has calculated the NPV of a new project as follows:

	Present value ($'000)
Sales revenue	4,000
Variable costs	(2,000)
Fixed costs	(500)
Corporation tax at 20%	(300)
Initial outlay	(1,000)
NPV	200

What is the sensitivity of the project decision to a change in sales volume?

☐ 12.5%

☐ 6.3%

☐ 10.0%

☐ 5.0%

(2 marks)

(Total = 10 marks)

125

Which of the following statements is correct?

☐ Tax-allowable depreciation is a relevant cash flow when evaluating borrowing to buy compared to leasing as a financing choice.

☐ Asset replacement decisions require relevant cash flows to be discounted by the after-tax cost of debt.

☐ If capital is rationed, divisible investment projects can be ranked by the profitability index when determining the optimum investment schedule.

☐ Government restrictions on bank lending are associated with soft capital rationing.   **(2 marks)**

126 PD Co is deciding whether to replace its delivery vans every year or every other year. The initial cost of a van is $20,000. Maintenance costs would be nil in the first year, and $5,000 at the end of the second year. Secondhand value would fall from $10,000 to $8,000 if it held onto the van for 2 years instead of just 1. PD Co's cost of capital is 10%.

How often should PD Co replace its vans, and what is the equivalent annual cost (EAC) of that option?

Replace every	EAC $
1	10,910
1	12,002
2	10,093
2	8,761

☐ ☐ ☐ ☐   **(2 marks)**

127 A lease versus buy evaluation has been performed. The management accountant performed the calculation by taking the saved initial outlay and deducting the tax-adjusted lease payments and the lost capital allowances. The accountant discounted the net cash flows at the post-tax cost of borrowing. The resultant net present value (NPV) was positive.

Assuming the calculation is free from arithmetical errors, what would the conclusion for this decision be?

☐ Lease is better than buy
☐ Buy is better than lease
☐ A further calculation is needed
☐ The discount rate was wrong so a conclusion cannot be drawn   **(2 marks)**

128 AB Co is considering either leasing an asset or borrowing to buy it, and is attempting to analyse the options by calculating the NPV of each. When comparing the two, AB Co is uncertain whether it should include interest payments in its option to 'borrow and buy' as it is a future, incremental cash flow associated with that option. AB Co is also uncertain which discount rate to use in the NPV calculation for the lease option.

How should AB Co treat the interest payments and what discount rate should it use?

	Include interest?	Discount rate
☐	Yes	After tax cost of the loan if they borrow and buy
☐	Yes	AB Co's weighted average cost of capital
☐	No	After-tax cost of the loan if they borrow and buy
☐	No	AB Co's weighted after cost of capital

(2 marks)

129   Which of the following is always true about capital rationing?

1   The profitability index is suitable for handling multiple-period capital rationing problems if projects are divisible.   ☐ ☐

2   Projects being divisible is an unrealistic assumption.   ☐ ☐

(2 marks)

The following information relates to questions 130 and 131.

NB Co is faced with an immediate capital constraint of $100m available to invest.

It is considering investing in four divisible projects:

	Initial cost $m	NPV $m
Project 1	40	4
Project 2	30	5
Project 3	50	6
Project 4	60	5

130   What is the NPV generated from the optimum investment programme?

$☐m

(2 marks)

131   What is the NPV generated from the optimum investment programme if the projects were indivisible?

$☐m

(2 marks)

132   Which of the following is potentially a benefit to the lessee if they lease as opposed to buy?

☐ Avoiding tax exhaustion
☐ Attracting lease customers that may not have been otherwise possible
☐ Exploiting a low cost of capital
☐ Potential future scrap proceeds

(2 marks)

133   A professional kitchen is attempting to choose between gas and electricity for its main heat source. Once a choice is made, the kitchen intends to keep to that source indefinitely. Each gas oven has an NPV of $50,000 over its useful life of 5 years. Each electric oven has an NPV of $68,000 over its useful life of 7 years. The cost of capital is 8%.

Which should the kitchen choose and why?

☐ Gas because its average NPV per year is higher than electric
☐ Electric because its NPV is higher than gas
☐ Electric because its equivalent annual benefit is higher
☐ Electric because it lasts longer than gas

(2 marks)

134   Which **TWO** of the following are typically benefits of a shorter replacement cycle?

☐ Higher scrap value
☐ Better company image and efficiency
☐ Lower annual depreciation
☐ Less time to benefit from owning the asset

(2 marks)

(Total = 20 marks)

Section B questions

Sensitivity analysis

The following scenario relates to questions 135–139.

A company is considering a project with the following cash flows.

Year	Initial investment $'000	Variable costs $'000	Cash inflows $'000	Net cash flows $'000
0	(11,000)			(11,000)
1		(3,200)	10,300	7,100
2		(3,200)	10,300	7,100

Cash flows arise from selling 1,030,000 units at $10 per unit. The company has a cost of capital of 9%.

The net present value (NPV) of the project is $1,490.

135   What is the sensitivity of the project to changes in sales volume (to 1 dp)?

    A   8.2%

    B   8.4%

    C   11.9%

    D   26.5%   **(2 marks)**

136   What is the discounted payback of the project?

    A   1.18 years

    B   1.25 years

    C   1.55 years

    D   1.75 years   **(2 marks)**

137   What is the internal rate of return (IRR) of the project (using discount rates of 15% and 20%)?

    A   18.9%

    B   21.2%

    C   24.2%

    D   44.3%   **(2 marks)**

138   **12/15**

Which of the following statements is true?

    A   The sensitivity of NPV to a change in sales volume can be calculated as NPV divided by the present value of future sales income.

    B   The certainty equivalent approach converts risky cash flows into riskless equivalent amounts which are discounted by a capital asset pricing model (CAPM) derived project-specific cost of capital.

    C   Using random numbers to generate possible values of project variables, a simulation model can generate a standard deviation of expected project outcomes.

    D   The problem with risk and uncertainty in investment appraisal is that neither can be quantified or measured.   **(2 marks)**

139   Which **TWO** of the following statements are true of the IRR and the NPV methods of appraisal?

1   IRR ignores the relative sizes of investments.

2   IRR is easy to use where there are non-conventional cash flows (eg cash flow changes from negative
       to positive and then back to negative over time).

3   NPV is widely used in practice.

4   IRR is technically superior to NPV.

A   1 and 2
B   1 and 3
C   2 and 4
D   3 and 4

(2 marks)

(Total = 10 marks)

Guilder Co

The following scenario relates to questions 140–144.

Guilder Co is appraising four different projects but is experiencing capital rationing in Year 0. No capital rationing is expected in future periods but none of the four projects that Guilder Co is considering can be postponed, so a decision must be made now. Guilder Co's cost of capital is 12%.

The following information is available.

Project	Outlay in Year 0 $	PV $	NPV $
Amster	100,000	111,400	11,400
Eind	56,000	62,580	6,580
Utrec	60,000	68,760	8,760
Tilbur	90,000	102,400	12,400

140 Arrange the projects in order of their preference to Guilder using the profitability index, with the most attractive first.

Order of preference (1st, 2nd etc)

Amster

Eind

Utrec

Tilbur

(2 marks)

141 Which of the following statements about Guilder Co's decision to use PI is true?

☐ The PI takes account of the absolute size of the individual projects.

☐ PI highlights the projects which are slowest in generating returns.

☐ PI can only be used if projects are divisible.

☐ PI allows for uncertainty about the outcome of each project.

(2 marks)

142 Several years later, there is no capital rationing and Guilder Co decides to replace an existing machine. Guilder Co has the choice of either a Super machine (lasting four years) or a Great machine (lasting three years).

The following present value table includes the figures for a Super machine.

	0	1	2	3	4
Maintenance costs		(20,000)	(29,000)	(32,000)	(35,000)
Investment and scrap	(250,000)				25,000
Net cash flow	(250,000)	(20,000)	(29,000)	(32,000)	10,000
Discount at 12%	1.000	0.893	0.797	0.712	0.636
Present values	(250,000)	(17,860)	(23,113)	(22,784)	(6,360)

Tax and tax-allowable depreciation should be ignored.

What is the equivalent annual cost (EAC) of the Super machine (to the nearest whole number)?

$ ☐

(2 marks)

143 Which of the following statements concerning Guilder Co's use of the EAC are true?

(1) The use of equivalent annual cost is appropriate in periods of high inflation.

(2) The EAC method assumes that the machine can be replaced by exactly the same machine in perpetuity.

☐ Both statements are true.

☐ Both statements are false.

☐ Statement 1 is true and statement 2 is false.

☐ Statement 1 is false and statement 2 is true. **(2 marks)**

144 The following potential cash flows are predicted for maintenance costs for the Great machine:

Year	Cash flow $	Probability
2	19,000	0.55
2	26,000	0.45
3	21,000	0.3
3	25,000	0.25
3	31,000	0.45

What is the expected present value of the maintenance costs for Year 2 (to the nearest whole number)?

$ ☐ **(2 marks)**

CBE style OT case Trecor Co (Specimen exam 2007, amended)

18 mins

The following scenario relates to questions 145–149.

Trecor Co plans to buy a machine costing $250,000 which will last for 4 years and then be sold for $5,000.
Net cash flows before tax are expected to be as follows.

	T_1	T_2	T_3	T_4
Net cash flow $	122,000	143,000	187,000	78,000

Depreciation is charged on a straight-line basis over the life of an asset.

145 Calculate the before-tax return on capital employed (accounting rate of return) based on the average investment (to the nearest whole percentage).

☐ %

(2 marks)

146 Are the following statements on return on capital employed (ROCE) true or false?

	True	False
If ROCE is less than the target ROCE then the purchase of the machine can be recommended.	☐	☐
ROCE can be used to compare two mutually exclusive projects.	☐	☐

(2 marks)

147 Trecor Co can claim tax-allowable depreciation on a 25% reducing balance basis. It pays tax at an annual rate of 30% one year in arrears.

What amount of tax relief would be received by Trecor in time 4 of a net present value (NPV) calculation?

$ ☐

(2 marks)

148 What is the payback period for the machine (to the nearest whole month)?

☐ year(s)   ☐ month(s)

(2 marks)

149 Which **TWO** of the following statements about the internal rate of return (IRR) are **TRUE**?

☐ IRR ignores the relative sizes of investments.
☐ IRR measures the increase in company value.
☐ IRR can incorporate discount rate changes during the life of the project.
☐ IRR and NPV sometimes give conflicting rankings over which project should be prioritised.

(2 marks)

(Total = 10 marks)

CBE style OT case BRT Co (6/11, amended)

18 mins

The following scenario relates to questions 150–154.

BRT Co has developed a new confectionery line that can be sold for $5.00 per box and that is expected to have continuing popularity for many years. The finance director has proposed that investment in the new product should be evaluated over a four-year time-horizon, even though sales would continue after the fourth year, on the grounds that cash flows after four years are too uncertain to be included.

The variable cost (in current price terms) will depend on sales volume, as follows.

Sales volume (boxes)	Less than 1 million	1–1.9 million	2–2.9 million	3–3.9 million
Variable cost ($ per box)	2.80	3.00	3.00	3.05

Forecast sales volumes are as follows.

Year		1	2	3	4
Demand (boxes)		0.7 million	1.6 million	2.1 million	3.0 million

Tax

Tax-allowable depreciation on a 25% reducing balance basis could be claimed on the cost of equipment. Profit tax of 30% per year will be payable one year in arrears. A balancing allowance would be claimed in the fourth year of operation.

Inflation

The average general level of inflation is expected to be 3% per year for the selling price and variable costs. BRT Co uses a nominal after-tax cost of capital of 12% to appraise new investment projects.

A trainee accountant at BRT Co has started a spreadsheet to calculate the net present value (NPV) of a proposed new project.

	A	B	C	D	E	F	G
1	Year	0	1	2	3	4	5
2		$'000	$'000	$'000	$'000	$'000	$'000
3	Inflated sales						
4	Inflated variable costs						
5	Fixed costs		(1,030)	(1,910)	(3,060)	(4,277)	
6	Net cash flow		556	1,485	1,530	2,308	
7	Taxation						
8	Tax benefits						
9	Working capital	(750)	(23)	(23)	(24)	750	
10	Investment	(2,000)					
11	Project cash flows						
12	Discount factor 12%	1.000	0.893	0.797	0.712	0.636	0.567
13	Present value						

150   What is the sales figure for Year 2 (cell D3 in the spreadsheet), to the nearest $'000?

$⬚'000

(2 marks)

151   What are the variable costs for Year 3 (cell E4 in the spreadsheet), to the nearest $'000?

$⬚'000

(2 marks)

152   What are the tax benefits generated by the tax-allowable depreciation on the equipment in Year 4 (cell F8), to the nearest $'000?

$⬚'000

(2 marks)

153 Which of the following statements about the project appraisal are true/false?

	True	False
The trainee accountant has used the wrong percentage for the cost of capital.	☐	☐
Ignoring sales after four years underestimates the value of the project.	☐	☐
The working capital figure in Year 4 is wrong.	☐	☐

(2 marks)

154 The trainee accountant at BRT Co has calculated the internal rate of return (IRR) for the project.

Are the following statements true or false?

1 When cash flow patterns are conventional, the NPV and IRR methods will give the same accept or reject decision.

2 The project is financially viable under IRR if it exceeds the cost of capital.

☐ Both statements are true.
☐ Both statements are false.
☐ Statement 1 is true and statement 2 is false.
☐ Statement 2 is true and statement 1 is false.

(2 marks)

(Total = 10 marks)

Section C questions

155 Calvic Co

36 mins

Calvic Co services custom cars and provides its clients with a courtesy car while servicing is taking place. It has a fleet of 10 courtesy cars which it plans to replace in the near future. Each new courtesy car will cost $15,000. The trade-in value of each new car declines over time as follows:

Age of courtesy car (years)	1	2	3
Trade-in value ($/car)	11,250	9,000	6,200

Servicing and parts will cost $1,000 per courtesy car in the first year and this cost is expected to increase by 40% per year as each vehicle grows older. Cleaning the interior and exterior of each courtesy car to keep it up to the standard required by Calvic's clients will cost $500 per car in the first year and this cost is expected to increase by 25% per year.

Calvic Co has a cost of capital of 10%. Ignore taxation.

Required

(a) Using the equivalent annual cost method, calculate whether Calvic Co should replace its fleet after one year, two years, or three years.
(12 marks)

(b) Explain how an organisation can determine the best way to invest available capital under capital rationing. Your answer should refer to single-period capital rationing, project divisibility and the investment of surplus funds.
(8 marks)

(Total = 20 marks)

156 Project E (6/14, amended)

36 mins

Project E is a strategically important project which the board of OAP Co has decided must be undertaken in order for the company to remain competitive, regardless of its financial acceptability. The project has a life of four years. Information relating to the future cash flows of this project are as follows:

Year	1	2	3	4
Sales volume (units)	12,000	13,000	10,000	10,000
Selling price ($/unit)	450	475	500	570
Variable cost ($/unit)	260	280	295	320
Fixed costs ($'000)	750	750	750	750

These forecasts are before taking into account of selling price inflation of 5.0% per year, variable cost inflation of 6.0% per year and fixed cost inflation of 3.5% per year. The fixed costs are incremental fixed costs which are associated with Project E. At the end of 4 years, machinery from the project will be sold for scrap with a value of $400,000. Tax-allowable depreciation on the initial investment cost of Project E is available on a 25% reducing balance basis and OAP Co pays corporation tax of 28% per year, one year in arrears. A balancing charge or allowance is available at the end of the fourth year of operation.

OAP Co has a nominal after-tax cost of capital of 13% per year. The initial investment for Project E is $5,000,000.

Required

(a) Calculate the nominal after-tax net present value of Project E and comment on the financial acceptability of this project.
(14 marks)

(b) Discuss the reasons why the board of OAP Co may decide to limit the funds that are available to finance projects.
(6 marks)

(Total = 20 marks)

157 AGD Co (FMC, 12/05, amended)   36 mins

AGD Co is a profitable company which is considering the purchase of a machine costing $320,000. If purchased, AGD Co would incur annual maintenance costs of $25,000. The machine would be used for 3 years and at the end of this period would be sold for $50,000. Alternatively, the machine could be obtained under a 3-year lease for an annual lease rental of $120,000 per year, payable in advance. The lease agreement would also provide insurance and maintenance for a three-year period. The lease also contains an annual break clause allowing the lease to be exited at the lessee's discretion.

AGD Co can claim tax-allowable depreciation on a 25% reducing balance basis. The company pays tax on profits at an annual rate of 30% and all tax liabilities are paid one year in arrears. AGD Co has an accounting year that ends on 31 December. If the machine is purchased, payment will be made in January of the first year of operation. If leased, annual lease rentals will be paid in January of each year of operation.

Required

(a) Using an after-tax borrowing rate of 7%, evaluate whether AGD Co should purchase or lease the new machine.

(12 marks)

(b) Discuss whether the lease may also provide non-financial benefits.   **(5 marks)**

(c) Explain the difference between risk and uncertainty in the context of investment appraisal.   **(3 marks)**

(Total = 20 marks)

158 Basril Co (FMC, 12/03, amended)   36 mins

Basril Co is reviewing investment proposals that have been submitted by divisional managers. The investment funds of the company are limited to $800,000 in the current year. Details of three possible investments, none of which can be delayed, are given below.

Project 1

An investment of $300,000 in workstation assessments. Each assessment would be on an individual employee basis and would lead to savings in labour costs from increased efficiency and from reduced absenteeism due to work-related illness. Savings in labour costs from these assessments in money terms are expected to be as follows:

Year	1	2	3	4	5
Cash flows ($'000)	85	90	95	100	95

Project 2

An investment of $450,000 in individual workstations for staff that is expected to reduce administration costs by $140,800 per annum in money terms for the next 5 years.

Project 3

An investment of $400,000 in new ticket machines. Net cash savings of $120,000 per annum are expected in current price terms and these are expected to increase by 3.6% per annum due to inflation during the 5-year life of the machines.

Basril Co has a money cost of capital of 12% and taxation should be ignored.

Required

(a) Determine the best way for Basril Co to invest the available funds and calculate the resultant net present value:

    (i)   On the assumption that each of the three projects is divisible   **(7 marks)**
    (ii) On the assumption that none of the projects are divisible   **(3 marks)**

(b) Explain how cash shortages can restrict the investment opportunities of a business.   **(5 marks)**

(c) Discuss the meaning of the term 'relevant cash flows' in the context of investment appraisal, giving examples to illustrate your discussion.   **(5 marks)**

(Total = 20 marks)

159 Degnis Co (Mar/June 16, amended)

Degnis Co is a company which installs kitchens and bathrooms to customer specifications. It is planning to invest $4,000,000 in a new facility to convert vans and trucks into motorhomes. Each motorhome will be designed and built according to customer requirements.

Degnis Co expects motorhome production and sales in the first four years of operation to be as follows.

Year	1	2	3	4
Motorhomes produced and sold	250	300	450	450

The selling price for a motorhome depends on the van or truck which is converted, the quality of the units installed and the extent of conversion work required.

Degnis Co has undertaken research into likely sales and costs of different kinds of motorhomes which could be selected by customers, as follows:

Motorhome type:	Basic	Standard	Deluxe
Probability of selection	20%	45%	35%
Selling price ($/unit)	30,000	42,000	72,000
Conversion cost ($/unit)	23,000	29,000	40,000

Fixed costs of the production facility are expected to depend on the volume of motorhome production as follows:

Production volume (units/year)	200–299	300–399	400–499
Fixed costs ($'000/year)	4,000	5,000	5,500

Degnis Co pays corporation tax of 28% per year, with the tax liability being settled in the year in which it arises. The company can claim tax-allowable depreciation on the cost of the investment on a straight-line basis over ten years.

Degnis Co evaluates investment projects using an after-tax discount rate of 11%.

Required

(a) Calculate the expected net present value of the planned investment for the first four years of operation.

(7 marks)

(b) After the fourth year of operation, Degnis Co expects to continue to produce and sell 450 motorhomes per year for the foreseeable future.

Required

Calculate the effect on the expected net present value of the planned investment of continuing to produce and sell motorhomes beyond the first four years and comment on the financial acceptability of the planned investment.

(3 marks)

(c) Critically discuss the use of probability analysis in incorporating risk into investment appraisal. (5 marks)

(d) Discuss the reasons why investment finance may be limited, even when a company has attractive investment opportunities available to it.

(5 marks)

(Total = 20 marks)

160 Warden Co (12/11, amended)

36 mins

Warden Co plans to buy a new machine. The cost of the machine, payable immediately, is $800,000 and the machine has an expected life of 5 years. Additional investment in working capital of $90,000 will be required at the start of the first year of operation. At the end of 5 years, the machine will be sold for scrap, with the scrap value expected to be 5% of the initial purchase cost of the machine. The machine will not be replaced.

Production and sales from the new machine are expected to be 100,000 units per year. Each unit can be sold for $16 per unit and will incur variable costs of $11 per unit. Incremental fixed costs arising from the operation of the machine will be $160,000 per year.

Warden Co has an after-tax cost of capital of 11% which it uses as a discount rate in investment appraisal. The company pays profit tax one year in arrears at an annual rate of 30% per year. Tax-allowable depreciation and inflation should be ignored.

Required

(a) Calculate the net present value of investing in the new machine and advise whether the investment is financially acceptable. **(8 marks)**

(b) Calculate the internal rate of return (IRR) of investing in the new machine and advise whether the investment is financially acceptable. **(4 marks)**

(c) (i) Explain briefly the meaning of the term 'sensitivity analysis' in the context of investment appraisal. **(2 marks)**

(ii) Using the IRR you calculated in part (b), calculate the sensitivity of the investment in the new machine to a change in selling price and to a change in discount rate, and comment on your findings. **(6 marks)**

(Total = 20 marks)

161 BQK Co (12/12, amended)

36 mins

BQK Co, a house-building company, plans to build 100 houses on a development site over the next 4 years. The purchase cost of the development site is $4,000,000, payable at the start of the first year of construction. Two types of house will be built, with annual sales of each house expected to be as follows:

Year	1	2	3	4
Number of small houses sold:	15	20	15	5
Number of large houses sold:	7	8	15	15

Houses are built in the year of sale. Each customer finances the purchase of a home by taking out a long-term personal loan from their bank. Financial information relating to each type of house is as follows:

	Small house	Large house
Selling price:	$200,000	$350,000
Variable cost of construction:	$100,000	$200,000

Selling prices and variable cost of construction are in current price terms, before allowing for selling price inflation of 3% per year and variable cost of construction inflation of 4.5% per year.

Fixed infrastructure costs of $1,500,000 per year in current price terms would be incurred. These would not relate to any specific house, but would be for the provision of new roads, gardens, drainage and utilities. Infrastructure cost inflation is expected to be 2% per year.

BQK Co pays profit tax one year in arrears at an annual rate of 30%. The company can claim tax-allowable depreciation on the purchase cost of the development site on a straight-line basis over the four years of construction.

BQK Co has a real after-tax cost of capital of 9% per year and a nominal after-tax cost of capital of 12% per year. New investments are required by the company to have a before-tax return on capital employed (accounting rate of return) on an average investment basis of 20% per year.

Required

(a) Calculate the net present value of the proposed investment and comment on its financial acceptability. Work to the nearest $1,000. **(13 marks)**

(b) Discuss the effect of a substantial rise in interest rates on the financing cost of BQK Co and its customers, and on the capital investment appraisal decision-making process of BQK Co. **(7 marks)**

(Total = 20 marks)

162 Uftin Co (12/14, amended)   36 mins

Uftin Co is a large company which is listed on a major stock market. The company has been evaluating an investment proposal to manufacture Product K3J. The initial investment of $1,800,000 will be payable at the start of the first year of operation. The following draft evaluation has been prepared by a junior employee.

Year	1	2	3	4
Sales (units/year)	95,000	100,000	150,000	150,000
Selling price ($/unit)	25	25	26	27
Variable costs ($/unit)	11	12	12	13

Note. The above selling prices and variable costs per unit have not been inflated.

	$'000	$'000	$'000	$'000
Sales revenue	2,475	2,605	4,064	4,220
Variable costs	(1,097)	(1,260)	(1,890)	(2,048)
Fixed costs	(155)	(155)	(155)	(155)
Interest payments	(150)	(150)	(150)	(150)
Cash flow before tax	1,073	1,040	1,869	1,867
Tax-allowable depreciation	(450)	(450)	(450)	(450)
Taxable profit	623	590	1,419	1,417
Taxation		(137)	(130)	(312)
Net cash flow	623	453	1,289	1,105
Discount at 12%	0.893	0.797	0.712	0.636
Present values	556	361	918	703

	$'000
Present value of cash inflows	2,538
Cost of machine	(1,800)
NPV	738

The junior employee also provided the following information:

(1) Relevant fixed costs are forecast to be $150,000 per year.

(2) Sales and production volumes are the same and no finished goods inventory is held.

(3) The corporation tax rate is 22% per year and tax liabilities are payable one year in arrears.

(4) Uftin Co can claim tax-allowable depreciation of 25% per year on a reducing balance basis on the initial investment.

(5) A balancing charge or allowance can be claimed at the end of the fourth year.

(6) It is expected that selling price inflation will be 4.2% per year, variable cost inflation will be 5% per year and fixed cost inflation will be 3% per year.

(7) The investment has no scrap value.

(8) The investment will be partly financed by a $1,500,000 loan at 10% per year.

(9) Uftin Co has a weighted average cost of capital of 12% per year.

Required

(a) Prepare a revised draft evaluation of the investment proposal and comment on its financial acceptability.

(11 marks)

(b) Explain any **TWO** revisions you have made to the draft evaluation in part (a) above. **(4 marks)**

(c) Discuss **TWO** ways of incorporating risk into the investment appraisal process. **(5 marks)**

(Total = 20 marks)

163 Hraxin Co (6/15, amended)   36 mins

Hraxin Co is appraising an investment project which has an expected life of four years and which will not be repeated. The initial investment, payable at the start of the first year of operation, is $5m. Scrap value of $500,000 is expected to arise at the end of 4 years.

There is some uncertainty about what price can be charged for the units produced by the investment project, as this is expected to depend on the future state of the economy. The following forecast of selling prices and their probabilities has been prepared:

Future economic state	Weak	Medium	Strong
Probability of future economic state	35%	50%	15%
Selling price in current price terms	$25 per unit	$30 per unit	$35 per unit

These selling prices are expected to be subject to annual inflation of 4% per year, regardless of which economic state prevails in the future.

Forecast sales and production volumes, and total nominal variable costs, have already been forecast, as follows:

Year	1	2	3	4
Sales and production (units)	150,000	250,000	400,000	300,000
Nominal variable cost ($'000)	2,385	4,200	7,080	5,730

Incremental overheads of $400,000 per year in current price terms will arise as a result of undertaking the investment project. A large proportion of these overheads relate to energy costs which are expected to increase sharply in the future because of energy supply shortages, so overhead inflation of 10% per year is expected.

The initial investment will attract tax-allowable depreciation on a straight-line basis over the four-year project life. The rate of corporation tax is 30% and tax liabilities are paid in the year in which they arise. Hraxin Co has traditionally used a nominal after-tax discount rate of 11% per year for investment appraisal.

Required

(a) Calculate the expected net present value of the investment project and comment on its financial acceptability. **(9 marks)**

(b) Distinguish between risk and uncertainty and briefly explain why they should be considered in the investment appraisal process. **(5 marks)**

(c) Critically discuss if sensitivity analysis will assist Hraxin Co in assessing the risk of the investment project. **(6 marks)**

(Total = 20 marks)

164 Vyxyn Co (Mar/Jun 17)

36 mins

Vyxyn Co is evaluating a planned investment in a new product costing $20m, payable at the start of the first year of operation. The product will be produced for four years, at the end of which production will cease. The investment project will have a terminal value of zero. Financial information relating to the investment project is as follows:

Year	1	2	3	4
Sales volume (units/year)	440,000	550,000	720,000	400,000
Selling price ($/unit)	26.50	28.50	30.00	26.00
Fixed cost ($/year)	1,100,000	1,121,000	1,155,000	1,200,00

These selling prices have not yet been adjusted for selling price inflation, which is expected to be 3.5% per year. The annual fixed costs are given above in nominal terms.

Variable cost per unit depends on whether competition is maintained between suppliers of key components. The purchasing department has made the following forecast:

Competition	Strong	Moderate	Weak
Probability	45%	35%	20%
Variable cost ($/unit)	10.80	12.00	14.70

The variable costs in this forecast are before taking account of variable cost inflation of 4.0% per year.

Vyxyn Co can claim tax-allowable depreciation on a 25% per year reducing balance basis on the full investment cost of $20m and pays corporation tax of 28% per year one year in arrears.

It is planned to finance the investment project with an issue of 8% loan notes, redeemable in ten years' time. Vyxyn Co has a nominal after-tax weighted average cost of capital of 10%, a real after-tax weighted average cost of capital of 7% and a cost of equity of 11%.

Required

(a) Discuss the difference between risk and uncertainty in relation to investment appraisal. **(3 marks)**

(b) Calculate the expected net present value of the investment project and comment on its financial acceptability and on the risk relating to variable cost. **(9 marks)**

(c) Critically discuss how risk can be considered in the investment appraisal process. **(8 marks)**

(Total = 20 marks)

165 Pelta Co (Sep/Dec 17)

36 mins

The directors of Pelta Co are considering a planned investment project costing $25m, payable at the start of the first year of operation. The following information relates to the investment project:

	Year 1	Year 2	Year 3	Year 4
Sales volume (units/year)	520,000	624,000	717,000	788,000
Selling price ($/unit)	30.00	30.00	30.00	30.00
Variable costs ($/unit)	10.00	10.20	10.61	10.93
Fixed costs ($/year)	700,000	735,000	779,000	841,000

This information needs adjusting to take account of selling price inflation of 4% per year and variable cost inflation of 3% per year. The fixed costs, which are incremental and related to the investment project, are in nominal terms. The year 4 sales volume is expected to continue for the foreseeable future.

Pelta Co pays corporation tax of 30% one year in arrears. The company can claim tax-allowable depreciation on a 25% reducing balance basis.

The views of the directors of Pella Co are that all investment projects must be evaluated over four years of operations, with an assumed terminal value at the end of the fourth year of 5% of the initial investment cost. Both net present value and discounted payback must be used, with a maximum discounted payback period of two years. The real after-tax cost of capital of Pelta Co is 7% and its nominal after-tax cost of capital is 12%.

Required

(a)	(i)	Calculate the net present value of the planned investment project.	**(9 marks)**
	(ii)	Calculate the discounted payback period of the planned investment project.	**(2 marks)**
(b)		Discuss the financial acceptability of the investment project.	**(3 marks)**
(c)		Critically discuss the views of the directors on Pelta Co's investment appraisal.	**(6 marks)**

(Total = 20 marks)

MCQ bank – Sources of finance

18 mins

166 Which of the following statements about bonds are true?

1 Unsecured bonds are likely to require a higher yield to maturity than equivalent secured bonds.

2 Convertible bonds give the borrower the right but not the obligation to turn the bond into a predetermined number of ordinary shares.

3 A Eurobond is a bond that is denominated in a currency which is not native to where the bond itself is issued.

A 1 and 2
B 1 and 3
C 2 and 3
D 1, 2 and 3

(2 marks)

167 According to the creditor hierarchy, list the following from high risk to low risk:

1 Ordinary share capital
2 Preference share capital
3 Trade payables
4 Bank loan with fixed and floating charges

A 1, 2, 3, 4
B 2, 1, 4, 3
C 1, 2, 4, 3
D 4, 1, 2, 3

(2 marks)

168 Alpha is a listed company with a share price of $2 per share. It announces a 1 for 4 rights issue at $1.60 per share.

What is the theoretical ex-rights price?

A $2.40
B $1.80
C $1.68
D $1.92

(2 marks)

169 Which of the following best describes the term 'coupon rate' as it applies to bonds?

A Return received taking into account capital repayment as well as interest payments
B Annual interest received as a percentage of the nominal value of the bond
C Annual interest received as a percentage of the ex interest market price of the bond
D Annual interest received as a percentage of the cum-interest market price of the bond

(2 marks)

170 Which of the following describes a sukuk?

A A bond in Islamic finance where the lender owns the underlying asset and shares in the risks and rewards of ownership

B Equity in Islamic finance where profits are shared according to a pre-agreed contract – dividends are not paid as such

C Trade credit in Islamic finance where a pre-agreed mark-up is agreed in advance for the convenience of paying later

D A lease in Islamic finance where the lessor retains ownership and the risk and rewards of ownership of the underlying asset

(2 marks)

(Total = 10 marks)

MCQ bank – Dividend policy

171 Which of the following are assumptions for Modigliani and Miller's dividend irrelevance theory?

1 Perfect capital markets
2 No taxes or tax preferences
3 No transaction costs
4 No inflation

A 1, 2 and 3 only
B 1, 2 and 4 only
C 2, 3 and 4 only
D 1, 2, 3 and 4

(2 marks)

172 In which of the following situations is a residual dividend most likely to be appropriate?

A A large publicly listed company

B A small family-owned private company where the majority of the shareholders use dividend income to pay their living costs

C A small listed company owned by investors seeking maximum capital growth on their investment

D In a tax regime where individuals pay less tax on dividend income than on capital gains   **(2 marks)**

173 In Modigliani and Miller's dividend irrelevance theory, the process of 'manufacturing dividends' refers to which of the following?

A Dividends from manufacturing businesses
B Investors selling some shares to realise some capital gain
C Creative accounting to allow dividends to be paid
D Investing plans designed to create regular returns to shareholders

(2 marks)

174   **12/14**

Which of the following statements is correct?

A A bonus issue can be used to raise new equity finance.
B A share repurchase scheme can increase both earnings per share and gearing.
C Miller and Modigliani argued that the financing decision is more important than the dividend decision.
D Shareholders usually have the power to increase dividends at annual general meetings of a company.

(2 marks)

175 Three companies (Sun Co, Moon Co and Nite Co) have the following dividend payments history:

Company	20X1	20X2	20X3
Sun Co – Dividend	100	110	121
Sun Co – Earnings	200	200	201
Moon Co – Dividend	50	150	25
Moon Co – Earnings	100	300	50
Nite Co – Dividend	nil	300	nil
Nite Co – Earnings	400	350	500

Which best describes their apparent dividend policies?

	Sun Co	Moon Co	Nite Co	
A	Constant growth	Constant payout	Residual	
B	Constant payout	Constant growth	Residual	
C	High payout	Residual	Constant payout	
D	Constant growth	Residual	Constant payout	**(2 marks)**

(Total = 10 marks)

MCQ bank – Gearing and capital structure

176   A summary of HM Co's recent statement of profit or loss is given below:

	$'000
Revenue	10,123
Cost of sales	(7,222)
Gross profit	2,901
Expenses	(999)
Profit before interest and tax	1,902
Interest	(1,000)
Tax	(271)
Profit after interest and tax	631

70% of cost of sales and 10% of expenses are variable costs.

What is HM Co's operational gearing?

A   7.87
B   0.71
C   2.61
D   0.40   **(2 marks)**

177   The following is an extract of ELW's statement of financial position.

	$m	$m
Total assets		1,000
$1 ordinary share capital	100	
Retained earnings	400	
Total equity	500	
Loan notes	500	
		1,000

The ordinary shares are currently quoted at $5.50, and loan notes are trading at $125 per $100 nominal.

What is ELW's financial gearing ratio (debt/debt+equity) using market values?

A   40%
B   56%
C   57%
D   53%   **(2 marks)**

178   **12/14**

The following are extracts from the statement of financial position of a company:

	$'000	$'000
Equity		
Ordinary shares	8,000	
Reserves	20,000	
		28,000
Non-current liabilities		
Bonds	4,000	
Bank loans	6,200	
Preference shares	2,000	
		12,200

	$'000	$'000
Current liabilities		
Overdraft	1,000	
Trade payables	1,500	
		2,500
Total equity and liabilities		42,700

The ordinary shares have a nominal value of 50 cents per share and are trading at $5.00 per share. The preference shares have a nominal value of $1.00 per share and are trading at 80 cents per share. The bonds have a nominal value of $100 and are trading at $105 per bond.

What is the market value based gearing of the company, defined as prior charge capital/equity?

A   15.0%
B   13.0%
C   11.8%
D   7.3%   **(2 marks)**

179   AB Co has an interest cover greater than one and gearing (debt/debt + equity) of 50%.

What will be the impact on interest cover and gearing of issuing shares to repay half the debt?

	Interest cover	*Gearing*
A	Rise	Rise
B	Rise	Fall
C	Fall	Rise
D	Fall	Fall

                                                                         (2 marks)

180   All else being equal, a poor set of results and lower dividends that aren't as bad as shareholders were expecting would probably have the following impact:

	P/E ratio	*Dividend yield*
A	Increase	Increase
B	Increase	Decrease
C	Decrease	Increase
D	Decrease	Decrease

                                                                         (2 marks)

181   The following are extracts from the statement of financial position of a company:

	$'000	$'000
Equity		
Ordinary shares	8,000	
Reserves	20,000	
		28,000
Non-current liabilities		
Bonds	4,000	
Bank loans	6,200	
Preference shares	2,000	
		12,200
Current liabilities		
Overdraft	1,000	
Trade payables	1,500	
		2,500
		42,700

The ordinary shares have a nominal value of 50 cents per share and are trading at $5.00 per share. The preference shares have a nominal value of $1.00 per share and are trading at 80 cents per share. The bonds have a nominal value of $100 and are trading at $105 per bond.

What is the market value based gearing of the company, defined as prior charge capital/equity?

A   15.0%
B   13.0%
C   11.8%
D   7.3%

(2 marks)

182   Which of the following are handicaps that young SMEs face in accessing funds?

1   Uncertainty and risk for lenders
2   Financial statements are not sufficiently detailed
3   Shares cannot be placed privately

A   1 and 3 only
B   1 and 2 only
C   2 and 3 only
D   1, 2 and 3

(2 marks)

183   The following statements relate to small and medium-sized enterprises (SMEs).

1   Medium-term loans are harder to obtain than longer-term loans for SMEs.
2   SMEs are prone to funding gaps.

Are the statements true or false?

A   Statement 1 is true and statement 2 is false.
B   Statement 2 is true and statement 1 is false.
C   Both statements are true.
D   Both statements are false.

(2 marks)

184   Private individuals or groups of individuals can invest directly into a small business.

What is this known as?

A   Reverse factoring
B   Supply chain finance
C   Venture capital
D   Business angel financing

(2 marks)

185   The following statements relate to supply chain finance (SCF).

1   SCF is considered to be financial debt.
2   SCF allows an SME to raise finance at a lower interest rate than would normally be available to it.

Are the statements true or false?

A   Statement 1 is true and statement 2 is false.
B   Statement 2 is true and statement 1 is false.
C   Both statements are true.
D   Both statements are false.

(2 marks)

(Total = 20 marks)

CBE style OTQ bank – The cost of capital

186 GG Co has a cost of equity of 25%. It has 4 million shares in issue, and has done for many years.

Its dividend payments in the years 20X9 to 20Y3 were as follows.

End of year	Dividends $'000
20X9	220
20Y0	257
20Y1	310
20Y2	356
20Y3	423

Dividends are expected to continue to grow at the same average rate into the future.

According to the dividend valuation model, what should be the share price at the start of 20Y4 (to 2 decimal places)?

$ _____ **(2 marks)**

187 IPA Co is about to pay a $0.50 dividend on each ordinary share. Its earnings per share was $1.50.

Net assets per share is $6. Current share price is $4.50 per share.

What is the cost of equity (to the nearest whole percentage)?

_____ % **(2 marks)**

188 Which of the following best describes systematic risk?

☐ The chance that automated processes may fail
☐ The risk associated with investing in equity
☐ The diversifiable risk associated with investing in equity
☐ The residual risk associated with investing in a well-diversified portfolio **(2 marks)**

189 A share in MS Co has an equity beta of 1.3. MS Co's debt beta is 0.1. It has a gearing ratio of 20% (debt : equity). The market premium is 8% and the risk-free rate is 3%. MS Co pays 30% corporation tax.

What is the cost of equity for MS Co?

_____ % **(2 marks)**

190 **12/14**

Are the following statements true or false?

		True	False
1	An increase in the cost of equity leads to a fall in share price.	☐	☐
2	Investors faced with increased risk will expect increased return as compensation.	☐	☐
3	The cost of debt is usually lower than the cost of preference shares.	☐	☐

(2 marks)

191 BRW Co has 10% redeemable loan notes in issue trading at $90. The loan notes are redeemable at a 10% premium in 5 years' time, or convertible at that point into 20 ordinary shares. The current share price is $2.50 and is expected to grow at 10% per annum for the foreseeable future. BRW Co pays 30% corporation tax.

What is the best estimate of the cost of these loan notes (to 1 decimal place)?

_____ % **(2 marks)**

192   IDO Co has a capital structure as follows.

	$m
10m $0.50 ordinary shares	5
Reserves	20
13% irredeemable loan notes	7
	32

The ordinary shares are currently quoted at $3.00, and the loan notes at $90. IDO Co has a cost of equity of 12% and pays corporation tax at a rate of 30%.

What is IDO Co's weighted average cost of capital (WACC)?

⬚ %

(2 marks)

193   Which of the following are assumed if a company's current WACC is to be used to appraise a potential project?

		True	False
1	Capital structure will remain unchanged for the duration of the project.	☐	☐
2	The business risk of the project is the same as the current business operations.	☐	☐
3	The project is relatively small in size.	☐	☐

(2 marks)

194
6/15

On a market value basis, GFV Co is financed 70% by equity and 30% by debt. The company has an after-tax cost of debt of 6% and an equity beta of 1.2. The risk-free rate of return is 4% and the equity risk premium is 5%.

What is the after-tax weighted average cost of capital of GFV Co? (to 1 decimal place)

⬚ %

195   An 8% irredeemable $0.50 preference share is being traded for $0.30 cum-div currently in a company that pays corporation tax at a rate of 30%.

What is the cost of capital for these preference shares (to 1 decimal place)?

⬚ %

(2 marks)

(Total = 20 marks)

CBE style OTQ bank – Capital structure

196   Alf Co's gearing is 1:1 debt : equity. The industry average is 1:5. Alf Co is looking to raise finance for investment in a new project and it is wondering whether to raise debt or equity.

Applying the traditional view, which of the following is true?

- [ ] It should take on debt finance, as to do so will save tax.
- [ ] It should take on equity finance, as their gearing is probably beyond optimal.
- [ ] It doesn't matter, as it won't affect the returns the projects generate.
- [ ] More information is needed before a decision can be made.

(2 marks)

197   Why do Modigliani and Miller (with tax) assume increased gearing will reduce the weighted average cost of capital (WACC)?

- [ ] Debt is cheaper than equity.
- [ ] Interest payments are tax deductible.
- [ ] Reduced levels of expensive equity capital will reduce the WACC.
- [ ] Financial risk is not pronounced at moderate borrowing levels.

(2 marks)

198   **6/15**

Are the following statements true or false?

		True	False
(1)	The asset beta reflects both business risk and financial risk	[ ]	[ ]
(2)	Total risk is the sum of systematic risk and unsystematic risk	[ ]	[ ]
(3)	Assuming that the beta of debt is zero will understate financial risk when ungearing an equity beta	[ ]	[ ]

(2 marks)

199   Director A believes there is an optimal balance of debt : equity whereas Director B does not believe that the gearing decision affects the value of the business.

Match the capital structure theory that best reflects each of directors's beliefs.

Theory
Traditional view
M&M (no tax)
M&M (with tax)
Pecking order

Name
Director A
Director B

(2 marks)

200   Pecking order theory suggests finance should be raised in which order?

- [ ] Internal funds, rights issue, debt
- [ ] Internal funds, debt, new equity
- [ ] Debt, internal funds, new equity
- [ ] Rights issue, internal funds, debt

(2 marks)

The following information relates to questions 201 and 202.

TR Co has a gearing level of 1:3 debt : equity. TR is considering diversifying into a new market without changing its existing gearing. B Co is already operating in the new market. B Co has an equity beta of 1.05 and a gearing level of 1:4 debt : equity. Both companies pay 30% corporation tax.

201   What is the asset beta relevant to TR for the new market (to 2 dp)?

☐

(2 marks)

202   The risk-free rate is 4% and the market premium is 4%.

What is TR Co's cost of equity for assessing the decision to diversify into the new market (to 1 decimal place)?

☐%

(2 marks)

203   Why is an asset beta generally lower than an equity beta?

☐ An equity beta also includes an element of financial risk.

☐ Returns from assets are tax deductible.

☐ Asset betas contain less business risk.

☐ Capital markets are generally more efficient than business operations.   **(2 marks)**

204   When should a project-specific cost of capital be used for investment appraisal?

☐ If new finance is required before the project can go ahead

☐ If the project is small

☐ If the project is different from current operations

☐ If the project is the same as current operations   **(2 marks)**

205   **12/15**

Leah Co is an all-equity financed company which wishes to appraise a project in a new area of business. Its existing equity beta is 1.2. The average equity beta for the new business area is 2.0, with an average debt/debt plus equity ratio of 25%. The risk-free rate of return is 5% and the market risk premium is 4%.

Ignoring taxation and using the capital asset pricing model, what is the risk-adjusted cost of equity for the new project?

☐ 8.6%

☐ 9.8%

☐ 11.0%

☐ 13.0%

(2 marks)

(Total = 20 marks)

Section B questions

CBE style OT case IML Co

18 mins

The following scenario relates to questions 206–210.

IML Co is an all-equity financed listed company. Nearly all its shares are held by financial institutions.

IML has recently appointed a new finance director who advocates using the capital asset pricing model as a means of evaluating risk and interpreting stock market reaction to the company.

The following initial information has been put forward by the finance director for a rival company operating in the same industry:

	Equity beta
AZT Co	0.7

The finance director notes that the risk-free rate is 5% each year and the expected rate of return on the market portfolio is 15% each year.

206 Calculate, using the capital asset pricing model, the required rate of return on equity of AZT Co.

☐ %

(2 marks)

207 During the year IML Co paid a dividend of 15c per share. At the year end share price was $3.15. Share price was $2.50 at the start of the year.

What is the total shareholder return over the period?

☐ %

(2 marks)

208 Calculate the equity beta of IML Co, assuming its required annual rate of return on equity is 17% and the stock market uses the capital asset pricing model to calculate the equity beta.

☐ %

(2 marks)

209 Which **TWO** of the following statements are true?

☐ If IML Co's share price moved at three times the market rate, its equity beta factor would be 3.0.

☐ The beta factor of IML Co indicates the level of unsystematic risk.

☐ The higher the level of systematic risk, the lower the required rate of return by IML Co.

☐ IML Co wants a return on a project to exceed the risk-free rate.

(2 marks)

210 Are the following statements true or false?

True   False

1   CAPM assumes that investors in IML Co hold a fully diversified portfolio.   ☐ ☐

2   If IML Co has a low price/earnings ratio, it will have a low cost of equity.   ☐ ☐

(2 marks)

(Total = 10 marks)

Section C questions

211 Bar Co (12/11, amended)

36 mins

Bar Co is a stock exchange listed company that is concerned by its current level of debt finance. It plans to make a rights issue and to use the funds raised to pay off some of its debt. The rights issue will be at a 20% discount to its current ex dividend share price of $7.50 per share and Bar Co plans to raise $90m. Bar Co believes that paying off some of its debt will not affect its price/earnings ratio, which is expected to remain constant.

STATEMENT OF PROFIT OR LOSS INFORMATION

	$m
Revenue	472.0
Cost of sales	423.0
Profit before interest and tax	49.0
Interest	10.0
Profit before tax	39.0
Tax	11.7
Profit after tax	27.3

STATEMENT OF FINANCIAL POSITION INFORMATION

	$m
Equity	
Ordinary shares ($1 nominal)	60.0
Retained earnings	80.0
	140.0
Long-term liabilities	
8% bonds ($100 nominal)	125.0
	265.0

The 8% bonds are currently trading at $112.50 per $100 bond and bondholders have agreed that they will allow Bar Co to buy back the bonds at this market value. Bar Co pays tax at a rate of 30% per year.

Required

(a) Calculate the theoretical ex-rights price per share of Bar Co following the rights issue. **(3 marks)**

(b) Calculate and discuss whether using the cash raised by the rights issue to buy back bonds is likely to be financially acceptable to the shareholders of Bar Co, commenting in your answer on the belief that the current price/earnings ratio will remain constant. **(7 marks)**

(c) Calculate and discuss the effect on the financial risk of Bar Co of using the cash raised by the rights issue to buy back bonds, as measured by its interest coverage ratio and its book value debt to equity ratio. **(4 marks)**

(d) Discuss the dangers to a company of a high level of gearing, including in your answer an explanation of the following terms:

(i) Business risk
(ii) Financial risk

(6 marks)

(Total = 20 marks)

212 YGV Co (6/10, amended)

YGV Co is a listed company selling computer software. Its profit before interest and tax has fallen from $5m to $1m in the last year and its current financial position is as follows:

	$'000	$'000
Non-current assets		
Property, plant and equipment	3,000	
Intangible assets	8,500	11,500
Current assets		
Inventory	4,100	
Trade receivables	11,100	15,200
Total assets		26,700
Equity		
Ordinary shares	10,000	
Reserves	7,000	17,000
Current liabilities		
Trade payables	5,200	
Overdraft	4,500	9,700
Total equity and liabilities		26,700

YGV Co has been advised by its bank that the current overdraft limit of $4.5m will be reduced to $500,000 in 2 months' time. The finance director of YGV Co has been unable to find another bank willing to offer alternative overdraft facilities and is planning to issue bonds on the stock market in order to finance the reduction of the overdraft. The bonds would be issued at their nominal value of $100 per bond and would pay interest of 9% per year, payable at the end of each year. The bonds would be redeemable at a 10% premium to their nominal value after 10 years. The finance director hopes to raise $4m from the bond issue.

The ordinary shares of YGV Co have a nominal value of $1.00 per share and a current market value of $4.10 per share. The cost of equity of YGV Co is 12% per year and the current interest rate on the overdraft is 5% per year.

Taxation is at an annual rate of 30%.

Other financial information:

Average gearing of sector (debt/equity, market value basis):   10%
Average interest coverage ratio of sector: 8 times

Required

(a) Calculate the after-tax cost of debt of the 9% bonds. **(4 marks)**

(b) Calculate the effect of using the bond issue to finance the reduction in the overdraft on:

    (i) The interest coverage ratio
    (ii) Gearing (debt/equity, market value basis) **(4 marks)**

(c) Evaluate the proposal to use the bond issue to finance the reduction in the overdraft and discuss alternative sources of finance that could be considered by YGV Co, given its current financial position. **(12 marks)**

(Total = 20 marks)

213 NN Co (12/10, amended)

36 mins

Assets	$m	$m	$m
Non-current assets			101
Current assets			
Inventory		11	
Trade receivables		21	
Cash		10	
			42
Total assets			143
Equity and liabilities			
Ordinary share capital		50	
Preference share capital		25	
Retained earnings		19	
Total equity			94
Non-current liabilities			
Long-term borrowings		20	
Current liabilities			
Trade payables	22		
Other payables	7		
Total current liabilities		29	
Total liabilities			49
Total equity and liabilities			143

NN Co has a cost of equity of 12%. The ordinary shares of the company have a nominal value of 50 cents per share and an ex div market value of $8.30 per share.

The long-term borrowings of NN Co consist of 7% bonds that are redeemable in 6 years' time at their nominal value of $100 per bond. The current ex interest market price of the bonds is $103.50.

The preference shares of NN Co have a nominal value of 50 cents per share and pay an annual dividend of 8%. The ex div market value of the preference shares is 67 cents per share.

NN Co pays profit tax at an annual rate of 25% per year.

Required

(a)	Calculate the after-tax cost of debt of NN Co.	**(4 marks)**
(b)	Calculate the weighted average after-tax cost of capital of NN Co.	**(6 marks)**
(c)	Discuss the factors to be considered in formulating the dividend policy of a stock exchange listed company.	
		(10 marks)

(Total = 20 marks)

214 AQR Co (6/11, amended)   36 mins

The finance director of AQR Co has heard that the market value of the company will increase if the weighted average cost of capital of the company is decreased. The company, which is listed on a stock exchange, has 100 million shares in issue and the current ex div ordinary share price is $2.50 per share. AQR Co also has in issue bonds with a book value of $60m and their current ex interest market price is $104 per $100 bond. The current after-tax cost of debt of AQR Co is 7% and the tax rate is 30%.

The recent dividends per share of the company are as follows.

Year	20X0	20X1	20X2	20X3	20X4
Dividend per share (cents)	19.38	20.20	20.41	21.02	21.80

The finance director proposes to decrease the weighted average cost of capital of AQR Co, and hence increase its market value, by issuing $40m of bonds at their nominal value of $100 per bond. These bonds would pay annual interest of 8% before tax and would be redeemed at a 5% premium to nominal value after 10 years.

Required

(a) Calculate the market value after-tax weighted average cost of capital of AQR Co in the following circumstances:

    (i)   Before the new issue of bonds takes place
    (ii)   After the new issue of bonds takes place

    Comment on your findings. **(12 marks)**

(b) Discuss the director's view that issuing traded bonds will decrease the weighted average cost of capital of AQR Co and thereby increase the market value of the company. **(8 marks)**

(Total = 20 marks)

215 BKB Co (12/12, amended)   36 mins

The statement of financial position of BKB Co provides the following information:

	$m	$m
Equity finance		
Ordinary shares ($1 nominal value)	25	
Reserves	15	40
Non-current liabilities		
7% convertible bonds ($100 nominal value)	20	
5% preference shares ($1 nominal value)	10	30
Current liabilities		
Trade payables	10	
Overdraft	15	25
Total liabilities		95

BKB Co has an equity beta of 1.2 and the ex dividend market value of the company's equity is $125m. The ex interest market value of the convertible bonds is $21m and the ex dividend market value of the preference shares is $6.25m.

The convertible bonds of BKB Co have a conversion ratio of 19 ordinary shares per bond. The conversion date and redemption date are both on the same date in five years' time. The current ordinary share price of BKB Co is expected to increase by 4% per year for the foreseeable future.

The overdraft has a variable interest rate which is currently 6% per year and BKB Co expects this to increase in the near future. The overdraft has not changed in size over the last financial year, although one year ago the overdraft interest rate was 4% per year. The company's bank will not allow the overdraft to increase from its current level.

The equity risk premium is 5% per year and the risk-free rate of return is 4% per year. BKB Co pays profit tax at an annual rate of 30% per year.

Required

(a)   Calculate the market value after-tax weighted average cost of capital of BKB Co, explaining clearly any assumptions you make.

(12 marks)

(b)   Discuss why market value weighted average cost of capital is preferred to book value weighted average cost of capital when making investment decisions.

(4 marks)

(c)   Discuss the attractions to a company of convertible debt compared to a bank loan of a similar maturity as a source of finance.

(4 marks)

(Total = 20 marks)

216 Fence Co (6/14, amended)   36 mins

The equity beta of Fence Co is 0.9 and the company has issued 10 million ordinary shares. The market value of each ordinary share is $7.50. The company is also financed by 7% bonds with a nominal value of $100 per bond, which will be redeemed in 7 years' time at nominal value. The bonds have a total nominal value of $14m. Interest on the bonds has just been paid and the current market value of each bond is $107.14.

Fence Co plans to invest in a project which is different to its existing business operations and has identified a company in the same business area as the project, Hex Co. The equity beta of Hex Co is 1.2 and the company has an equity market value of $54m. The market value of the debt of Hex Co is $12m.

The risk-free rate of return is 4% per year and the average return on the stock market is 11% per year. Both companies pay corporation tax at a rate of 20% per year.

Required

(a)   Calculate the current weighted average cost of capital of Fence Co.

(7 marks)

(b)   Calculate a cost of equity which could be used in appraising the new project.

(4 marks)

(c)   Explain the difference between systematic and unsystematic risk in relation to portfolio theory and the capital asset pricing model.

(4 marks)

(d)   Explain the limitations of the capital asset pricing model.

(5 marks)

(Total = 20 marks)

217 Tinep Co (12/14, amended)

Tinep Co is planning to raise funds for an expansion of existing business activities and in preparation for this the company has decided to calculate its weighted average cost of capital. Tinep Co has the following capital structure:

	$m	$m
Equity		
Ordinary shares	200	
Reserves	650	
		850
Non-current liabilities		
Loan notes		200
		1,050

The ordinary shares of Tinep Co have a nominal value of 50 cents per share and are currently trading on the stock market on an ex dividend basis at $5.85 per share. Tinep Co has an equity beta of 1.15.

The loan notes have a nominal value of $100 and are currently trading on the stock market on an ex interest basis at $103.50 per loan note. The interest on the loan notes is 6% per year before tax and they will be redeemed in six years' time at a 6% premium to their nominal value.

The risk-free rate of return is 4% per year and the equity risk premium is 6% per year. Tinep Co pays corporation tax at an annual rate of 25% per year.

Required

(a) Calculate the market value weighted average cost of capital and the book value weighted average cost of capital of Tinep Co, and comment briefly on any difference between the two values. **(9 marks)**

(b) Discuss the factors to be considered by Tinep Co in choosing to raise funds via a rights issue. **(6 marks)**

(c) Explain the nature of a scrip (share) dividend and discuss the advantages and disadvantages to a company of using scrip dividends to reward shareholders. **(5 marks)**

(Total = 20 marks)

218 Grenarp Co (6/15, amended)

Grenarp Co is planning to raise $11,200,000 through a rights issue. The new shares will be offered at a 20% discount to the current share price of Grenarp Co, which is $3.50 per share. The rights issue will be on a 1 for 5 basis and issue costs of $280,000 will be paid out of the cash raised. The capital structure of Grenarp Co is as follows:

	$m	$m
Equity		
Ordinary shares (par value $0.50)	10	
Reserves	75	
		85
Non-current liabilities		
8% loan notes		30
		115

The net cash raised by the rights issue will be used to redeem part of the loan note issue. Each loan note has a nominal value of $100 and an ex interest market value of $104. A clause in the bond issue contract allows Grenarp Co to redeem the loan notes at a 5% premium to market price at any time prior to their redemption date. The price/earnings ratio of Grenarp Co is not expected to be affected by the redemption of the loan notes.

The earnings per share of Grenarp Co is currently $0.42 per share and total earnings are $8,400,000 per year. The company pays corporation tax of 30% per year.

Required

(a) Evaluate the effect on the wealth of the shareholders of Grenarp Co of using the net rights issue funds to redeem the loan notes.

(8 marks)

(b) Discuss whether Grenarp Co might achieve its optimal capital structure following the rights issue. **(7 marks)**

(c) Discuss **THREE** sources and characteristics of long-term debt finance which may be available to Grenarp Co.

(5 marks)

(Total = 20 marks)

219 Dinla Co (Mar/Jun 16, amended)   36 mins

Dinla Co has the following capital structure.

	$'000	$'000
Equity and reserves		
Ordinary shares	23,000	
Reserves	247,000	
		270,000
Non-current liabilities		
5% preference shares	5,000	
6% loan notes	11,000	
Bank loan	3,000	
		19,000
		289,000

The ordinary shares of Dinla Co are currently trading at $4.26 per share on an ex dividend basis and have a nominal value of $0.25 per share. Ordinary dividends are expected to grow in the future by 4% per year and a dividend of $0.25 per share has just been paid.

The 5% preference shares have an ex dividend market value of $0.56 per share and a nominal value of $1.00 per share. These shares are irredeemable.

The 6% loan notes of Dinla Co are currently trading at $95.45 per loan note on an ex interest basis and will be redeemed at their nominal value of $100 per loan note in 5 years' time.

The bank loan has a fixed interest rate of 7% per year.

Dinla Co pays corporation tax at a rate of 25%.

Required

(a) Calculate the after-tax weighted average cost of capital of Dinla Co on a market value basis.   **(8 marks)**

(b) Discuss the connection between the relative costs of sources of finance and the creditor hierarchy.

(3 marks)

(c) Discuss the circumstances under which the current weighted average cost of capital of a company could be used in investment appraisal and indicate briefly how its limitations as a discount rate could be overcome.

(5 marks)

(d) Explain the differences between Islamic finance and other conventional finance.   **(4 marks)**

(Total = 20 marks)

220 Tufa Co (Sep/Dec 17)

The following statement of financial position information relates to Tufa Co, a company listed on a large stock market which pays corporation tax at a rate of 30%.

	$m	$m
Equity and liabilities		
Share capital	17	
Retained earnings	15	
Total equity		32
Non-current liabilities		
Long-term borrowings	13	
Current liabilities	21	
Total liabilities		34
Total equity and liabilities		66

The share capital of Tufa Co consists of $12m of ordinary shares and $5m of irredeemable preference shares.

The ordinary shares of Tufa Co have a nominal value of $0.50 per share, an ex dividend market price of $7.07 per share and a cum dividend market price of $7.52 per share. The dividend for 20X7 will be paid in the near future. Dividends paid in recent years have been as follows:

Year	20X6	20X5	20X4	20X3
Dividend ($/share)	0.43	0.41	0.39	0.37

The 5% preference shares of Tufa Co have a nominal value of $0.50 per share and an ex dividend market price of $0.31 per share.

The long-term borrowings of Tufa Co consists $10m of loan notes and a $3m bank loan. The bank loan has a variable interest rate.

The 7% loan notes have a nominal value of $100 per loan note and a market price of $102.34 per loan note. Annual interest has just been paid and the loan notes are redeemable in four years' time at a 5% premium to nominal value.

Required

(a) Calculate the after-tax weighted average cost of capital of Tufa Co on a market value basis. **(11 marks)**

(b) Discuss the circumstances under which it is appropriate to use the current WACC of Tufa Co in appraising an investment project. **(3 marks)**

(c) Discuss THREE advantages to Tufa Co of using convertible loan notes as a source of long-term finance.
(6 marks)
(Total = 20 marks)

221 Dartig Co (12/08, amended)

36 mins

Dartig Co is a stock market listed company that manufactures consumer products and it is planning to expand its existing business. The investment cost of $5m will be met by a 1 for 4 rights issue. The current share price of Dartig Co is $2.50 per share and the rights issue price will be at a 20% discount to this. The finance director of Dartig Co expects that the expansion of existing business will allow the average growth rate of earnings per share over the last four years to be maintained into the foreseeable future.

The earnings per share and dividends paid by Dartig over the last four years are as follows:

	20X3	20X4	20X5	20X6	20X7
Earnings per share (cents)	27.7	29.0	29.0	30.2	32.4
Dividend per share (cents)	12.8	13.5	13.5	14.5	15.0

Dartig Co has a cost of equity of 10%. The price/earnings ratio of Dartig Co has been approximately constant in recent years.

Note. Ignore issue costs.

Required

(a) Calculate the theoretical ex-rights price per share prior to investing in the proposed business expansion.

(4 marks)

(b) Calculate the expected share price following the proposed business expansion using the price/earnings ratio method.

(4 marks)

(c) Discuss whether the proposed business expansion is an acceptable use of the finance raised by the rights issue, and evaluate the expected effect on the wealth of the shareholders of Dartig Co. **(6 marks)**

(d) Using the information provided, calculate the ex div share price predicted by the dividend growth model and discuss briefly why this share price differs from the current market price of Dartig Co. **(6 marks)**

(Total = 20 marks)

PART F: BUSINESS VALUATIONS

Questions 222 to 266 cover Business valuations, the subject of Part F of the BPP Financial Management Study Text.

MCQ bank – Business valuations

36 mins

222 ML Ltd is an unlisted accountancy firm owned by three shareholders. One of the shareholders has asked for an independent valuation of the company to be performed.

Which of the following is a valid reason for an independent valuation to be required?

A   The stock market is thought to be weak form efficient.

B   The realisable value of inventory is felt to be underestimated in the latest financial statements.

C   To evaluate a takeover bid by Company X which is offering to buy ML Ltd in exchange for shares in Company X.

D   The latest published statement of financial position was 11 months ago.   **(2 marks)**

6/15

223

The following financial information relates to QK Co, whose ordinary shares have a nominal value of $0.50 per share:

	$m	$m
Non-current assets		120
Current assets		
Inventory	8	
Trade receivables	12	20
Total assets		140
Equity		
Ordinary shares	25	
Reserves	80	105
Non-current liabilities		20
Current liabilities		15
Total equity and liabilities		140

On an historic basis, what is the net asset value per share of QK Co?

A $2.10 per share
B $2.50 per share
C $2.80 per share
D $4.20 per share   **(2 marks)**

224 ELW Co recently paid a dividend of $0.50 a share. This is $0.10 more than three years ago. Shareholders have a required rate of return of 10%.

Using the dividend valuation model and assuming recent dividend growth is expected to continue, what is the current value of a share?

A $23.41
B $5.00
C $38.48
D $10.48   **(2 marks)**

Cant Co has a cost of equity of 10% and has forecast its future dividends as follows:

Current year: No dividend
Year 1: No dividend
Year 2 $0.25 per share
Year 3: $0.50 per share and increasing by 3% per year in subsequent years

What is the current share price of Cant Co using the dividend valuation model?

A $7.35
B $5.57
C $6.11
D $6.28

(2 marks)

226   Jo Co is a company which is financed by equity only. It has just paid a dividend of $60m and earnings retained and invested were 60%. Return on investments is 20% and the cost of equity is 22%.

What is the market value of the company (to the nearest whole million)?

A $300m
B $272m
C $305m
D $672m

(2 marks)

227   DD Co's P/E ratio is 12. Its competitor's earnings yield is 10%.

When comparing DD Co to its competitor, which of the following is correct?

	Earnings yield	P/E ratio
A	Higher	Higher
B	Higher	Lower
C	Lower	Higher
D	Lower	Lower

(2 marks)

Black Co has in issue 5% irredeemable loan notes, nominal value of $100 per loan note, on which interest is shortly to be paid. Black Co has a before-tax cost of debt of 10% and corporation tax is 30%.

What is the current market value of one loan note?

A $55
B $50
C $76
D $40

(2 marks)

A company has 7% loan notes in issue which are redeemable in 7 years' time at a 5% premium to their nominal value of $100 per loan note. The before-tax cost of debt of the company is 9% and the after-tax cost of debt of the company is 6%.

What is the current market value of each loan note?

A $92.67
B $108.90
C $89.93
D $103.14

(2 marks)

230

A company has in issue loan notes with a nominal value of $100 each. Interest on the loan notes is 6% per year, payable annually. The loan notes will be redeemed in eight years' time at a 5% premium to nominal value. The before-tax cost of debt of the company is 7% per year.

What is the ex interest market value of each loan note?

A $94.03
B $96.94
C $102.91
D $103.10

(2 marks)

231   NCW Co is considering acquiring the ordinary share capital of CEW Co. CEW Co has for years generated an annual cash inflow of $10m. For a one-off investment of $6m in new machinery, earnings for CEW Co can be increased by $2m per annum. NCW Co has a cost of capital of 10%.

What is the value of CEW Co?

A $114 million
B $120 million
C $100 million
D $94 million

(2 marks)
(Total = 20 marks)

CBE style OTQ bank – Market efficiency

232 WC Co announces that it decided yesterday to invest in a new project with a huge positive net present value. The share price doubled yesterday.

What does this appear to be evidence of?

- [ ] A semi-strong form efficient market
- [ ] A strong form efficient market
- [ ] Technical analysis
- [ ] A weak form efficient market

(2 marks)

233 PX Co is considering making a takeover bid for JJ Co. Both companies are large listed sportswear retailers that sell to the general public.

The shares of both PX Co and JJ Co are regularly traded and their share prices react quickly to new information.

Which of the following is likely to be needed to allow PX Co to make sure that its bid is not too high?

- [ ] No information is needed because the stock market is semi-strong form efficient
- [ ] Estimates of the present value of the synergies that are likely to result from the takeover
- [ ] An aged accounts receivable summary
- [ ] The latest published statement of JJ Co's financial position

(2 marks)

234 Sarah decides to plot past share price movements to help spot patterns and create an investment strategy.

What does Sarah believe the stock market is?

- [ ] Completely inefficient
- [ ] Weak form efficient
- [ ] Semi-strong form efficient
- [ ] Strong form efficient

(2 marks)

235 Which of the following is evidence that stock markets are semi-strong form efficient?

- [ ] Repeating patterns appear to exist.
- [ ] Attempting to trade on consistently repeating patterns is unlikely to work.
- [ ] The majority of share price reaction to news occurs when it is announced.
- [ ] Share price reaction occurs before announcements are made public.

(2 marks)

236 Are the following statements true or false?

	True	False
Fundamental analysis values shares according to the expected future cash flows and risk of a business.	[ ]	[ ]
Technical analysis predicts future share price movements based on past share price movements and patterns.	[ ]	[ ]

(2 marks)

(Total = 10 marks)

Section B questions

Phobis Co (12/07, amended)

18 mins

The following scenario relates to questions 237–241.

Phobis Co is considering a bid for Danoca Co. Both companies are stock market listed and are in the same business sector. Financial information on Danoca Co, which is shortly to pay its annual dividend, is as follows:

Number of ordinary shares	5 million
Ordinary share price (ex div basis)	$3.30
Earnings per share	40.0c
Dividend payout ratio	60%
Dividend per share one year ago	23.3c
Dividend per share two years ago	22.0c
Average sector earnings yield	10%

237   Calculate the value of Danoca Co using the earnings yield method.

    A $2m
    B $5m
    C $16.5m
    D $20m   **(2 marks)**

238   Are the following statements true or false?

    1   If the P/E ratio of Danoca Co is lower than the average sector P/E ratio then the market does not view the growth prospects of Danoca very favourably.

    2   If the P/E ratio of Danoca Co is higher than the average sector ratio then an acquisition by Phobis Co could result in improved financial performance of Danoca Co.

    A   Statement 1 is true and statement 2 is false.
    B   Both statements are true.
    C   Statement 1 is false and statement 2 is true.
    D   Both statements are false.   **(2 marks)**

239   Using a cost of equity of 13% and a dividend growth rate of 4.5%, calculate the value of Danoca Co using the dividend growth model.

    A $14.75m
    B $5.00m
    C $2.95m
    D $16.50m   **(2 marks)**

240   Calculate the market capitalisation of Danoca Co.

    A $14.75m
    B $16.50m
    C $5.00m
    D $20.00m   **(2 marks)**

241 Which **TWO** of the following are true?

1 Under weak form hypothesis of market efficiency, share prices reflect all available information about past changes in share price.

2 If a stock market displays semi-strong efficiency then individuals can beat the market.

3 Behavioural finance aims to explain the implications of psychological factors on investor decisions.

4 Random walk theory is based on the idea that past share price patterns will be repeated.

A 1 and 2
B 1 and 3
C 2 and 4
D 3 and 4

(2 marks)

(Total = 10 marks)

GWW Co

The following scenario relates to questions 242–246.

GWW Co is a listed company which is seen as a potential target for acquisition by financial analysts. The value of the company has therefore been a matter of public debate in recent weeks and the following financial information is available:

Year	20Y2	20Y1	20Y0	20X9
Profit after tax ($m)	10.1	9.7	8.9	8.5
Total dividends ($m)	6.0	5.6	5.2	5.0

STATEMENT OF FINANCIAL POSITION INFORMATION FOR 20Y2

	$m	$m
Non-current assets		91.0
Current assets		
Inventory	3.8	
Trade receivables	4.5	8.3
Total assets		99.3
Equity finance		
Ordinary shares	20.0	
Reserves	47.2	67.2
Non-current liabilities		
8% bonds		25.0
Current liabilities		7.1
Total liabilities		99.3

The shares of GWW Co have a nominal (par) value of 50c per share and a market value of $4.00 per share. The business sector of GWW Co has an average price/earnings ratio of 17 times.

The expected net realisable values of the non-current assets and the inventory are $86.0m and $4.2m respectively. In the event of liquidation, only 80% of the trade receivables are expected to be collectible.

242   What is the value of GWW Co using market capitalisation (equity market value)?

    A $20m
    B $40m
    C $80m
    D $160m   (2 marks)

243   What is the value of GWW Co using the net asset value (liquidation basis)?

    A $58.9m
    B $61.7m
    C $62.6m
    D $99.3m   (2 marks)

244   What is the value of GWW Co using the price/earnings ratio method (business sector average price/earnings ratio)?

    A $1.7m
    B $61.7m
    C $160m
    D $171.7m   (2 marks)

245 An investor believes that they can make abnormal returns by studying past share price movements.

   In terms of capital market efficiency, to which of the following does the investor's belief relate?

   A   Fundamental analysis
   B   Operational efficiency
   C   Technical analysis
   D   Semi-strong form efficiency   **(2 marks)**

246 Assume that GWW Co's P/E ratio is 15. Its competitor's earnings yield is 6.25%.

   When comparing GWW Co to its competitor, which of the following is correct?

	Earnings yield of GWW	P/E ratio of GWW
A	Higher	Higher
B	Higher	Lower
C	Lower	Higher
D	Lower	Lower

   (2 marks)

CBE style OT case Corhig Co (6/12, amended)   18 mins

The following scenario relates to questions 247–251.

Corhig Co is a company that is listed on a major stock exchange. The company has struggled to maintain profitability in the last two years due to poor economic conditions in its home country and as a consequence it has decided not to pay a dividend in the current year. However, there are now clear signs of economic recovery and Corhig Co is optimistic that payment of dividends can be resumed in the future. Forecast financial information relating to the company is as follows:

Year	1	2	3
Earnings ($'000)	3,000	3,600	4,300
Dividends ($'000)	nil	500	1,000

The current average price/earnings ratio of listed companies similar to Corhig Co is five times.

The company is optimistic that earnings and dividends will increase after Year 3 at a constant annual rate of 3% per year.

247   Using Corhig Co's forecast earnings for Year 1 and the average P/E ratio of similar companies, what is the value of Corhig Co using the price/earnings ratio method?

$\boxed{}$m   **(2 marks)**

248   Are the following statements true or false?

	True	False
A P/E valuation using average earnings of $3.63m would be more realistic than the P/E ratio method calculated above	☐	☐
Using the average P/E ratio of similar companies is appropriate in this situation	☐	☐

(2 marks)

249   Assuming that the cost of equity is 12%, what is the present value of Corhig Co's Year 2 dividend?

$\boxed{}$ **(2 marks)**

250   Corhig Co plans to raise debt in order to modernise some of its non-current assets and to support the expected growth in earnings. This additional debt would mean that the capital structure of the company would change and it would be financed 60% by equity and 40% by debt on a market value basis. The before-tax cost of debt of Corhig Co would increase to 6% per year. In order to stimulate economic activity the Government has reduced the tax rate for all large companies to 20% per year.

Assuming that the revised cost of equity is 14%, what is the revised weighted average after-tax cost of capital of Corhig Co following the new debt issue? (Give your answer to 2 dp.)

$\boxed{}$%   **(2 marks)**

251   Match the description of the risk to the type of risk.

	Business	Financial	Systematic
Risk linked to the extent to which the company's profits depend on fixed, rather than variable, costs	☐	☐	☐
Risk that shareholder cannot mitigate by holding a diversified investment portfolio	☐	☐	☐
Risk that shareholder return fluctuates as a result of the level of debt the company undertakes	☐	☐	☐

(2 marks)

(Total = 10 marks)

CBE style OT case Close Co (12/11, amended)

18 mins

The following scenario relates to questions 252–256.

Recent financial information relating to Close Co, a stock market listed company, is as follows.

	$m
Profit after tax (earnings)	66.6
Dividends	40.0

STATEMENT OF FINANCIAL POSITION INFORMATION

	$m	$m
Non-current assets		595
Current assets		125
Total assets		720
Equity		
Ordinary shares ($1 nominal)	80	
Retained earnings	410	
		490
Non-current liabilities		
6% bank loan	40	
8% bonds ($100 nominal)	120	
		160
Current liabilities		70
Total equity and liabilities		720

Financial analysts have forecast that the dividends of Close Co will grow in the future at a rate of 4% per year. This is slightly less than the forecast growth rate of the profit after tax (earnings) of the company, which is 5% per year. The finance director of Close Co thinks that, considering the risk associated with expected earnings growth, an earnings yield of 11% per year can be used for valuation purposes.

Close Co has a cost of equity of 10% per year.

252 Calculate the value of Close Co using the net asset value method.

$ [   ] m

(2 marks)

253 Calculate the value of Close Co using the dividend growth model (DGM).

$ [   ] m

(2 marks)

254 Calculate the value of Close Co using the earnings yield method (in millions to 1 dp).

$ [   ] m

(2 marks)

255 The DGM has been used by financial analysts to value Close Co.

Are the following statements about the DGM true or false?

	True	False
It is very sensitive to changes in the growth rate.	☐	☐
It can only be used if dividends have been paid or are expected to be paid.	☐	☐

(2 marks)

256 Close Co is considering raising finance via convertible bonds.

Which of the following statements is correct about the current market value of a convertible bond where conversion is expected?

☐ The sum of the present values of the future interest payments + the present value of the bond's conversion value

☐ The sum of the present values of the future interest payments − the present value of the bond's conversion value

☐ The higher of the sum of the present values of the future interest payments and the present value of the bond's conversion value

☐ The lower of the sum of the present values of the future interest payments and the present value of the bond's conversion value

(2 marks)

(Total = 10 marks)

CBE style OT case WAW Co

The following scenario relates to questions 257–261.

WAW Co is an unlisted company that has performed well recently. It has been approached by a number of companies in the industry as a potential acquisition target.

The directors of WAW Co are looking to establish an approximate valuation of the company.

Recent information on the earnings per share and dividend per share of WAW Co is as follows:

Year to September	20X3	20X4	20X5	20X6
Earnings $m	6	6.5	7.0	7.5
Dividend $m	2.4	2.6	2.8	3.0

WAW Co has an estimated cost of equity of 12% and $5m ordinary shares in issue with a par value of $0.50.

There has been no change in the number of ordinary shares in issue over this period.

WAW Co pays corporation tax at a rate of 20%.

Listed companies similar to WAW Co have a price/earnings ratio of 15.

257 What is the value of a share in WAW Co using the dividend growth model?

    A $5.07
    B $4.79
    C $7.55
    D $15.10   **(2 marks)**

258 Which of the following statements are problems in using the dividend growth model to value a company?

    1   It is difficult to estimate future dividend growth.
    2   It cannot be used for unlisted companies as they do not have a cost of equity.
    3   It is inaccurate to assume that dividend growth will be constant.
    4   It does not adjust for the value of holding a controlling interest in a company.

    A   1 and 3
    B   1, 2 and 3
    C   1, 3 and 4
    D   1, 2, 3 and 4   **(2 marks)**

259 What is the value of WAW Co using the price/earnings ratio method?

    A $56.25 per share
    B $11.25 per share
    C $22.50 per share
    D $45.00 per share   **(2 marks)**

260 A high price/earnings ratio is usually seen as an indication that:

    A   The company's earnings are expected to be risky
    B   The dividend payout is excessive
    C   The share price is overstated
    D   The company is expected to grow   **(2 marks)**

261 Which of the following statements are true about WAW Co's dividend policy?

1 Shareholders achieve steady dividend growth.
2 The dividend payout ratio is constant.
3 The dividend cover is 2.5.
4 Shareholders are indifferent between reinvesting in the business and the payment of a dividend.

A 1, 2 and 3
B 1, 2 and 4
C 1 and 3
D 2, 3 and 4

(2 marks)

(Total = 10 marks)

CBE style OT case DFE Co

18 mins

The following scenario relates to questions 262–266.

DFE Co is hoping to invest in a new project. DFE Co's gearing is slightly above the industry average, so when seeking finance for the new project DFE Co opts for equity finance.

The board of DFE Co recently appointed a media liaison officer as they believe the timing and method of public announcements (such as the investment in a large project) is important in managing the value of DFE Co's shares.

DFE Co has 8% convertible loan notes in issue which are redeemable in 5 years' time at their nominal value of $100 per loan note. Alternatively, each loan note could be converted after 5 years into 70 equity shares with a nominal value of $1 each.

The equity shares of DFE Co are currently trading at $1.25 per share and this share price is expected to grow by 4% per year. The before-tax cost of debt of DFE Co is 10% and the after-tax cost of debt of DFE Co is 7%.

262   What is the capital structure theory that DFE Co appears to subscribe to?

☐ Traditional view
☐ Modigliani-Miller (no tax)
☐ Modigliani-Miller (with tax)
☐ Residual view   **(2 marks)**

263   How efficient does the DFE Co board believe the markets to be?

☐ Completely inefficient
☐ Weak form efficient
☐ Semi-strong form efficient
☐ Strong form efficient   **(2 marks)**

264   What is the current market value of each convertible loan note (to 2 dp)?

$☐   **(2 marks)**

265   In relation to DFE Co hedging interest rate risk, which of the following statements is correct?

☐ The flexible nature of interest rate futures means that they can always be matched with a specific interest rate exposure.
☐ Interest rate options carry an obligation to the holder to complete the contract at maturity.
☐ Forward rate agreements are the interest rate equivalent of forward exchange contracts.
☐ Matching is where a balance is maintained between fixed rate and floating rate debt.   **(2 marks)**

266   Which of the following could cause the interest yield curve to steepen?

1   Increased uncertainty about the future
2   Heightened expectations of an increase in interest rates
3   The expectation that interest rate decreases will happen earlier than previously thought

☐ 1 and 2 only
☐ 1, 2 and 3
☐ 2 and 3 only
☐ 1 only   **(2 marks)**

(Total = 10 marks)

PART G: RISK MANAGEMENT

Questions 267 to 306 cover Risk management, the subject of Part G of the BPP Financial Management Study Text.

MCQ bank – Foreign currency risk

36 mins

267   Exporters Co is concerned that the cash received from overseas sales will not be as expected due to exchange rate movements.

What type of risk is this?

A   Translation risk
B   Economic risk
C   Credit risk
D   Transaction risk

(2 marks)

268   The current euro/US dollar exchange rate is €1 : $2. ABC Co, a Eurozone company, makes a $1,000 sale to a US customer on credit. By the time the customer pays, the euro has strengthened by 20%.

What will the euro receipt be?

A   €416.67
B   €2,400
C   €600
D   €400

(2 marks)

269   The current forward rate for the US dollar/euro is $/€ 1.9950– 2.0010.

What will a $2,000 receipt be translated to at the forward rate?

A   €4,002
B   €999.5
C   €998
D   €4,008

(2 marks)

270   3/16

Which of the following derivative instruments are characterised by a standard contract size?

1   Futures contract
2   Exchange-traded option
3   Forward rate agreement
4   Swap

A   1 and 2
B   2 and 3
C   3 and 4
D   1 and 4

(2 marks)

271   A US company owes a European company €3.5m due to be paid in 3 months' time. The spot exchange rate is $1.96 – $2 : €1 currently. Annual interest rates in the two locations are as follows:

	Borrowing	Deposit
US	8%	3%
Europe	5%	1%

What will be the equivalent US$ value of the payment using a money market hedge?

A $6,965,432
B $6,979,750
C $7,485,149
D $7,122,195

(2 marks)

272   In comparison to forward contracts, which **TWO** of the following are true in relation to futures contracts?

1   They are more expensive.
2   They are only available in a small amount of currencies.
3   They are less flexible.
4   They may be an imprecise match for the underlying transaction.

A   1, 2 and 4 only
B   2 and 4 only
C   1 and 3 only
D   1, 2, 3 and 4   **(2 marks)**

A company whose home currency is the dollar ($) expects to receive 500,000 pesos in 6 months' time from a customer in a foreign country. The following interest rates and exchange rates are available to the company:

Spot rate   15.00 peso per $
Six-month forward rate   15.30 peso per $

	Home country	Foreign country
Borrowing interest rate	4% per year	8% per year
Deposit interest rate	3% per year	6% per year

Working to the nearest $100, what is the 6-month dollar value of the expected receipt using a money market hedge?

A $32,500
B $33,700
C $31,800
D $31,900   **(2 marks)**

274   The current spot rate for the US$ to the European € is $2 : €1. Annual interest rates in the two countries are 8% in the US, and 4% in Europe.

What is the three months forward rate (to four decimal places) likely to be?

A $1.9804 : €1
B $2.0198 : €1
C $1.9259 : €1
D $2.0769 : €1   **(2 marks)**

Handria is a country that has the peso for its currency and Wengry is a country that has the dollar ($) for its currency.

The current spot exchange rate is 1.5134 pesos = $1.

Using interest-rate differentials, the one year forward exchange rate is 1.5346 pesos = $1.

The currency market between the peso and the dollar is assumed perfect and the International Fisher Effect holds.

Which of the following statements is true?

A   Wengry has a higher forecast rate of inflation than Handria.
B   Handria has a higher nominal rate of interest than Wengry.
C   Handria has a higher real rate of interest than Wengry.
D   The forecast future spot rate of exchange will differ from the forward exchange rate.   **(2 marks)**

An investor plans to exchange $1,000 into euros now, invest the resulting euros for 12 months, and then exchange the euros back into dollars at the end of the 12-month period. The spot exchange rate is €1.415 per $1 and the euro interest rate is 2% per year. The dollar interest rate is 1.8% per year.

Compared to making a dollar investment for 12 months, at what 12-month forward exchange rate will the investor make neither a loss nor a gain?

A   €1.223 per $1
B   €1.412 per $1
C   €1.418 per $1
D   €1.439 per $1

(2 marks)
(Total = 20 marks)

MCQ bank – Interest rate risk

277   Which is the best definition of basis risk?

A   Interest rates on deposits and on loans are revised at different times.
B   Interest rates on deposits and loans move by different amounts.
C   Interest rates move.
D   The bank base rate might move with a knock-on effect to other interest rates.   **(2 marks)**

278   **6/15**

Which of the following statements are correct?

(1)   The general level of interest rates is affected by investors' desire for a real return
(2)   Market segmentation theory can explain kinks (discontinuities) in the yield curve
(3)   When interest rates are expected to fall, the yield curve could be sloping downwards

A   1 and 2 only
B   1 and 3 only
C   2 and 3 only
D   1, 2 and 3   **(2 marks)**

279   **6/16**

Which of the following statements concerning the causes of interest rate fluctuations is correct?

A   Liquidity preference theory suggests that investors want more compensation for short-term lending than for long-term lending.

B   According to expectations theory, the shape of the yield curve gives information on how inflation rates are expected to influence interest rates in the future.

C   An inverted yield curve can arise if government policy is to keep short-term interest rates high in order to bring down inflation.

D   Market segmentation theory suggests long-term interest rates depend on how easily investors can switch between market segments of different maturity.   **(2 marks)**

280   Interest rates are currently 5%. ADB Co needs a $4m 6-month loan in 3 months' time and buys a 3–9 forward rate agreement (FRA) at 8%. When ADB Co signs the loan it agrees to a rate of 7%.

What is the payment or receipt ADB Co will make or receive under the FRA?

A   ADB pays the bank $40,000
B   ADB pays the bank $20,000
C   ADB receives $40,000 from the bank
D   ADB received $20,000 from the bank   **(2 marks)**

281   **6/15**

Which of the following statements are correct?

(1)   Interest rate options allow the buyer to take advantage of favourable interest rate movements

(2)   A forward rate agreement does not allow a borrower to benefit from a decrease in interest rates

(3)   Borrowers hedging against an interest rate increase will buy interest rate futures now and sell them at a future date

A   1 and 2 only
B   1 and 3 only
C   2 and 3 only
D   1, 2 and 3   **(2 marks)**

(Total = 10 marks)

Rose Co (6/15, amended)

The following scenario relates to questions 282–286.

Rose Co expects to receive €750,000 from a credit customer in the European Union in 6 months' time. The spot exchange rate is €2.349 per $1 and the 6-month forward rate is €2.412 per $1. The following commercial interest rates are available to Rose Co:

	Deposit rate	Borrow rate
Euros	4.0% per year	8.0% per year
Dollars	2.0% per year	3.5% per year

Rose Co does not have any surplus cash to use in hedging the future euro receipt. It also has no euro payments to make.

Rose Co is also considering using derivatives such as futures, options and swaps to manage currency risk.

In addition, Rose Co is concerned about the possibility of future interest rate changes and wants to understand how a yield curve can be interpreted.

282 What could Rose Co do to reduce the risk of the euro value dropping relative to the dollar before the €750,000 is received?

    A   Deposit €750,000 immediately
    B   Enter into an interest rate swap for 6 months
    C   Enter into a forward contract to sell €750,000 in 6 months
    D   Matching payments and receipts to the value of €750,000   **(2 marks)**

283 What is the dollar value of a forward market hedge in six months' time?

    A $310,945
    B $319,285
    C $1,761,750
    D $1,809,000   **(2 marks)**

284 If Rose Co used a money market hedge, what would be the percentage borrowing rate for the period?

    A   1.75%
    B   2.00%
    C   4.00%
    D   8.00%   **(2 marks)**

285 Which of the following statements is correct?

    A   Once purchased, a currency futures contract has a range of settlement dates.

    B   Currency swaps can be used to hedge exchange rate risk over longer periods than the forward market.

    C   Banks will allow forward exchange contracts to lapse if they are not used by a company.

    D   Currency options are paid for when they are exercised.   **(2 marks)**

286   Which of the following statements is correct?

   A   Governments can keep interest rates low by selling short-dated government bills in the money market.

   B   The normal yield curve slopes upward to reflect increasing compensation to investors for being unable to use their cash now.

   C   The yield on long-term loan notes is lower than the yield on short-term loan notes because long-term debt is less risky for a company than short-term debt.

   D   Expectations theory states that future interest rates reflect expectations of future inflation rate movements.

                                                                                        (2 marks)

                                                                                   (Total = 10 marks)

Edwen Co

18 mins

The following scenario relates to questions 287–291.

Edwen Co is based in Country C, where the currency is the C$. Edwen is expecting the following transactions with suppliers and customers who are based in Europe.

One month: Expected receipt of 240,000 euros
One month: Expected payment of 140,000 euros
Three months: Expected receipts of 300,000 euros

A one-month forward rate of 1.7832 euros per $1 has been offered by the company's bank and the spot rate is 1.7822 euros per $1.

Other relevant financial information is as follows:

Three-month European borrowing rate   1.35%

Three-month Country C deposit rate   1.15%

Assume that it is now 1 April.

287 What are the expected dollar receipts in one month using a forward hedge (to the nearest whole number)?

    A $56,079
    B $56,110
    C $178,220
    D $178,330   **(2 marks)**

288 What are the expected dollar receipts in three months using a money market hedge (to the nearest whole number)?

    A $167,999
    B $296,004
    C $166,089
    D $164,201   **(2 marks)**

289 Edwen Co is expecting a fall in the value of the C$.

What is the impact of a fall in a country's exchange rate?

    1   Exports will be given a stimulus.
    2   The rate of domestic inflation will rise.

    A   1 only
    B   2 only
    C   Both 1 and 2
    D   Neither 1 nor 2   **(2 marks)**

290 Edwen Co is considering a currency futures contract.

Which of the following statements about currency futures contracts are true?

    1   The contracts can be tailored to the user's exact requirements.
    2   The exact date of receipt or payment of the currency does not have to be known.
    3   Transaction costs are generally higher than other hedging methods.

    A   1 and 2 only
    B   1 and 3 only
    C   2 only
    D   3 only   **(2 marks)**

291 Do the following features apply to forward contracts or currency futures?

    1   Contract price is in any currency offered by the bank

    2   Traded over the counter

    A   Both features relate to forward contracts.

    B   Both features relate to currency futures.

    C   Feature 1 relates to forward contracts and feature 2 relates to currency futures.

    D   Feature 2 relates to forward contracts and feature 1 relates to currency futures.   **(2 marks)**

(Total = 10 marks)

CBE style OT case Zigto Co (6/12, amended)   18 mins

The following scenario relates to questions 292–296.

Zigto Co is a medium-sized company whose ordinary shares are all owned by the members of one family. The domestic currency is the dollar. It has recently begun exporting to a European country and expects to receive €500,000 in 6 months' time. The company plans to take action to hedge the exchange rate risk arising from its European exports.

Zigto Co could put cash on deposit in the European country at an annual interest rate of 3% per year, and borrow at 5% per year. The company could put cash on deposit in its home country at an annual interest rate of 4% per year, and borrow at 6% per year. Inflation in the European country is 3% per year, while inflation in the home country of Zigto Co is 4.5% per year.

The following exchange rates are currently available to Zigto Co:

Current spot exchange rate	2.000 euro per $
Six-month forward exchange rate	1.990 euro per $
One-year forward exchange rate	1.981 euro per $

Zigto Co wants to hedge its future euro receipt.

Zigto Co is also trying to build an understanding of other types of currency risk and the potential impact of possible future interest rate and inflation rate changes.

292   What is the dollar value of a forward exchange contract in six months' time (to the nearest whole number)?

$☐

(2 marks)

293   What is the dollar value of a money market hedge in six months' time (to the nearest whole number)?

$☐

(2 marks)

294   What is the one-year expected (future) spot rate predicted by purchasing power parity theory (to three dp)?

☐

(2 marks)

295   Are the following statements true or false?

		True	False
1	Purchasing power parity tends to hold true in the short term.	☐	☐
2	Expected future spot rates are based on relative inflation rates between two countries.	☐	☐
3	Current forward exchange rates are based on relative interest rates between two countries.	☐	☐

(2 marks)

296   Are the following statements true or false?

		True	False
1	Transaction risk affects cash flows.	☐	☐
2	Translation risk directly affects shareholder wealth.	☐	☐
3	Diversification of supplier and customer base across different countries reduces economic risk.	☐	☐

(2 marks)
(Total = 10 marks)

CBE style OT case PGT Co

The following scenario relates to questions 297–301.

PGT Co, whose home currency is the dollar ($), trades with both customers and suppliers in the European Union where the local currency is the euro (€). PGT Co has the following transactions due within the next six months:

	Receipts	Payments
3 months	1,000,000 euros	400,000 euros
6 months	500,000 dollars	300,000 euros

The finance director at PGT Co is concerned about the exchange rate due to uncertainty in the economy. He would like to hedge the exchange rate risk and has gathered the following information:

Spot rate (euro per $1)   1.7694 – 1.8306
Three-month forward rate (euro per $1)   1.7891 – 1.8510

PGT Co also has a 12 million loan in dollars. There is increased uncertainty in the economy regarding future interest rates due to impending elections which could lead to a change in political leadership and direction. PGT has never previously managed interest rate risk, but given the uncertainty the finance director is considering using a forward rate agreement.

The following commercial interest rates are currently available to PGT Co:

	Deposit rate	Borrow rate
Euros	4%	8%
Dollars	2%	3.5%

Assume that PGT Co does not have any surplus cash.

297 What is the three-month dollar receipt of a forward market hedge? (to the nearest whole number)?

$[   ]

(2 marks)

298 What is the cost in six months' time of a money market hedge? (to the nearest whole number)?

$[   ]

(2 marks)

299 Which of the following statements about a forward rate agreement (FRA) is/are true?

		True	False
1	FRAs can be used to manage interest rate risk on borrowings but not interest rate risk on investments.	☐	☐
2	FRAs are over the counter contracts.	☐	☐
3	The user of an FRA has the option to let the contract lapse if the rate is unfavourable.	☐	☐

(2 marks)

300 Which of the following statements are true if interest rate parity theory is used to forecast the forward value of the dollar for the transaction in six months' time (assuming interest rates stay the same)?

☐ The value of the dollar will be forecast to rise compared to the spot rate – leading to a fall in the cost of the transaction.

☐ The value of the dollar will be forecast to rise compared to the spot rate – leading to a rise in the cost of the transaction.

☐ The value of the dollar will be forecast to fall compared to the spot rate – leading to a rise in the cost of the transaction.

☐ The value of the dollar will be forecast to fall compared to the spot rate – leading to a fall in the cost of the transaction.

(2 marks)

301 Which of the following statements are true in relation to purchasing power parity?

		True	False
1	The theory holds in the long term rather than the short term.	☐	☐
2	The exchange rate reflects the different cost of living in two countries.	☐	☐
3	The forward rate can be found by multiplying the spot rate by the ratio of the real interest rates of the two countries.	☐	☐

(2 marks)
(Total = 10 marks)

CBE style OT case TGA Co

The following scenario relates to questions 302–306.

TGA Co's sales are exported to a European country and are invoiced in euros.

TGA Co expects to receive €500,000 from export sales at the end of 3 months. A forward rate of €1.687 per $1 has been offered by the company's bank and the spot rate is €1.675 per $1.

Other relevant financial information is as follows:

Short-term dollar borrowing rate   5% per year
Short-term dollar deposit rate   4% per year

TGA Co can borrow short term in the euro at 9% per year.

Assume there are 365 days in each year.

302   What could TGA Co do to reduce the risk of the euro value dropping relative to the dollar before the €500,000 is received?

    1   Deposit €500,000 immediately
    2   Enter into a forward contract to sell €500,000 in 3 months
    3   Enter into an interest rate swap for 3 months

  ☐   1 or 2 only
  ☐   2 only
  ☐   3 only
  ☐   1, 2 or 3   **(2 marks)**

303   What is the dollar value of a forward market hedge (to the nearest whole number)?

  $ ☐   **(2 marks)**

304   What is the dollar value of a money market hedge?

  ☐ $284,814
  ☐ $292,761
  ☐ $294,858
  ☐ $297,770

                                                            (2 marks)

305   TGA Co is considering futures contracts.

Which of the following statements are true of futures contracts?

                                                 True   *False*

Transactions costs are lower than other hedging methods.   ☐   ☐
They can be tailored to TGA Co's exact requirements.   ☐   ☐

                                                            (2 marks)

306 The following statements refer to types of foreign currency risk.

1 The risk that TGA Co will make exchange losses when the accounting results of its foreign branches are expressed in the home currency

2 The risk that exchange rate movements will affect the international competitiveness of TGA Co

What types of risk do the statements refer to?

	Economic	Translation	Transaction
Statement 1	☐	☐	☐
Statement 2	☐	☐	☐

(2 marks)

(Total = 10 marks)

Answers

MCQ bank – Financial management and financial objectives

1   **B**   80c

	$
Profit before tax	2,628,000
Less tax	788,000
Profit after tax	1,840,000
Less preference dividend (6% × 4,000,000)	240,000
Earnings attributable to ordinary shareholders	1,600,000
Number of ordinary shares	2,000,000
EPS = 1,600,000/2,000,000 =	80c

Syllabus area A3(d)(i)

2   **A**   D is true for a profit seeking organisation but would not be relevant to a not for profit organisation. However, financial management is also relevant to a not for profit organisation.

B is a definition of management accounting.

C is a definition of financial accounting.

Syllabus area A1(b)

3   **B** $\text{P/E ratio} = \dfrac{\text{MV ex div}}{\text{EPS}} = \dfrac{\$3.60}{60c} = 6$

MV ex div = 3.72 – 0.12 = 3.60. The ex div price is used because it reflects the underlying value of the share after the dividend has been paid.

Syllabus area A3(d)

4   **D**   Mean growth in earnings per share =

$$\sqrt[3]{\frac{35.7}{30.0}} - 1 = 0.06 \text{ or } 6\%$$

Notes on incorrect answers:

Dividend payout is dividend/earnings, this does not deliver the value of 40%.

Mean growth in dividends per share =

$$\sqrt[3]{\frac{15.0}{13.0}} - 1 = 0.05 \text{ or } 5\%$$

Total shareholder return can be calculated as:

$(P_1 - P_0 + D_1)/P_0$

P_0 is the share price at the beginning of the year 3 = \$2.25

P_1 is the share price at the end of period – this is unknown so TSR cannot be calculated.

Syllabus area A3(d)

5   **D**   Financial management decisions cover investment decisions, financing decisions (Options B and C) and dividend decisions (Option A).

Syllabus area A1(a)

CBE style OTQ bank – Financial management and financial objectives

6   **$3.60**

$$\text{Shareholder return} = \frac{P_1 - P_0 + D_1}{P_0}$$

$$\therefore 0.25 = \frac{P_1 - 3.00 + 0.15}{3.00}$$

$$\therefore 0.75 = P_1 - 3.00 + 0.15$$

$$\therefore P_1 = 3.60$$

Syllabus area A3(d)

7   **Minimisation of risk**.

Corporate governance best practice aims to **manage** risk to desired and controlled levels, not to minimise risk. Running a business implies taking calculated risks in anticipation of a commensurate return.

Syllabus area A3(e)(ii)

8   Statement 1 is false. Maximising market share is not a financial objective.

Statement 2 is true. The primary financial objective of any profit-making company is to maximise shareholder wealth.

Statement 3 is true. Financial objectives should be quantifiable. These include, for example, target values for earnings per share, dividend per share and gearing which are all quantifiable measures.

Syllabus area A2(b)

9   **Efficiency has increased but effectiveness has decreased**.

Economy is the cost of inputs (for example teacher salaries). This is not mentioned in the question.

Efficiency is the ratio of inputs to outputs. Each teacher (input) is now teaching more students, so efficiency has increased.

Effectiveness is the quality of outputs. The output in this example is exam results, which have suffered – hence effectiveness is reduced.

Syllabus area A4(c)

10   **36.4%**

Shareholder return $= (P_1 - P_0 + D_1)/P_0$.
$\therefore$ shareholder return $= (0.75 + 0.25)/(3.50 - 0.75)$
                            $= 36.4\%$

Syllabus area A3(d)(ii)

11   Statement 1 is true. The economist's concept of profits is broadly in terms of cash, whereas accounting profits may not equate to cash flows.

Statement 2 is false. Profit does not take account of risk.

Statement 3 is true. Accounting profit can be manipulated to some extent by choices of accounting policies.

Syllabus area A2(b)

12
'Cost per successfully treated patient' relates to efficiency. Efficiency measures relate the resources used to the output produced (getting as much as possible for what goes in).

'Proportion of patients readmitted after unsuccessful treatment' relates to effectiveness. Effectiveness means getting done, by means of economy and efficiency, what was supposed to be done.

'Cost per operation' relates to economy (spending money frugally), as does 'Percentage change in doctors' salaries compared with previous year'.

Syllabus area A4(c)

13
The correct answer is:

Return on equity can be defined as profit before interest and tax divided by shareholders' funds – this is NOT true as return on equity can be defined as profit **AFTER** interest and tax divided by shareholders' funds

Syllabus area A3(d)

14
The correct answer is: **8.0%**

Dividend yield is compares dividend paid over a year to the current ex-div share price. Dividend for the year is $0.08 + $0.06= $0.14

Ex div share price (representing the amount of money being invested in the share) = $1.83 – $0.08 = $1.75.

$0.14/1.75 \times 100 = 8.0\%$

Syllabus area A3(d)

15
Statement 2 is true and statement 1 is false.

The financial management function is responsible for making decisions relating to investment (statement 2) but will also have primary responsibility for cash flow forecasting (statement 1). Financial reporting control cash flow reporting but not forecasting.

Syllabus area A1(a)

ABC Co

16   B

	20X8	*20X7*
ROCE (PBIT/Long-term capital)	$14,749/($53,900) = 27.4%	$13,506/($52,587) = 25.7%

Percentage increase $= \dfrac{27.4 - 25.7}{25.7} = 6.6\%$

17   D   19.8%

Operating profit margin $= \dfrac{\text{PBIT}}{\text{Sales}} = \dfrac{\$14{,}749}{\$74{,}521} = 19.8\%$

18   D   The total shareholder return is $(P_1 - P_0 + D_1)/P_0 = (8.82 - 7.41 + 0.34)/7.41 = 23.6\%$.

19   A   Statement 1 is true and statement 2 is false.

The shareholders of ABC would probably be reasonably pleased with the performance over the two years. (For example, share price has increased by 19% ((8.82 – 7.41)/7.41 × 100%).) However, salaries and wages have only increased by 2.4% ((20,027 – 19,562)/19,562 × 100%), which is below the rate of inflation, so employees may be less pleased with the situation. So statement 1 is true.

Statement 2 is false. The financial risk that the shareholders are exposed to does not appear to be a problem area as gearing has decreased from 49.9% to 35.1% and interest cover is more than sufficient.

20 **B**   All of the statements support the theory. Accounting profits can be manipulated to some extent by choices of accounting policies. Profit does not take account of risk. Shareholders will be very interested in the level of risk, and maximising profits may be achieved by increasing risk to unacceptable levels. Profits on their own take no account of the volume of investment that it has taken to earn the profit. Profits must be related to the volume of investment to have any real meaning. Profits are reported every year (with half-year interim results for quoted companies). They are measures of short-term historic performance, whereas a company's performance should ideally be judged over a longer term and future prospects considered as well as past profits.

MCQ bank – Financial management environment

21 C Fiscal policy is the balance of government taxation and spending. A contractionary fiscal policy implies a government budget surplus – the Government is reducing demand by withdrawing higher amounts from the economy by way of higher taxation and/or spending less. 'B' would be the result of an expansionary fiscal policy. 'A' may happen as a result of an expansionary policy as an economy 'booms'. 'D' may happen following a contractionary fiscal policy, although lower inflation and interest rates are only a secondary effect. As an economy enters recession, inflationary pressure may decrease and interest rates may be reduced to encourage borrowing. However, as these are not directly due to fiscal policy, C is the more direct and immediate impact.

Syllabus area B1(c)

22 A Monetary policy manages demand by influencing the supply of money (including the availability of credit) and interest rates. An expansionary policy implies low interest rates to encourage borrowing and investment, and to discourage saving. It also implies an increased availability of credit to encourage spending and the stimulation of demand in an economy. Tax rates are a tool of fiscal policy, so C and D are incorrect. B would be the result of a contractionary monetary policy.

Syllabus area B1(c)

23 A As an economy approaches its peak, inflation increases because price increases 'soak up' high demand as productivity peaks. Unemployment is low so businesses struggle to fill vacancies. B is incorrect – export demand is affected by foreign demand, not domestic, and growth rates are unlikely to be increasing as the economy reaches its peak – they will decrease. C describes a recession. D is incorrect because as an economy peaks a contractionary fiscal policy is likely to be employed implying lower government spending and higher taxation.

Syllabus area B1(c)

24 D Statement 2 is correct as lending is securitised.

Statement 1 is incorrect as money markets are markets for short-term capital, of less than a year.

Statement 3 is incorrect, the money markets are mainly used by large companies.

Syllabus area B3(c)

25 A Rationale: Debts lose 'real' value with inflation: a company that owes a lot of money would effectively pay less (in real terms) over time. The other organisations would suffer because inflation would make exports relatively expensive and imports relatively cheap; business might be lost due to price rises; and the cost of implementing price changes would be high.

Syllabus area B1(d)

MCQ bank – Financial management environment

26 C Dividend creation benefits the intermediaries' investors, not their customers/borrowers.

Syllabus area B2(b)

27 C Certificate of deposit, commercial paper and treasury bill. Money markets focus on short-term financial instruments. A corporate bond is a long-term source of finance, hence is a capital market instrument. Certificates of deposit and commercial paper are short-term private sector lending/borrowing. A treasury bill is short-term government borrowing.

Syllabus area B3(c)

28 D A letter of credit involves a selling company and a buying company (who use the letter of credit reduce the credit risk of the selling company). Options A and C are incorrect as these would be done by the buying company's bank. Option B would be done by the selling company's bank.

Syllabus area B2(a)

29 **C** Eurobonds by definition are bonds issued in a currency other than the domestic currency of the country of issue. The prefix 'Euro' does not refer to the continent Europe or the European currency the euro.

Syllabus area B2(d)

30 **D** Ordinary shares are riskiest as all other investors are preferential to ordinary shareholders. Preference shares are riskier than corporate bonds as preference shares are paid after corporate bonds – bonds imply a contractual right to receive a predefined level of return. Treasury bills are short-term government borrowing hence are the lowest risk of all.

Syllabus area B2(d)

MCQ bank – Financial management environment

31 Statement 1 is true.

Statement 2 is false. The reverse yield gap refers to yields on shares being lower than on low-risk debt. A reverse yield gap can occur because shareholders may be willing to accept lower returns on their investments in the short term, in anticipation that they will make capital gains in the future.

Statement 3 is true. Disintermediation means borrowers dealing with lenders directly and has led to a reduction in the role of financial intermediaries.

Syllabus area B2(b)

32 Statements 2 and 4 only

Fiscal policy is action by the Government to spend money, or to collect money in taxes with the purpose of influencing the condition of the national economy.

Statement 1 is incorrect. Decreasing interest rates relates to monetary policy.

Statement 2 is correct. Reducing taxation relates to fiscal policy.

Statement 3 is incorrect. This is government policy on intervention to influence the exchange rate.

Statement 4 is correct. Spending money on public works is an example of fiscal policy.

Syllabus area B1(b/c)

33 All statements are correct.

Syllabus area B3

34 Statement 1 is incorrect: a capital market securities like a share, is an asset to a buyer.

Statements 2 and 3 are correct.

Syllabus area B2

35

Statement 1 – incorrect: it is fiscal policy that involves changing tax rates

Statement 2 – correct: in a floating rate system the exchange rate is determined by demand and supply.

Statement 3 – incorrect: it is monetary policy that seeks to influence the economy and economic growth by increasing or decreasing interest rates

Syllabus area B1(b)

36   **Both statements are true**.

If a government spends more, for example, on public services such as hospitals, without raising more money in taxation, it will increase expenditure in the economy and raise demand. Although the second statement appears to contradict the first, it is also true. After the government has kick-started demand (as in statement 1) then it should be able to repay the borrowing it has taken on as tax receipts rise due to higher economic activity.

Syllabus area B1(c)

37   **UK exporters to the US will suffer. UK importers from the US will benefit**.

A weakening dollar implies, for example, an exchange rate that moves from, say, $1:£1 to $2:£1. A UK exporter will therefore receive less £ sterling for their $ revenue. However, a UK company importing from the US will benefit by way of a lower £ cost for any given $ price they need to pay for their imports.

Syllabus area B1(b)

38   Options 1, 2 and 3 are all situations which may require regulation, because they are all examples of where the free market has failed.

Syllabus area B1(d)

39   **Low & stable inflation, achievement of a balance between exports and imports**.

The four main objectives of macroeconomic policy relate to economic growth, stable inflation, unemployment and the balance of payments (balance between exports and imports). Equitable income distribution is a social/political issue. Recycling is an environmental issue.

Syllabus area B1(a)

40   **Increasing public expenditure, decreasing taxation**.

Rationale: increasing public spending and cutting taxes should both increase the level of consumer spending which will stimulate economic activity.

Notes on incorrect answers:

Increasing the exchange rate will increase the price of exported goods and lower the price of imported goods; this is likely to lead to a fall in domestic economic activity. Increasing interest rates will cut investment (by companies) and consumer expenditure, even if only after a time lag.

Syllabus area B1(b)

MCQ bank – Working capital

41   **D** $3.151m

Current raw material inventory =

15/365 × purchases of (0.5 × $100m) = **$2.055m**

Current WIP inventory

= 35/365 × cost of goods sold $100m = **$9.589m**

Current finished goods inventory

= 40/365 × cost of goods sold $100m = **$10.959m**

A reduction of 5 days in raw material inventory =

5/15 × 2.055 = **$0.685m**

A reduction of 4 days in WIP inventory

= 4/35 × 9.589 = **$1.096m**

A reduction of 5 days in finished goods inventory

= 5/40 × 10.959 = **$1.370m**

Total reduction = 0.685 + 1.096 + 1.370 = **$3.151m**

Syllabus area C3(a)

42   **C**   Both the cash operating cycle and reported profits will reduce.

Receivables paying sooner will reduce receivables days and hence reduce the length of the cash operating cycle. The cost of the discount (approximately 2% per month as they pay a month earlier than usual) outweighs the interest saved on the overdraft (at 10% per annum this is less than 1% per month) hence the net effect will be reduced profit.

Syllabus area C2(d)

43   **A**   36.5 days

Current ratio = current assets/current liabilities = 2

Here   = ($3m + inventory)/$2m = 2

So inventory = $1m

If cost of sales is $10m then inventory days = (1/10) × 365 = 36.5 days

Syllabus area C3(a)

44   **D**   Reduction in receivables = $4,500,000 × 30/360 × 35% = $131,250

Alternatively: average receivables days will fall to (60 × 0.65) + (30 × 0.35) = 49.5 days which is a reduction of 10.5 days; $4,500,000 × 10.5/360 = $131,250.

Interest saved at 10% = $131,250 × 0.1 = $13,125
Cost of discount = $4,500,000 × 35% × 1% = $15,750
Net cost = $13,125 – $15,750 = $2,625

$1,875 is incorrectly arrived at by using 25% based on total customers instead of credit customers.

Syllabus area C2(d)

45   B   Inventory = $15,000,000 \times \dfrac{60}{360}$ = $2,500,000

Trade receivables = $27,000,000 \times \dfrac{50}{360}$ = $3,750,000

Trade payables = $15,000,000 \times \dfrac{45}{360}$ = $1,875,000

Net investment required = 2,500,000 + 3,750,000 – 1,875,000 = $4,375,000

Syllabus area C3(a)

CBE style OTQ bank – Managing working capital

46   **1,600**

Annual demand = 40×250 = 10,000 ball bearings = D

Order cost = $64 = C_o

Holding cost per year per unit = 25% of $2 = $0.50 = C_h

$$\text{EOQ} = \sqrt{\frac{2C_0D}{C_h}}$$

$$= \sqrt{\frac{2 \times 64 \times 10,000}{0.5}}$$

= 1,600 ball bearings

Syllabus area C2(c)

47   **$22,219**

Total cost = Annual purchase costs + annual ordering cost + annual holding cost.

Annual purchase cost = 10,000 units × $2 = $20,000

Annual ordering cost = number of orders × cost per order = (10,000/250) × $50 = $2,000

Annual holding cost = Average inventory level × cost to hold per unit per annum

= [(250/2) + 50] × $1.25 = $218.75

Total cost = $20,000 + $2,000 + $218.75 = $22,218.75 = $22,219 (to nearest $).

Syllabus area C2(c)

48   **1,2 and 3**

Statement 1 is correct. If a business is profitable then an increase in sales should translate to more working capital.

Statement 2 is correct. The greater the cash operating cycle, the greater the working capital investment need is. Greater working capital means more cash tied up and therefore not earning profit.

Statement 3 is correct. Overtrading (or undercapitalisation) is where a business is overreliant on short-term finance to support its operations. It is trying to do too much too quickly with little long-term capital.

Syllabus area C1(b/c)

49 **$114,521 cost**

The current collection period is $4/20 \times 365 = 73$ days.

Therefore a reduction to 60 days would be a reduction of 13 days.

Hence $13/365 \times \$20m = \$712,329$ reduction in receivables.

Finance cost saving $= \$712,329 \times 12\% = \$85,479$

Cost of discount $= 1\% \times \$20m = \$200,000$ per annum

Net cost $= \$200,000 - \$85,479 = \$114,521$

Syllabus area C2(d)

50 **2 only**

Statement 1 is incorrect because it is factoring with **no recourse** that provides insurance against bad debts

Syllabus area C2(d)

51 **Commercial paper**

Commercial paper is a source of finance and not directly applicable to the management of foreign debts.

Syllabus area C2(d)

52 **$28,500**

The cost is (total sales $\times$ 1.5%) + \$6,000 = ($1.5m \times 1.5\%$) + \$6,000 = \$28,500

Non-recourse means that the factor carries the risk of the bad debts.

Syllabus area C2(d)

53 'Assumes a small number of close suppliers' relates to just-in-time (JIT). It is not a drawback of EOQ.

Syllabus area C2(c)

54 'Increased risk of bad debts' relates to receivables, not payables.

Syllabus area C2(e)

55 **Lower inventory holding costs, more frequent deliveries**

Inventory shortages are the most likely problem with a JIT inventory ordering system as inventory is held at a minimal level. Ordering costs should rise because deliveries are more frequent.

Syllabus area C2(c)

CBE style OTQ bank – Working capital finance

56 **$290,084**

Receipts for March:

	$
50% March sales for cash (50% × $150,000)	75,000
80% × February credit sales less 4% discount (50% × 80% × $501,500 × 96%)	192,576
15% × January credit sales (50% × 15% × $300,100)	22,508
	290,084

Syllabus area C2(b)

57   **55,000**

Optimum cash conversion =

$$\sqrt{\frac{2 \times 400 \times 150,000}{(0.05 - 0.001)}} = \$54.772$$

55,000 to the nearest '000.

Syllabus area C2(f)

58   **They are all true.**

Miller Orr defines the difference between the upper limit and lower limit as the 'spread'.

TB Co's spread is $10m - $1m = $9m.

Miller Orr also defines the return point as the lower limit plus a third of the spread. In this case:

$1 + [(1/3) \times 9] = \$4m$

When the upper limit is reached, sufficient securities are purchased to reduce the cash balance back to the return point. In this case $10m - $4m = $6m. Therefore statement 1 is correct.

When the lower limit is reached, sufficient securities are sold to increase the cash balance back up to the return point. In this case $4m - $1 = $3m. Therefore statement 2 is correct.

The spread is calculated as:

$$3\left[\frac{\frac{3}{4} \times \text{transaction cost} \times \text{variance of cash flows}}{\text{interest rate}}\right]^{\frac{1}{3}}$$

An increase in variance will therefore increase the spread. Therefore statement 3 is correct.

Syllabus area C2(f)

59   **More short-term finance is used because it is cheaper, although it is risky**.

Aggressive working capital finance means using more short-term finance (and less long-term). Short-term finance is cheaper but it is risky – it may not be renewed when required and finance rates may change when they are renewed. C describes a conservative financing policy. D is describing a more aggressive working capital investment policy (not finance).

Syllabus area C3(b)

60   **Rate risk and renewal risk**

Rate risk refers to the fact that when short-term finance is renewed, the rates may vary when compared to the previous rate. This risk is less with long-term finance as it is renewed less frequently.

Renewal risk refers to the fact that finance providers may not renew the source of finance when it matures. This risk will be more acute with short-term finance as it needs renewing more often.

Short-term finance tends to be more flexible than long-term finance (eg overdraft, or supplier credit) so 'inflexibility' is incorrect. Maturity mismatch is not a risk specifically related to short-term finance so is incorrect.

Syllabus area C3(b)

PKA Co

61 **B** 1 and 2 only. The two main objectives of working capital management are to ensure the business has sufficient liquid resources to continue the business and to increase its profitability. These two objectives will often conflict because liquid assets give the lowest returns. Statement 3 is therefore not correct.

62 **A** 10,000 units

Minimum inventory level = reorder level − (average usage × average lead time)
Average usage per week = 625,000 units/50 weeks = 12,500 units
Average lead time = 2 weeks
Reorder level = 35,000 units
Minimum inventory level = 35,000 − (12,500 × 2) = 10,000 units

63 **D** 25,000 units

Economic order quantity

$$EOQ = \sqrt{\frac{2C_0D}{C_h}} = \sqrt{\frac{2 \times 250 \times 625,000}{0.5}} = 25,000 \text{ units}$$

64 **A** 1 and 2 only. The key to reducing the percentage of bad debts is to assess the creditworthiness of customers. Since the industry average accounts receivable period is 75 days, PKA needs to be careful not to lose business as a result of over-stringent credit control action (such as legal action). A good approach would be to encourage early payment, for example, through early settlement discounts.

65 **C** 2 and 3 only. With-recourse factoring does not remove the risk of bad debts. A factor should be able to accelerate receipts so that they are in line with PKA's terms of trade.

Plot Co

66 **D** $5,454 per year

Cost of current ordering policy

Total cost = order costs + holding costs
Ordering cost = 12 × $267 = $3,204 per year
Note. One order per month
Monthly order = monthly demand = 300,000/12 = 25,000 units
Buffer inventory = 25,000 × 0.4 = 10,000 units
Average inventory excluding buffer inventory = 25,000/2 = 12,500 units
Average inventory including buffer inventory = 12,500 + 10,000 = 22,500 units
Holding cost = 22,500 × 0.1 = $2,250 per year
Total cost = $3,204 + $2,250 = $5,454 per year

67 **B** $5,004 per year

Cost of ordering policy using economic order quantity (EOQ)

$EOQ = \sqrt{(2 \times C_o \times D)/C_h}$
$EOQ = \sqrt{(2 \times 267 \times 300,000)/0.10} = 40,025$ per order
Number of orders per year = 300,000/40,025 = 7.5 orders per year
Order cost = 7.5 × 267 = $2,003
Average inventory excluding buffer inventory = 40,025/2 = 20,013 units
Average inventory including buffer inventory = 20,013 + 10,000 = 30,013 units
Holding cost = 30,013 × 0.1 = $3,001 per year
Total cost = $2,003 + $3,001 = $5,004 per year

68 **B** Current receivables = $10m × (60/365) = $1,643,835.

Overdraft interest charge per annum relating to current receivables = $1,643,835 × 10% = $164,383.50 pa

Interest saved when half customers pay cash = 0.5 × $164,383.50 = $82,191.75 per year

Annual cost of the discount = 0.5 × $10m × 2% = $100,000

Net cost of offering the early settlement discount = $100,000 – $82,191.75 = $17,808.25 cost per year

69 **C** Both statements are true.

In terms of working capital finance, organisations can have a conservative (mainly long-term finance) or aggressive (mainly short-term finance) approach. The former is likely to be low risk but expensive, the latter more risky but cheaper (as short-term finance is low risk from an investor's perspective).

Poor financial management of working capital can lead to cash flow difficulties or even the failure of a business. Good working capital management can also create profits and minimise costs, and this ultimately adds to the wealth of shareholders – a key objective in the vast majority of businesses.

70 **D** The two symptoms of overtrading are increasing levels of inventory and current liabilities. Trade receivables increase during overtrading so statement 1 is not a symptom. Most of the increase in assets is financed by credit rather than long-term borrowings so statement 3 is not a symptom.

Gorwa Co

71 **20X7 30.53 times**

	20X7
Sales/net working capital	37,400/(9,200 – 7,975) = 30.53 times

72 **12 days**

20X6 days = 2,400/23,781 × 365 = 36.8
20X7 days = 4,600/34,408 × 365 = 48.8
Increase = 12 days

73 **Both statements are true.**

	20X7	20X6
Inventory days	4,600/34,408 × 365 = 49 days	2,400/23,781 × 365 = 37 days
Receivables days	4,600/37,400 × 365 = 45 days	2,200/26,720 × 365 = 30 days

74 **The correct answers are: Inventory turnover slows down and the current ratio falls.**

Another symptom of overtrading is a rapid growth in sales revenue (not a rapid reduction). The payment period to accounts payables lengthens as the business takes longer to pay amounts due.

75 **Non-current assets are sold.**

The other events may have limited or no effect on net working capital. Cash will rise to offset the increase in current liabilities if payments to suppliers are delayed. Cash will increase if credit is reduced, offsetting the fall in receivables. Cash will fall (or liabilities will rise) if inventories increase.

Cat Co

76 **$907,400**

Current cost = purchase cost + order cost + holding cost

Purchase cost = 120,000 units × $7.50 = $900,000 per year

Order costs = number of orders × fixed order cost = (120,000/10,000) × $200 = $2,400 per year

Holding cost = average inventory level × cost per unit per year = (10,000/2) × $1 = $5,000

Total current cost = $900,000 + $2,400 + $5,000 = $907,400.

Syllabus area C2(c)

77 **$901,400**

The cost = purchase cost + order cost + holding cost

Purchase cost = 120,000 units × $7.50 × (1 − 3.6%) = $867,600 per year

Order costs = number of orders × fixed order cost = (120,000/30,000) × $200 = $800 per year

Holding cost = average inventory level × cost per unit per year = (30,000/2) × $2.20 = $33,000

Total cost = $867,600 + $800 + $33,000 = $901,400.

Syllabus area C2(c)

78 **$89,041**

If the credit period is reduced to 60 days, receivables will become
(60/365) × $25 million = $4,109,589.

This is ($5 million − $4,109,589 =) $890,411 lower than before, saving interest of
10% × $890,411 = $89,041 per year.

This interest is saved as lower receivables implies more money (lower overdraft) in the bank.

Syllabus area C2(d)

79 **Statements 1 and 3 are correct.**

Statement 1 is correct. Sufficient working capital should be maintained to ensure bills can be paid on time; however, working capital (receivables, inventory, payables) do not earn a return as such, so excessive working capital is undesirable – spare cash for example should be temporarily placed to earn a return (provided risk is low).

Statement 2 is incorrect. A conservative approach to working capital investment implies aiming to keep relatively high levels of working capital. The reason for this is generally to reduce risk (less risk of inventory shortages, give customers plenty of time to pay, pay supplier cash) but it is expensive – it is money tied up not directly earning a return – hence will decrease profitability, not increase it.

Statement 3 is correct. Too much or too little working capital leads to poor business performance. Too much reduces profitability, too little is risky. Hence managing it to an appropriate level is important for a business if it is to be successful.

Statement 4 is incorrect. The two objectives of working capital management are to ensure the business has sufficient liquid resources and increase profitability. These objectives will often conflict as liquid assets give the lowest returns.

Syllabus area C1(b)

80 **Statement 2 only relates to an aggressive approach.**

Statement 1 relates to a conservative approach to financing working capital. Statement 2 relates to an aggressive approach.

Syllabus area C3(b)

81 APX Co

Text references. Financial intermediaries are covered in Chapter 3. Forecasting and working capital financing are covered in Chapters 4, 5 and 6.

Top tips. This question covers the key skills of forecasting financial statements as well as using and interpreting provided financial information. Part (c) requires a quick, relevant discussion of financial intermediaries which will be straightforward if you can remember the key terminology.

Part (a) may throw you as it requires a forecast financial position statement and statement of profit and loss. However, the format is provided in the question and the workings require logical manipulation of the accounting ratios provided. Fill in as many figures as you can and you will gain a mark for each correct calculation.

Easy marks. This question may look daunting initially but there are plenty of easy marks available if you tackle it logically and move on quickly if you get stuck.

Marking scheme

			Marks
(a)	Gross profit	1	
	Net profit	1	
	Profit before tax	1	
	Retained profit	1	
	Inventory	1	
	Trade receivables	1	
	Trade payables	1	
	Reserves	1	
	Overdraft	1	
	Layout and format	1	
		Maximum	9
(b)	Working capital financing policies	2–3	
	Financial analysis	1–2	
	Working capital financing policy of company	2–3	
		Maximum	6
(c)	Relevant discussion on financial intermediaries		5
			20

(a) (i) Forecast statement of profit or loss

	$m
Revenue (16.00m × 1.084)	17.344
Cost of sales (17.344m – 5.203m)	12.141
Gross profit (17.344m × 30%)	5.203
Other expenses (5.203m – 3.469m)	1.734
Net profit (17.344m × 20%)	3.469
Interest (10m × 0.08) + 0.140m	0.940
Profit before tax	2.529
Tax (2.529m × 0.3)	0.759
Profit after tax	1.770
Dividends (1.770m × 50%)	0.885
Retained profit	0.885

(ii) Forecast statement of financial position

	$m	$m
Non-current assets		22.00
Current assets		
Inventory (12.141m × (110/365))	3.66	
Trade receivables (17.344m × (65/365))	3.09	
		6.75
Total assets		28.75

	$m	$m
Equity finance		
Ordinary shares	5.00	
Reserves (7.5m + 0.885m)	8.39	
		13.39
Long-term bank loan		10.00
		23.39
Current liabilities		
Trade payables (12.141m × (75/365))	2.49	
Overdraft (28.75m – 23.39m – 2.49 = balancing figure)	2.87	
		5.36
Total liabilities		28.75

(b) **Working capital financing policy**

Working capital financing policies can be described as **conservative**, **moderate** or **aggressive**, depending on the extent to which fluctuating current assets and permanent current assets are financed by short-term sources of finance.

Permanent current assets are the amount required to meet long-term minimum needs and sustain normal trading activity, for example inventory and the average level of accounts receivable.

Fluctuating current assets are the current assets which vary according to normal business activity, for example due to seasonal variations.

A **conservative** working capital financing policy uses **long-term** funds to finance non-current assets and permanent current assets, as well as a proportion of fluctuating current assets.

An **aggressive** working capital financing policy uses **short-term** funds to finance fluctuating current assets and a proportion of permanent current assets as well. This is riskier but potentially more profitable.

A **balance** between risk and return might be best achieved by a moderate policy, which uses long-term funds to finance long-term assets (non-current assets and permanent current assets) and short-term funds to finance short-term assets (fluctuating current assets).

The current statement of financial position shows that APX Co uses **trade payables** and an **overdraft** as sources of **short-term** finance. 89% (100 × 4.1/4.6) of current assets are financed from short-term sources and only 11% are financed from long-term sources. This appears to be a **very aggressive** working capital financing policy which carries significant risk. For example, if the bank called in the overdraft, APX Co might have to resort to more expensive short-term financing.

The **forecast** statement of financial position shows a **reduced** reliance on short-term finance. 79% (100 × 5.36/6.75) of current assets are now financed from short-term sources and 21% are financed from long-term sources. This reduces the risk of the working financing capital policy.

Further moves away from an aggressive policy would be hampered by a lack of ability to pay interest on more long-term debt. The forecast **interest coverage ratio** is only 3.7 times (3.469/0.94). Alternatively, APX Co could consider an **increase in equity funding** to decrease reliance on short-term finance.

(c) **Role of financial intermediaries**

Financial intermediaries provide a **link** between investors who have surplus cash and borrowers who have a need for finance.

Financial intermediaries **aggregate** invested funds. This means that they group together the small amounts of cash provided by individual investors, so that borrowers who need large amounts of cash have a convenient and readily accessible route to obtain necessary funds.

Financial intermediaries **reduce** the risk for individual lenders by **pooling**. They will assume the risk of loss on short-term funds borrowed by business organisations. Such losses are shared among lenders in general.

Financial intermediaries also offer **maturity transformation**, in that they bridge the gap between the wish of most lenders for **liquidity** and the desire of most borrowers for loans over longer periods.

82 Pangli Co

Examining team

Marking scheme

				Marks
(a)	(i)	Cost of sales	0.5	
		Inventory days	0.5	
		Receivables days	0.5	
		Cash operating cycle	0.5	
				2
	(ii)	Inventory 31 January	0.5	
		Receivables 31 January	1	
		Payables 31 January	1	
		Overdraft 31 January	1.5	
				4
	(iii)	Current ratio 1 January	2	
		Current ratio 31 January	2	
				4
(b)		First technique	2	
		Second technique	2	
		Third technique	2	
		Fourth technique	2	
		Fifth technique	2	
				10
				20

(a) (i)   The cash operating cycle can be calculated by adding inventory days and receivables days, and subtracting payables days.

Cost of sales = $3,500,000 \times (1 - 0.4)$ = $2,100,000

Inventory days = $360 \times 455,000/2,100,000$ = 78 days
Trade receivables days = $360 \times 408,350/3,500,000$ = 42 days
Trade payables days = $360 \times 186,700/2,100,000$ = 32 days

Cash operating cycle of Pangli Co = 78 + 42 − 32 = 88 days

(ii)   Inventory at end of January 20X7 = 455,000 + 52,250 = $507,250

At the start of January 20X7, 100% of December 20X6 receivables will be outstanding ($300,000), together with 40% of November 20X6 receivables ($108,350 = 40% × 270,875), a total of $408,350 as given.

	$
Trade receivables at start of January 20X7	408,350
Outstanding November 20X6 receivables paid	(108,350)
December 20X6 receivables, 60% paid	(180,000)
January 20X7 credit sales	350,000
Trade receivables at end of January 20X7	470,000

	$
Trade payables at start of January 20X7	186,700
Payment of 70% of trade payables	(130,690)
January 20X7 credit purchases	250,000
Trade payables at end of January 20X7	306,010

	$
Overdraft at start of January 20X7	240,250
Cash received from customers	(288,350)
Cash paid to suppliers	130,690
Interest payment	70,000
Operating cash outflows	146,500
Overdraft expected at end of January 20X7	299,090

(iii)   Current assets at start of January 20X7 = 455,000 + 408,350 = $863,350
Current liabilities at start of January 20X7 = 186,700 + 240,250 = $426,950
Current ratio at start of January 20X7 = 863,350/426,950 = 2.03 times

Current assets at end of January 20X7 = 507,250 + 470,000 = $977,250
Current liabilities at end of January 20X7 = 306,010 + 299,090 = $605,100
Current ratio at end of January 20X7 = 977,250/605,100 = 1.62 times

(b)   Pangli Co could use the following techniques in managing trade receivables: assessing creditworthiness; managing accounts receivable; collecting amounts owing; offering early settlement discounts: using factoring and invoice discounting; and managing foreign accounts receivable.

Assessing creditworthiness

Pangli Co can seek to reduce its exposure to the risks of bad debt and late payment by assessing the creditworthiness of new customers. In order to do this, the company needs to review information from a range of sources. These sources include trade references, bank references, credit reference agencies and published accounts. To help it to review this information, Pangli Co might develop its own credit scoring process. After assessing the creditworthiness of new customers, Pangli Co can decide on how much credit to offer and on what terms.

Managing accounts receivable

Pangli Co needs to make sure that its credit customers abide by the terms of trade agreed when credit was granted following credit assessment. The company wants its customers to settle their outstanding accounts on time and also to keep to their agreed credit limits. Key information here will be the number of overdue accounts and the degree of lateness of amounts outstanding. An aged receivables analysis can provide this information.

Pangli Co also needs to make sure that its credit customers are aware of the outstanding invoices on their accounts. The company will therefore remind them when payment is due and regularly send out statements of account.

Collecting amounts owing

Ideally, credit customers will pay on time and there will be no need to chase late payers. There are many ways to make payment in the modern business world and Pangli Co must make sure that its credit customers are able to pay quickly and easily. If an account becomes overdue, Pangli Co must make sure it is followed up quickly. Credit control staff must assess whether payment is likely to be forthcoming and if not, a clear policy must be in place on further steps to take. These further steps might include legal action and using the services of a debt collection agency.

Offering early settlement discounts

Pangli Co can encourage its credit customers to settle outstanding amounts by offering an early settlement discount. This will offer a reduction in the outstanding amount (the discount) in exchange for settlement before the due date. For example, if the credit customer agreed to pay in full after 40 days, an early settlement discount might offer a 2% discount for settling after 25 days. Pangli Co must weigh the benefit of offering such an early settlement discount against the benefit expected to arise from its use by credit customers. One possible benefit might be a reduction in the amount of interest the company pays on its overdraft. Another possible benefit might be matching or bettering the terms of trade of a competitor.

Using factoring and invoice discounting

Pangli Co might use a factor to help manage its accounts receivable, either on a recourse or non-recourse basis. The factor could offer assistance in credit assessment, managing accounts receivable and collecting amounts owing. For a fee, the factor could advance a parcentage of the face value of outstanding invoices. The service offered by the factor would be tailored to the needs of the company.

Invoice discounting is a service whereby a third party, usually a factor, pays a percentage of the face value of a collection of high value invoices. When the invoices are settled, the outstanding balance is paid to the company, less the invoice discounter's fee.

Managing foreign accounts receivable

Foreign accounts receivable can engender increased risk of non-payment by customers and can increase the value of outstanding receivables due to the longer time over which foreign accounts receivable are outstanding. Pangli Co could reduce the risk of non-payment by assessing creditworthiness, employing an export factor, taking out export credit insurance, using documentary credits and entering into countertrade agreements. The company could reduce the amount of investment in foreign accounts receivable through using techniques such as advances against collections and negotiating or discounting bills of exchange

Examining team's note: Only five techniques were required to be discussed.

83 WQZ Co

Text references. Receivables management is covered in Chapter 5.

Top tips. For parts (a) and (b) it is important to set up the calculations in a way that makes it easy for the marker to follow.

In part (c) it is important that the answer focuses on the question about factors affecting trade receivables management rather than talking about methods of reducing trade receivables balances.

Easy marks. The discussion of factors in formulating a trade receivables management policy should provide easy marks.

ACCA examining team's comments. For part (a) a number of answers failed to gain full marks because they did not calculate the change in inventory management costs, even after correctly calculating these costs under the current ordering policy and after applying the EOQ model. Poorer answers showed a lack of understanding of the relationship between ordering costs and holding costs, and an inability to calculate these costs. Feedback from markers indicated that some answers to part (b) were disorganised, with unlabelled calculations and a lack of explanation. It is important to help the marking process by labelling calculations, explaining workings and using correct notation, eg '$ per year', '$m', 'days' and so on.

Marks

(a) Current policy:

Annual ordering cost		0.5
Annual holding cost		0.5
Total annual cost		1
EOQ policy:		
Annual order size		1
Annual ordering cost and holding cost		1
Change in inventory management cost		1
		5

(b)

Reduction in trade receivables		2
Financing cost saving		1
Cost of early settlement discount		1
Comment on net benefit		2
Maximum early settlement discount		1
		7

(c) Relevant discussion

8

20

(a) **Current policy**

Order size = 10% × 160,000 = 16,000 units per order

Number of orders = 160,000/16,000 = 10 orders per year

Annual ordering cost = 10 × 400 = $4,000

Average inventory = 5,000 + 16,000/2 = 13,000 units

Holding cost of average inventory = 13,000 × 5.12 = $66,560 per year

Total annual cost = $4,000 + $66,560 = $70,560

EOQ model

Order size = $\sqrt{\dfrac{2 \times 400 \times 160,000}{5.12}}$ = 5,000 units per order

Number of orders = 160,000/5,000 = 32 orders per year

Annual ordering cost = 32 × 400 = $12,800

Average inventory = 5,000 + 5,000/2 = 7,500 units

Holding cost of average inventory = 7,500 × 5.12 = $38,400 per year

Total annual cost = $12,800 + $38,400 = $51,200

Cost savings from EOQ method

70,560 − 51,200 = $19,360 per year

Note. Since the holding cost of buffer stock is a common cost to both models, this could have been omitted from the calculations. Full marks could still be gained from this approach.

(b) **Change of receivables policy**

Receivables payment period is currently $(18/87.6) \times 365 = 75$ days

Under the new policy only 25% will pay in 30 days, so the revised payment period would be

$(0.25 \times 30) + (0.75 \times 60) = 52.5$ days

Current trade receivables = $18m

Revised level using the revised payment period = $87.6 \times (52.5/365) = \$12.6m$

Reduction in receivables = $18 - 12.6 = \$5.4m$

Short-term finance cost is 5.5%

Finance cost savings = $5.4m \times 0.055 = \$297,000$

Administration savings = $753,000

Total savings = 297,000 + 753,000 = $1,050,000

Cost of the discount = credit sales $\times$ % customers taking discount $\times$ discount %

Cost of the discount = $87.6m \times 0.25 \times 0.01 = \$219,000$

Benefit of the discount = $1,050,000 - 219,000 = \$831,000$

The proposed change in receivables management should be accepted, although this does depend on the forecast cost savings being achieved.

Maximum discount

25% of the customers will take the discount. Therefore the total sales value affected by the discount will be 25% of $87.6m, which is $21.9m.

The maximum discount will be where the costs equal the benefits of $1,050,000. This would occur at:

$1.05/21.9 = 0.048 = 4.8\%$

(c) The policy on the management of trade receivables will depend on a number of factors.

The level of trade receivables

If there is a substantial amount of capital tied up in trade receivables, then the policy may be aimed at reducing the level of investment by not granting credit as freely as before or shortening the credit terms.

The cost of trade credit

Where the cost of trade credit (including opportunity costs) is high, a company will want to reduce the level of investment in trade receivables.

Competitor trade terms

Unless a company can differentiate itself from its competitors, it will need to at least match the credit terms offered by its competitors to avoid a loss of customers.

Liquidity needs

Where a company needs to improve its liquidity it may want to reduce credit terms or consider debt factoring or invoice discounting.

Risk appetite

A company may be prepared to risk higher levels of bad debts by offering credit terms that are relatively relaxed as this will increase sales volume.

Expertise in credit management

If a company lacks expertise in credit management, particularly in monitoring the level of receivables, then it may choose to factor its debts.

84 Bold Co

Marking scheme

			Marks
(a)	Explanation of cash operating cycle	1–2	
	Cash operating cycle and working capital policy	2–3	
	Cash operating cycle and business operation	2–3	
	Other relevant discussion	1–2	
		Maximum	8
(b)	Inventory days	1	
	Receivables days	1	
	Payables days	1	
	Cash operating cycle	1	
			4
(c)	Revised trade receivables	1	
	Reduction in trade receivables	1	
	Reduction in finance cost	1	
	Administration costs	0.5	
	Saving in bad debts	0.5	
	Interest on advance	1	
	With-recourse factor fee	0.5	
	Net benefit of with-recourse offer	0.5	
	Without-recourse factor fee	0.5	
	Elimination of bad debts	1	
	Net benefit of non-recourse offer	0.5	
			8
			20

(a) The cash operating cycle is the period of time which elapses between the point at which cash begins to be expended on the production of a product and the collection of cash from a customer. The cash operating cycle in a manufacturing business equals the average time that raw materials remain in inventory less the average period of credit taken from suppliers plus the average time taken to produce the goods plus the average time taken by customers to pay for the goods.

There is a relationship between the cash operating cycle and the level of investment in working capital. If the turnover periods for inventories and accounts receivable lengthen, or the payment period to accounts payable shortens, then the operating cycle will lengthen and the investment in working capital will increase. The length of the cash operating cycle depends on the working capital policy which will determine the level of investment in working capital and also the nature of the business operations.

Working capital policy

The level of investment in working capital depends on the company's working capital policy. Two companies with similar business operations may have significantly different levels of investment depending on whether they adopt a conservative or an aggressive approach. An aggressive policy involves having lower levels of inventory and trade receivables and will therefore mean there is a shorter cash operating cycle. A conservative policy involves having higher levels of inventory and trade receivables and will give rise to a longer cash operating cycle. The longer cash operating cycle will mean profitability is less than under the aggressive approach, but it reduces risk such as the risk of a stock-out.

Nature of business operations

Business operations will have a significant effect on the cash operating cycle. A business supplying services may have very low levels of inventory whereas a manufacturer may have very high levels of inventory. A retailer who operates mainly using cash sales will have a significantly lower level of trade receivables than a company which conducts most of its sales by offering credit terms.

(b)　Inventory days = 4,500/16,400 × 365 = 100 days
　　　Trade receivables days = 3,500/21,300 × 365 = 60 days
　　　Trade payables days = 3,000/16,400 × 365 = 67 days
　　　Cash operating cycle = 100 + 60 − 67 = 93 days

(c)　**With-recourse offer**

Since the factor will reduce trade receivables days to 35 the trade receivables figure will change.

Revised trade receivables /$21,300,000 × 365 days = 35 days
Revised trade receivables = 35/365 × $21,300,000
Revised trade receivables under factoring = $2,042,466
Reduction in trade receivables = $3,500,000 − $2,042,466 = $1,457,534

	$
Finance cost saving ($1,457,534 × 7%)	102,027
Administration cost saving	40,000
Bad debt saving ($21,300,000 × (0.009 − 0.006))	63,900
	205,927
Additional interest on advance (2,042,466 × 0.8 × 0.02)	(32,679)
Net benefit	173,248
Factor fee (21,300,000 × 0.0075)	(159,750)
	13,498

Non-recourse offer

As the offer is without recourse, bad debts are reduced to zero as the factor will bear these. Therefore Bold Co will gain a benefit of a further 0.6% of revenue.

	$
Net benefit of with-recourse offer	173,248
Non-recourse factor fee (21,300,000 × 0.0125)	(266,250)
Net cost before adjusting for bad debts	(93,002)
Elimination of bad debts ($21,300,000 × 0.006)	127,800
Net benefit	34,798

85 Wobnig Co

Marking scheme

			Marks
(a)	Rapid increase in revenue	1–2	
	Increase in trade receivables days	1–2	
	Decrease in profitability	1–2	
	Rapid increase in current assets	1–2	
	Increased dependence on short-term finance	2–3	
	Decrease in liquidity	2–3	
	Conclusion as regards overtrading	1	
	Maximum		12
(b)	Working capital investment policy	3–4	
	Working capital financing policy	5–6	
	Maximum		8
			20

(a)   Signs of overtrading:

Rapid increase in sales revenue: Wobnig Co's sales revenue has increased by 40% from $10,375k in 20X0 to $14,525k in 20X1. This rapid growth in revenue is not supported by a similar increase in long-term financing, which has only increased by 4.7% ($16,268k in 20X1 compared to $15,541k in 20X0).

Rapid increase in current assets: Wobnig Co's current assets have also nearly doubled, increasing from $2,826k in 20X0 to $5,349k in 20X1 (89%). This is striking, given that long-term financing has only increased by 4.7%. Trade receivables have increased by 85% ($1,734k in 20X0 and $3,200k in 20X1), and inventory levels have increased by 97% ($2,149k from $1,092k in 20X0).

Increase in inventory days: Linked to the above, inventory turnover has slowed noticeably, from 60 days in 20X0 to 75 days in 20X1, well above the industry average of 55 days. This may indicate that Wobnig Co is expecting further increases in sales volumes in the future.

Increase in receivable days: Perhaps a matter of greater concern is the fact that trade receivables are being paid much more slowly. Receivable days have increased from 61 days in 20X0 to 80 days in 20X1, again significantly above the industry average. It could be that in order to encourage sales, Wobnig Co has offered more favourable credit terms to its customers. However, the increase in receivable days may also indicate that Wobnig Co is lacking sufficient resources to effectively manage its receivables, and/or that its customers may be unable to settle their debts on time, as they are struggling financially.

Reduction in profitability: Although Wobnig Co's sales revenue has increased by 40% over the past year, its profit before interest and tax (PBIT) has only increased by 8.9%. The net profit margin has actually decreased, from 36% in 20X0 to 28% in 20X1. This may be due partly to the company selling at lower margins to increase sales volumes, but most likely points to increased costs of sales and operating costs.

With the additional costs associated with holding larger inventories, and increasing financing costs from overdrafts (see below), the company's profitability is likely to suffer even more in the future.

Increase in current liabilities: Wobnig Co is increasingly financed through current liabilities, which has increased by 131% (from $1,887k in 20X0 to $4,365k in 20X1) while long-term financing has increased only marginally by 4.7%. The sales revenue/net working capital ratio has increased from 11 times to 15 times in 20X1. In particular, overdraft has increased by 500% from 20X0 to 20X1. Payables days have lengthened from 90 days to 100 days, indicating that Wobnig Co is finding it more difficult to settle trade debts.

All of this will put further strain on financing costs, eroding the distributable profits. The company's interest expense has increased from $292k to $355k.

Reduced liquidity: The cause of Wobnig Co's increasing dependence on overdrafts and lengthening payables days lies in its reduced liquidity. Wobnig Co's current ratio has reduced from 1.5 times to 1.2 times, compared to the industry average of 1.7 times. The more sensitive quick ratio has reduced from 0.9 times to 0.7 times, against the average of 1.1 times. Wobnig Co does not yet have a liquid deficit, though, as its current assets still exceed its current liabilities.

Conclusion

From the trends discussed above, we can conclude that Wobnig Co is overtrading.

Workings

Ratio	Formula	20X1	20X0
Net profit margin	PBIT/Revenue × 100%	28%	36%
Current ratio	Current assets/current liabilities	1.2 times	1.5 times
Quick ratio	(Current assets − inventory)/current liabilities	0.7 times	0.9 times
Inventory days	Inventory/cost of sales × 365	75 days	60 days
Receivables days	Trade receivables/revenue × 365	80 days	61 days
Payables days	Trade payables/cost of sales × 365	100 days	90 days
Net working capital	Current assets − current liabilities	$984,000	$949,000
Revenue/net working capital	Revenue/net working capital	15 times	11 times

(Note that the Revenue/net working capital ratio can also be calculated excluding cash balances or overdraft.)

(b)   Working capital investment policy dictates how much a company chooses to invest in current assets. Working capital financing policy, on the other hand, determines how a company funds its day to day operations: with short-term or long-term sources. The working capital investment policy is therefore an investment decision, while the working capital financing policy is a financing decision.

Both working capital investment policy and working capital financing policy are described in terms of conservative, moderate and aggressive. However, these terms mean different things in the contexts of investment and financing.

In the context of working capital investment, a conservative policy aims to reduce the risk of system breakdown by holding high levels of working capital: generous credit terms for customers, high levels of inventory and quick payment of suppliers. This approach can result in a high financing cost and may give rise to cash flow problems. By contrast, an aggressive approach reduces financing cost and increases profitability by cutting inventories, collecting debts early from customers and delaying payment to suppliers.

In the context of working capital financing, current assets are divided into permanent current assets (the level of current assets that supports a standard level of business activity) and fluctuating assets (the level of current assets that rise and fall due to unexpected business demands). A conservative policy is one that uses long-term funding to finance most of the assets of the company, calling upon short-term financing only when fluctuations in current assets push total assets above a certain level. An aggressive policy, by contrast, is one that finances all fluctuating current assets and some permanent current assets out of short-term sources. This approach presents a greater risk of liquidity issues, but allows for lower financing costs. This is because short-term finance is cheaper than long-term finance.

Working capital investment and working capital financing therefore describe two different aspects of working capital management. In fact, it is possible for a company to adopt an aggressive working capital investment policy and a conservative working capital financing policy, or vice versa.

86 KXP Co

Text references. Early settlement discounts, the effect of a change in credit policy, bulk discounts and the factors to be considered in managing trade receivables are all covered in Chapter 5. The optimum level of cash to be held is covered in Chapter 6.

Top tips. The calculations in parts (a) and (b) should pose no problems if you work through them logically.

Easy marks. Parts (a) and (b) contain straightforward calculations. For parts (c) and (d), plan your answers into clearly defined points first, and avoid repeating yourself.

ACCA examining team's comments. In part (a), weaker answers showed a lack of understanding of how the receivables days ratio links credit sales for a period with the trade receivables balance at the end of the period. Some answers, for example, tried to calculate the revised trade receivables balance by applying changed receivables days ratios to current receivables, instead of applying them to credit sales. In part (b), perhaps because information on holding cost and order cost was provided in the question, many candidates calculated the economic order quantity (EOQ). The question made no reference to the EOQ and an EOQ calculation was not necessary. For part (c), many answers failed to gain reasonable marks because they did not discuss factors. For example, some answers explained the workings of the Baumol and Miller-Orr cash management models. The question did not ask for a discussion of these models and such answers gained little or no credit.

Marking scheme

			Marks
(a)	Revised trade receivables	0.5	
	Reduction in trade receivables	0.5	
	Reduction in financing cost	1	
	Cost of early settlement discount	1	
	Net cost of change in receivables policy	1	
	Comment on findings	1	
			5
(b)	Current annual ordering cost	0.5	
	Current holding cost	0.5	
	Total cost of current inventory policy	0.5	
	Revised cost of materials	0.5	
	Revised number of orders	0.5	
	Revised ordering cost	0.5	
	Revised holding cost	0.5	
	Net benefit of bulk purchase discount	0.5	
	Comment on assumptions	1	
			5
(c)	Transactions need for cash	1–2	
	Precautionary need for cash	1–2	
	Speculative need for cash	1–2	
	Other relevant discussion	1–2	
		Maximum	5
(d)	Credit analysis	1–2	
	Credit control	1–2	
	Receivables collection	1–2	
	Cost and benefits of trade receivables policy	1–2	
		Maximum	5
			20

(a) **Cost/benefit of changing trade receivables policy**

Receivables paying within 30 days = 50% × $15m × 30/365 = $616,438

Receivables paying after 45 days = 30% × $15m × 45/365 = $554,795

Total receivables changing their payment patterns = $616,438 + $554,795 = $1,171,233

Original value of these receivables = 80% × $2,466k = $1,972,800

Reduction in receivables = **$801,567**

Cost of early payment discount = 50% × $15m × 1% = $75,000

Reduction in financing cost = $801,567 × 6% = $48,094

Net cost of changing trade receivables policy = $75,000 − $48,094 = **$26,906**

Alternative calculation for the reduction in receivables

Current receivable days = $2,466k/$15,000k × 365 = 60 days

Receivable days under new trade receivables policy = 50% × 30 + 30% × 45 + 20% × 60 = 40.5 days

Decrease in receivable days = 60 − 40.5 = 19.5 days

Reduction in receivables = $15m × 19.5/365 = **$801,370** (difference due to rounding)

Conclusion

The benefit of the new trade receivables policy is outweighed by the associated costs. KXP Co should not adopt the proposed policy. However, the analysis currently excludes bad debts and assumes constant sales throughout the year – the company may need to take these into account. Given that receivables on average are failing to meet the credit period, KXP Co may still want to consider how the trade receivables policy may be changed in order to encourage earlier payment.

(b) Total annual cost of inventory policy = cost of materials + ordering cost + holding cost

Current policy

Annual ordering cost = 12 × $150 = $1,800

Annual holding cost = $0.24 × (15,000/2) = $1,800

Total annual cost = $540,000 + $1,800 + $1,800 = $543,600

Proposed policy

Annual cost of materials = $540,000 × 98% = $529,200

KXP Co currently requires 180,000 units of Product Z per year (12 × 15,000).

To benefit from the bulk discount, KXP Co needs to order 30,000 units each time. This means KXP Co will make 6 orders per year (180,000/30,000).

Revised annual ordering cost = 6 × $150 = $900

Revised annual holding cost = $0.24 × (30,000/2) = $3,600

Total annual cost = $529,200 + $900 + $3,600 = $533,700

Net benefit

Net benefit of taking bulk purchase discount = $543,600 − $533,700 = $9,900

Conclusion

The analysis shows that the bulk discount should be accepted. However, KXP Co may wish to evaluate the appropriateness of a number of key assumptions first:

- Demand for Product Z is constant throughout the year, and does not change from year to year.
- Ordering costs and holding costs are both constant throughout the year.

BPP
LEARNING MEDIA

(c) The optimum level of cash to be held by a company depends on the following factors:

The level of cash required for the company's operations

This includes holding enough cash to:

(i) Pay for the transactions expected to occur during the period (including the payment of suppliers, and finance costs). This can be achieved by drawing up a cash budget.

(ii) Cover unexpected expenditure and account for uncertainty in the cash budget. In addition to the cash needs forecasted in the cash budget, the company needs to have a precautionary 'buffer' for unexpected events. This can be estimated based on previous experience.

The availability of finance

Not all sources of finance may be available to a company. A small or medium-sized company, for example, may not be able to obtain or extend bank loans as easily. An unlisted company will find it very difficult, and expensive, to raise funds through issuing securities. Where it is difficult and/or expensive to raise new finance, a company will need to hold more cash.

The availability and attractiveness of other uses for the cash

The amount of cash that a company holds will also depend on whether there are other, more attractive ways to use the cash. Instead of holding cash for no return, a company usually has the option of putting the cash in a deposit account with a bank, investing it in short- or long-term debt instruments, or investing in equity shares of listed companies. The extent to which the company will consider these alternative uses depends on the amount of investment required, the expected level of return (interest, dividends or capital growth), the term to maturity and the ease of realising the investment.

A company may also wish to hold cash in order to be able to take advantage of an unexpected speculative opportunity when it arises.

(d) Factors to consider in formulating a trade receivables management policy

The total credit

Each company must determine the level of total credit it is willing to offer. This involves finding a balance between maximising revenue from customers, and minimising the finance costs associated with funding the period of credit and also minimising bad debts.

Allowing a long period of credit may attract more sales, but the company may suffer from high finance costs. A short period of credit will reduce the need for additional finance, but the company may lose out on sales opportunities.

The cost of the additional finance – be it bank overdraft interest, loans or equity – must be considered.

Credit control

Companies need to have a policy in place for assessing the creditworthiness of customers. Verifying that new customers are creditworthy before concluding the sale reduces the risk of customer default.

This may involve requiring references for new customers, checking credit ratings through a credit rating agency, and offering a lower level of credit for new customers. A credit rating system may be devised to determine the appropriate level of credit to offer to new customers based on their characteristics (such as age and occupation).

Collection

A credit policy can only be maintained if it is policed effectively and the amounts owing collected. The company will need to monitor customers' payment records to ensure that the credit limits are maintained. An aged receivables analysis should be performed on a regular basis. Any breaches of credit limits should be brought to the attention of the credit controller.

Factors which would influence how tightly a company polices its credit policy include the number of customers requiring more credit, and the extent to which the company is exposed to accounts receivable.

The associated costs of collection, either internal or external, also need to be considered. The costs of collection should not be greater than the amount collected.

Changes to the credit policy

The credit policy needs to be reviewed regularly and revised as economic conditions and customer payment patterns change. The company may wish to assess whether it is beneficial to offer an early payment discount to encourage customers to pay earlier, or extend the credit period to encourage custom. The associated costs and impact on the company's working capital must be considered. Only when the financial benefit of the change in policy outweighs the additional costs should the change go ahead.

87 CSZ Co

Text references. The working capital cycle and liquidity ratios are covered in Chapter 4.

Top tips. There are two requirements in part (a) and two requirements in part (b). Make sure that you don't accidentally miss out some of the requirements. You may have been thrown by the mention of a negative working capital cycle but, if you think about what the cycle actually means, you should be able to see that a negative cycle is possible.

Easy marks. There are easy marks for calculations in part (a) and part (b) if you know the liquidity ratios.

ACCA examining team's comments. The examining team commented that in part (a), many students incorrectly stated that the working capital cycle should be positive. Many students gained good marks in part (b). For part (c) some students discussed at length possible reasons for the changes in inventory, trade payables, trade receivables and so on, often writing as though the changes had occurred rather than having been forecast. The only discussion that was specifically required was in the area of working capital financing. This emphasises the need to read the question requirement carefully and to respond directly to what is required.

Marking scheme

			Marks
(a)	Inventory days	0.5	
	Trade receivables days	0.5	
	Trade payables days	0.5	
	Working capital cycle	0.5	
	Discussion of working capital cycle	4	
			6
(b)	Cost of sales	0.5	
	Inventory	0.5	
	Trade receivables	0.5	
	Current assets	0.5	
	Current liabilities	0.5	
	Target quick ratio	1	
	Net working capital cycle	0.5	
	Target sales/net working capital ratio	1	
			5
(c)	Trade payables	1	
	Overdraft	1	
	Analysis of current asset and liability positions	1–3	
	Comparison of current asset and liability positions	1–3	
	Discussion of change in financing policy	1–3	
	Maximum	9	
			20

(a)

				Days
Inventory days	$= \dfrac{\text{Average inventory}}{\text{Cost of sales}} \times 365$	$\dfrac{5,700}{26,000} \times 365$	$=$	80
A/cs receivable days	$= \dfrac{\text{Trade receivables}}{\text{Credit sales revenue}} \times 365$	$\dfrac{6,575}{40,000} \times 365$	$=$	60
A/cs payable days	$= \dfrac{\text{Trade payables}}{\text{Cost of sales}} \times 365$	$\dfrac{2,137}{26,000} \times 365$	$=$	(30)
		Working capital cycle:		110

The working capital cycle is the **period of time** which elapses between the point at which **cash begins to be expended** on the production of a product and the **collection of cash from a customer**. Therefore CSZ Co starts spending 110 days (on average) before cash is collected from the customer.

A **negative** working capital cycle would mean that CSZ Co was **paid by customers before** it started to **spend cash** on the **production**. This can sometimes occur. For example, supermarkets often receive payment for goods before they have paid for them.

A business does **not normally have a choice** on whether its working capital cycle is positive or negative because it depends on the inventory, receivables and payables days and these usually **depend** on the **nature of the business**. The length of the working capital cycle is usually **similar between** businesses in the **same sector**.

(b) Quick ratio $= \dfrac{\text{Current assets less inventories}}{\text{Current liabilities}} = \dfrac{8,219}{5,073+3,616} = 0.95$ times

Inventory days $= \dfrac{\text{Inventory}}{\text{Cost of sales}} \times 365 \therefore \dfrac{\text{Inventory}}{24,000} \times 365 = 60 \therefore$ Inventory = \$3,945

Receivables days $= \dfrac{\text{Receivables}}{\text{Sales}} \times 365 \therefore \dfrac{\text{Receivables}}{40,000} \times 365 = 75 \therefore$ Receivables = \$8,219

Payables days $= \dfrac{\text{Payables}}{\text{Cost of sales}} \times 365 \therefore \dfrac{\text{Payables}}{24,000} \times 365 = 55 \therefore$ Payables = \$3,616

Current ratio $= \dfrac{3,945+8,219}{3,616+\text{overdraft}} = 1.4 \therefore$ overdraft = \$5,073

Net current assets at the end of March 20X5 $= \$3,945k + \$8,219k - \$3,616k - \$5,073k$

$= \$3,475,000$

Target sales = \$40m

Target ratio of sales to net working capital = 40,000/3,475 = 11.5 times

Note that the sales/net working capital ratio can also be calculated excluding cash balances or overdraft.

(c) The current liabilities at the end of March 20X5, calculated in part (b), can be divided into trade payables and the forecast overdraft balance.

Trade payables using target trade payables days = 24,000,000 × 55/365 = \$3,616,438.

The overdraft (balancing figure) = 8,688,846 − 3,616,438 = \$5,072,408

Comparing current assets and current liabilities:

	March 20X4		March 20X5	
	\$'000	\$'000	\$'000	\$'000
Inventory	5,700		3,945	
Trade receivables	6,575	12,275	8,219	12,164
Overdraft	2,137		3,616	
	4,682	6,819	5,072	8,688
Net current assets		5,456		3,476

The overdraft as a percentage of current liabilities will fall from 69% (4,682/6,819) to 58% (5,702/8,688). Even though the overdraft is expected to increase by 8.3%, current liabilities are expected to increase by 27.4% (8,688/6,819). Most of this increase is expected to be carried by trade payables, which will rise by 69.2% (3,616/2,317), with trade payables days increasing from 30 days to 55 days.

At the end of March 20X4, current liabilities were 56% of current assets (100 × 6,819/12,275), suggesting that 44% of current assets were financed from a long-term source. At the end of March 20X5, current liabilities are expected to be 71% of current assets (100 × 8,688/12,164), suggesting that 29% of current assets are finance from a long-term source. This increasing reliance on short-term finance implies an aggressive change in the working capital financing policy of CSZ Co.

88 Flit Co

Text references. Cash flow forecasts and short-term investments are covered in Chapter 6. The current ratio is covered in Chapter 4.

Top tips. Part (a) requires you to read the scenario carefully and be methodical. You need to set out your workings separately and think about timings carefully. Part (b) is fairly straightforward. Note that the question says that no inventories are held. Part (c) is worth three marks so should take you over five minutes. In part (e), don't forget to explain your findings.

Easy marks. There are easy marks for calculations in part (a) by following the proforma approach. There are four easy marks available in part (e) for simply using the Miller-Orr formulae given to you in the exam.

Marking scheme

		Marks	
(a)	Monthly receivables	1	
	Loan	0.5	
	Raw materials	1	
	Variable costs	1	
	Machine	0.5	
	Closing balances	1	
			5
(b)	Closing finished goods inventory	0.5	
	Revised holding and ordering costs	0.5	
	Inventory cost if discount is taken	0.5	
	Benefit if bulk purchase discount taken	0.5	
			2
(c)	Temporary nature of short-term cash surplus	1	
	Investment should have no risk of capital loss	1	
	Shares are not suitable for investment	1	
			3
(d)	Discussion of Baumol model 2–3 marks per valid point	Maximum	5
(e)	Calculation of spread	1	
	Calculation of upper limit	1	
	Calculation of return point	1	
	Explanation of findings	2	
			5
			20

(a)

	Jan $'000	Feb $'000	Mar $'000
Sales revenue (W1)	960	1,000	1,092
Loan income			300
Total cash receipts	960	1,000	1,392
Production costs (W2)	500	520	560
Variable overheads (W3)	130	140	150
Machine purchase			400
Total cash payments	630	660	1,110
Net surplus	330	340	282
Opening balance	40	370	710
Closing balance	370	710	992

Workings

1   Sales

Month of sale				Cash received
Dec	1,200 units × $800	=	$960,000	Jan
Jan	1,250 units × $800	=	$1,000,000	Feb
Feb	1,300 units × $800 × 1.05	=	$1,092,000	Mar

2   Production costs

Month of production				Cash paid
Dec	1,250 units × 2 units × $200	=	$500,000	Jan
Jan	1,300 units × 2 units × $200	=	$520,000	Feb
Feb	1,400 units × 2 units × $200	=	$560,000	Mar

3   Variable overheads

Month of production				Cash paid
Jan	1,300 units × $100	=	$130,000	Jan
Feb	1,400 units × $100	=	$140,000	Feb
Mar	1,500 units × $100	=	$150,000	Mar

(b) $Current\ ratio = \dfrac{current\ assets}{current\ liabilities}$

Current assets

Inventory = finished goods for April sales of 1,500 units

Cost of production = materials + variable costs = $400 + $100 = $500 per unit

1,500 units × $500 = $750,000

Cash = $992,000

Trade receivables = March 1,400 units × $800 × 1.05 = $1,176,000

Current liabilities

Trade payables = cash owed for March raw materials = 1,500 units × 2 units × $200 = $600,000

∴ Current ratio = $\dfrac{\$750,000 + \$992,000 + \$1,176,000}{\$600,000}$ = 4.9 times

(c) When investing a surplus the company should consider the following.

Liquidity. Shares are not quickly and easily converted into cash.

Profitability. The company should seek to obtain a good return for the risk incurred. A good return on shares usually means a long-term investment. However, the surplus is only temporary.

Safety. Share values can go down as well as up which could lead to capital losses.

The question states that the surplus is a short-term surplus. Investing in shares is therefore inappropriate. A deposit account with a bank would be more appropriate.

(d) **The Baumol model and cash management**

A number of different cash management models indicate the **optimum amount of cash** that a company should hold. One such model is based on the idea that deciding on optimum cash balances is like deciding on optimum inventory levels, and suggests the optimum amount to be transferred regularly from investments to current account.

We can distinguish two types of cost which are involved in obtaining cash:

(i) The **fixed cost** represented, for example, by the issue cost of equity finance or the cost of negotiating an overdraft

(ii) The **variable cost** (opportunity cost) of keeping the money in the form of cash

The Baumol approach has the following drawbacks for companies such as Flit Co.

(i) In reality, it is unlikely to be **possible** to **predict amounts required** over future periods with much certainty.

(ii) No **buffer inventory** of cash is allowed for. There may be costs associated with running out of cash.

(iii) There may be other **normal costs** of holding cash, which increase with the average amount held.

(iv) It assumes **constant transaction costs** and **interest rates**.

(e) **Determination of spread**

Daily interest rate = 5.11/365 = 0.014% per day

Variance = (standard deviation)^2
so variance of cash flows = 1,000 × 1,000 = $1,000,000 per day

Transaction cost = $18 per transaction

Spread = 3 × ((0.75 × transaction cost × variance)/interest rate)1/3

= 3 × ((0.75 × 18 × 1,000,000)/0.00014)1/3 = 3 × 4,585.7 = $13,757

Lower limit = $7,500

Upper limit = $(7,500 + 13,757) = $21,257

Return point = $7,500 + ($13,757/3) = $12,086

Relevance of the values

The Miller-Orr model takes account of **uncertainty** in relation to cash flows. The cash balance of Renpec Co is allowed to vary between the lower and upper **limits** calculated by the model.

If the cash balance reaches an **upper limit** the firm **buys sufficient securities** to return the cash balance to a normal level (called the 'return point'). When the cash balance reaches a lower limit, the firm sells securities to bring the balance back to the return point.

The Miller-Orr model therefore helps Renpec Co to decrease the risk of running out of cash, while avoiding the loss of profit caused by having unnecessarily high cash balances.

89 Widnor Co

Marking scheme

			Marks
(a)	Reduction in trade receivables	1	
	Reduction in financing cost	1	
	Reduction in administration costs	1	
	Saving in bad debts	1	
	Increase in financing cost	1	
	Factor's annual fee	1	
	Advice on acceptance of factor's offer	1	
			7
(b)	Bank and other references	1	
	Credit rating	1	
	Other relevant discussion	1	
			3
(c)	Relevant discussion 2–3 marks per valid point	Maximum	10
			20

(a)   The factor's offer will be financially acceptable to Widnor Co if it results in a net benefit rather than a net cost.

	$
Current trade receivables	4,458,000
Revised trade receivables = 26,750,000 × 35/360 =	2,600,694
Reduction in trade receivables	1,857,306

	$	$
Reduction in financing cost = 1,857,306 × 0.05 =	92,865	
Saving in bad debts = 26,750,000 × 0.01 × 0.7 =	187,250	
Reduction in administration costs	50,000	
Benefits		330,115
Increase in financing cost = 2,600,694 × 0.8 × 0.07 – 0.05 =	41,611	
Factor's annual fee = 26,750,000 × 0.0075 =	200,625	
Costs		(242,236)
Net benefit		87,879

The factor's offer is therefore financially acceptable.

(b)   The creditworthiness of potential customers can be assessed from a range of different sources of information. References are useful in this respect, and potential customers should supply a bank reference and a trade or other reference when seeking credit on purchases. Another source of information is the credit rating of the potential customer, which can be checked by a credit rating agency or credit reference agency. For larger potential customers, a file can be opened where additional information can be located, evaluated and stored, such as the annual report and accounts of the potential customer, press releases and so on.

(c)   **Risks arising from granting credit to foreign customers**

Foreign debts raise the following special problems. When goods are sold abroad, the customer might ask for credit. Exports take time to arrange, and there might be complex paperwork. Transporting the goods can be slow, if they are sent by sea. These **delays in foreign trade** mean that exporters often build up **large investments** in inventories and accounts receivable. These working capital investments have to be financed somehow.

The **risk of bad debts** can be greater with foreign trade than with domestic trade. If a foreign customer refuses to pay a debt, the exporter must pursue the debt in the customer's own country, where procedures will be subject to the laws of that country.

How risks can be managed and reduced

A company can reduce its investment in foreign accounts receivable by insisting on **earlier payment** for goods. Another approach is for an exporter to arrange for a **bank to give cash for a foreign debt**, sooner than the exporter would receive payment in the normal course of events. There are several ways in which this might be done.

Where the exporter asks their bank to handle the collection of payment (of a bill of exchange or a cheque) on their behalf, the bank may be prepared to make an **advance** to the exporter against the collection. The amount of the advance might be 80% to 90% of the value of the collection.

Negotiation of bills or cheques is similar to an advance against collection, but would be used where the bill or cheque is payable outside the exporter's country (for example in the foreign buyer's country).

Discounting bills of exchange is where a bank buys the bill before it is due and credits the value of the bill after a discount charge to the company's account.

Export factoring could be considered where the exporter pays for the specialist expertise of the factor in order to reduce bad debts and the amount of investment in foreign accounts receivable.

Documentary credits provide a method of payment in international trade, which gives the exporter a secure risk-free method of obtaining payment. The buyer (a foreign buyer, or a domestic importer) and the seller (a domestic exporter or a foreign supplier) first of all agree a contract for the sale of the goods, which provides for payment through a documentary credit. The buyer then requests a bank in their country to issue a letter of credit in favour of the exporter. The issuing bank, by issuing its letter of credit, guarantees payment to the beneficiary.

Countertrade is a means of financing trade in which goods are exchanged for other goods.

Export credit insurance is insurance against the risk of non-payment by foreign customers for export debts. If a credit customer defaults on payment, the task of pursuing the case through the courts will be lengthy, and it might be a long time before payment is eventually obtained.

Premiums for export credit insurance are, however, very high and the potential benefits might not justify the cost.

MCQ bank – Investment decisions

90   **C**   49%

Return on capital employed = Average annual accounting profits/Average investment

Average annual accounting profits = (16,500 + 23,500 + 13,500 – 1,500)/4 = $13,000 pa.

Note accounting profits are **after** depreciation so no adjustment is required.

Average investment = (initial investment + scrap)/2 = ($46,000 + $7,000)/2 = $26,500

ROCE = 13,000/26,500 = 49%

Syllabus area D1(d)

91   **A**   Payback period is the amount of time taken to repay the initial investment.

Time		Profit	Depreciation*	Cash flow	Cumulative cash flow
		$	$	$	$
0	Investment			(46,000)	(46,000)
1	Cash inflow	16,500	9,750	26,250	(19,750)
2	Cash inflow	23,500	9,750	33,250	13,500

* Depreciation = ($46,000 – $7,000)/4

Payback period = 1 + (19,750/33,250) = 1.59 years or 1 year 7 months to the nearest month.

Syllabus area D1(b)

92   **B**   1 is correct as there is no 'cut-off' point (unlike the payback period calculation).

2 is incorrect. ROCE is profit based.

3 is correct, and may well help explain ROCE's use in the real world.

Syllabus area D1(d)

93   **B**   The $1,000 is sunk. If the chemical is used in a new project it would save SW Co $400 that it would otherwise have to spend to dispose of the chemical. This equates to an effective net cash inflow (or, more precisely, the avoidance of an outflow) of $400. Thus the project appraisal should show an inflow of $400 in relation to using this chemical.

Syllabus area D1(a)

94   **C** $20,000

We assume BLW Co would choose the cheapest source of labour.

Cost to buy in = $20 × 1,000 hours = $20,000

Cost to divert existing labour = lost contribution + labour cost ie
($10 + $15) × 1,000 hours = $25,000

The cheapest alternative is therefore to buy in at a cost of $20,000.

To calculate how the existing BLW Co project would suffer as a result of diverting labour, the current labour cost is added back to the lost contribution to give the full impact of diverting labour away from its current role.

Syllabus area D1(a)

95   **A** $14,000. The current rental cost is $5,000. The net new rental cost, should the project proceed, would be ($17,000 + $5,000 – $3,000) = $19,000, so an increment of $19,000 – $5,000 = $14,000.

Syllabus area D1(a)

96 **C** Option A is a benefit, not a drawback. Option B is incorrect. The payback period does not take account of the time value of money. D is incorrect. The calculation is not based on profit. On the assumption that the basic reason for approving a project is that it will increase shareholder wealth, a major drawback of the payback period is that it does not attempt to measure the impact on shareholder wealth should the project go ahead.

Syllabus area D1(b)

97 **C**

Time $m	Cash flow	d.f. 15%	PV $m	d.f. 20%	PV $m
0	(6.5)	1.000	(6.500)	1.000	(6.500)
1	2.4	0.870	2.088	0.833	1.999
2	3.1	0.756	2.344	0.694	2.151
3	2.1	0.658	1.382	0.579	1.216
4	1.8	0.572	1.030	0.482	0.868
			0.344		(0.266)

IRR = 15 + [(5 × 0.344)/(0.344 + 0.266)] = 15 + 2.82 = 17.8%

Syllabus area D1(f)

98 **D** 5%. A payback of 20 years suggests net annual inflow of 50,000/20 = $2,500 per annum.

Return on capital employed (ROCE) = Average annual accounting profit/Average investment.

Average annual accounting profit = $2,500 cash inflows less depreciation.

Depreciation = 50,000/40 = $1,250 per year.

So average annual accounting profit = $2,500 – $1,250 = $1,250.

Average investment = ($50,000 + 0)/2 = $25,000.

Therefore ROCE = $1,250/$25,000 = 0.05 or 5% per annum.

Syllabus area D1(d)

99 **B** The cost should not feature in the project appraisal as the accountant is paid anyway, ie his salary is not incremental.

Syllabus area D1(a)

MCQ bank – Investment appraisal using DCF

100 **D** The present value of the annuity = $7,000 × AF_{3-7}

where AF_{3-7} is the 10% annuity factor from years 3–7 inclusive.

AF_{3-7} = AF_{1-7} – AF_{1-2}

= 4.868 – 1.736 (from tables)

= 3.132

Therefore the present value = $7,000 × 3.132 = $21,924

Syllabus area D1(e)

101 **C** Option 1

Step 1 Calculate the future value of the perpetuity using the cost of capital

$90,000/0.1 = $900,000

Step 2 Discount it back to today using a discount factor of 10% at the end of year 2

PV = $900,000 × 0.826 = $743,400

Option 2

The present value of the lump sum = $910,000 × DF_1

Where DF_1 is the 1 year 10% discount factor from tables = 0.909

So present value of lump sum = $910,000 × 0.909 = $827,180

The lump sum should be chosen because it has a higher net present value.

Syllabus area D1(e)

102 C Remember that a cash outlay or receipt which occurs at the beginning of a time period is taken to occur at the end of the previous year. Therefore an inflow of $12,000 in advance for 5 years (ie starting now) is taken to occur in years 0, 1, 2, 3 and 4.

NPV at 10%:

Time		$	DF 10%	PV $
0	Investment	(40,000)	1	(40,000)
0–4	Net cash inflows	12,000	1 + 3.17 = 4.17	50,040
5	Decommissioning	(15,000)	0.621	(9,315)
	Net present value			725

= $700 to the nearest $100

Syllabus area D1(e)

103 A 12%

$$IRR = a + \left[\frac{NPV_a}{NPV_a - NPV_b} \times (b-a) \right]\%$$

where a = lower % discount rate

b = higher % discount rate

NPV_A = NPV at a%

NPV_B = NPV at b%

NPV at 10% = $725 (see question above)

NPV at 15%:

Time		$	DF 15%	PV $
0	Investment	(40,000)	1	(40,000)
0–4	Net cash inflows	12,000	1 + 2.855 = 3.855	46,260
5	Decommissioning	(15,000)	0.497	(7,455)
	Net present value			(1,195)

Therefore IRR = 10% + [(725/(725 + 1,195)) × (15% − 10%)] = 11.9% (12% to the nearest whole %)

Syllabus area D1(f)

104 D The project with the highest NPV will maximise shareholder wealth as NPV directly measures the impact on shareholder wealth.

Syllabus area D1(g)

105 C It takes into account the time value of money and it considers the whole project.

Statement 1 is not an advantage. The decision rule depends on the shape of the IRR curve. There could be several IRRs and whether the IRR needs to be higher or lower than the cost of capital depends on the project cash flows.

Statement 2 is an advantage. IRR is a discounting technique hence takes into account the time value of money.

Statement 3 is a disadvantage. The 'reinvestment assumption' is a flaw in IRR. There is no reason to suppose that funds generated early on in a project will be reinvested at the IRR after that point. The funds may well be distributed elsewhere.

Statement 4 is an advantage. Unlike the payback period, the IRR considers **all** of the future incremental cash flows associated with a decision in its calculation.

Syllabus area D1(f)

106 **C** The NPV will decrease and there will be no change to the IRR.

A higher cost of capital will discount future inflows more heavily, reducing the NPV of the project. The cost of capital does not feature in the calculation of the IRR, only in the decision rule that follows the calculation.

Syllabus area D1(e)(f)

107 **B** The net present value of the agreement is $26,496, hence:

$26,496	= ($a \times AF_{1-4}$) + 10,000	Where AF_{1-4} is the 4 year 8% annuity factor
$16,496	= $a \times 3.312$	(from tables)
$a	= $16,496/3.312$	
	= $4,981$	

Syllabus area D1(e)

108 **A** The IRR formula requires two NPV calculations at different rates to estimate the IRR.

B is inaccurate. Linear interpolation is still an estimate. It is not 100% precise.

C is inaccurate. There may be more than one IRR. It depends on whether the cash flows are conventional or not.

D is not necessarily true. For example, an unusual project with an initial large inflow followed by years of outflows will have a positive slope.

Syllabus area D1(h)

109 **A** The present value of the holiday home = $1.5m \times$ (DF for time 5 at 10%) = $1.5m \times 0.621$ = $931,500

Therefore the present value of the annuity = $931,500.

$931,500 = $a \times AF_{0-4}$

Where AF_{0-4} is the annuity factor from time 0 to time 4

$AF_{0-4} = 1 + AF_{1-4}$	= 1 + 3.170 = 4.170	
So $931,500	= $a \times 4.170$	
$a	= $931,500/4.170$	
	= $223,381 or $223,400 to the nearest $100	

Syllabus area D1(e)

MCQ bank – Allowing for tax and inflation

110 **C** The asset is purchased on 31 December 20X4 (T0) so the first portion of tax-allowable depreciation is accounted for on that date (as this is the end of the year). The amount of the depreciation would be $1m \times 25\%$ = $250,000.

Claiming this allowance will save ($250,000 \times 30\%$ =) $75,000 tax when it is paid at T1 (one-year delay) hence the present value = $75,000 \times DF_1$ = $75,000 \times 0.909$ = $68,175.

Syllabus area D2(b)

111 **B** As tax is paid one year in arrears, the $20,000 and associated tax are treated separately:

PV of perpetuity: $20,000 \times 1/0.1$	=	$200,000
Less PV of tax: ($20,000 \times 30\%$) $\times (AF_{2-\infty})$		
$AF_{2-\infty} = (1/0.1) - DF_1$ = 10 − 0.909 = 9.091		
PV of tax = $20,000 \times 30\% \times 9.091$	=	$(54,546)
After tax	=	$145,454

Syllabus area D2(b)

112 C

	Working capital required (10% × sales)	Increments = cash flow	Discount factor 10%	Present value
	$			
T0	10,000	(10,000)	1	(10,000.00)
T1	12,500	(2,500)	0.909	(2,272.50)
T2	10,500	2,000	0.826	1,652.00
T3	0	10,500	0.751	7,885.50
				(2,735.00)

Syllabus area D1(e)

113 A The working capital required will inflate year on year, then the inflated amount will be 'returned' at the end of the project:

	Working capital required (with 10% inflation)	Increments = cash flow	Discount factor 12%	Present value
	$			
T0	100,000	(100,000)	1	(100,000)
T1	110,000	(10,000)	0.893	(8,930)
T2	0	110,000	0.797	87,670
				(21,260)

Syllabus area D2(a)

114 C $58,175. As not all cash flows will inflate at the same rate, cash flows will be inflated where necessary and discounted using the money rate.

$(1 + \text{money rate}) = (1.08) \times (1.02) = 1.1016$ so m = 10% to the nearest whole percentage

Nominal income = $100,000 × (1 + income inflation) = $100,000 × 1.1 = $110,000

Nominal expenses = $35,000 (zero inflation)

Therefore NPV = [(110,000 − 35,000) × DF$_1$] − 10,000   where DF$_1$ = the 1 year 10% discount factor (tables)

= (75,000 × 0.909) − 10,000 = $58,175

Syllabus area D2(a)

115 C In order to use the perpetuity factor (1/r) the annual amount must be constant, so the calculation needs to be done in real terms.

The money cost of capital is given in the question, so the real rate needs to be calculated using:

$(1 + r) \times (1 + h) = (1 + i)$ where r = real rate, h = inflation, i = money rate, so

$(1 + r) \times (1.02) = (1.102)$

$(1 + r) = 1.102/1.02 = 1.08$ or 8%.

The perpetuity factor from T2-∞ = (1/r) − DF1 = (1/0.08) − 0.926 = 11.574

Therefore the present value = 10,000 × 11.574 = $115,740

Syllabus area D2(a)

116 A Increased expectation of inflation will have two effects.

(1) Higher expected nominal cash flow
(2) Higher nominal discount rate

These will cancel each other out exactly.

Syllabus area D2(a)

117 B $(1 + r) \times (1 + h) = (1 + i)$ where r = real rate, h = inflation, i = money rate, so

$(1 + r) \times (1.04) = (1.10)$

$(1 + r) = 1.10/1.04 = 1.058$ or 5.8%.

Syllabus area D2(a)

118 D   The value of the tax-allowable depreciation is $150,000 \times 100\% \times 30\% = \$45,000$ receivable immediately so the net initial outlay = 150,000 – 45,000 = $105,000.

The future value of 105,000 in 2 years' time (note…'receivable in 2 years…')

$= 105,000 \times 1.1^2 = \$127,050$.

The revenue is taxable, so the pre-tax contract revenue needs to be 127,050/(1 – 0.3) = $181,500.

Syllabus area D2(b)

119 D   The inflation included in the money cost of capital is required by the investors to compensate them for the loss of general purchasing power their money will suffer in the future as a result of investing in the business.

Syllabus area D2(a)

CBE style OTQ bank – Project appraisal and risk

120   **Statements 1 & 3 are correct, statement 2 is incorrect**

Statement 2 is incorrect because the expected net present value is the value expected to occur if an investment project with several possible outcomes is undertaken **many times**.

Syllabus area D3(c)

121   **$11,100**

Total cash flow $	Joint probability	EV of cash flow $
36,000	0.1125	4,050
14,000	0.0375	525
32,000	0.4500	14,400
10,000	0.1500	1,500
16,000	0.1875	3,000
(6,000)	0.0625	(375)
		23,100
Less initial investment		(12,000)
EV of the NPV		11,100

Syllabus area D3(c)

122   **Just under three years**

Adjusted payback period is payback period based on discounted cash flows:

Time	Cash flow $	DF 8%	Discounted cash flow $	Cumulative discounted cash flow
0	(100,000)		(100,000)	(100,000)
1	40,000	0.926	37,040	(62,960)
2	40,000	0.857	34,280	(28,680)
3	40,000	0.794	31,760	3,080

Syllabus area D3(d)

123 **70%** To force an NPV = 0, the 4-year annuity factor, AF_{1-4} = 110,000/40,000 = 2.75

Proof: the NPV calculation would be $(2.75 \times 40,000) - 110,000 = 0$

From tables, the 4-year annuity factor closest to 2.75 is 2.743, corresponding to a discount rate of 17%.

In terms of sensitivity: (17 – 10)/10 = 70% sensitivity

The cost of capital can therefore increase by 70% before the NPV becomes negative.

Note. Alternatively the IRR could be estimated to find the 17% instead of tables.

NPV when cost of capital is 18% = $-110,000 + (40,000 \times 2.69) = (2,400)$

$$IRR = 0.1 + \frac{16,800}{16,800 + 2,400} \times (0.18 - 0.1) = 17\%$$

Syllabus area D3(b)

124 Correct answer:

Sensitivity = $200,000/((4,000,000 - 2,000,000) \times 0.8) \times 100 =$ **12.5%**

A change in sales volume affects sales revenue and variable costs, but not fixed costs. The sensitivity of the NPV to a change in contribution must therefore be calculated. However, a change in contribution will cause a change in the corporation tax liability, so it is essential that the after-tax contribution be considered.

Contribution = $4,000,000 - 2,000,000 = \$2,000,000$

After-tax contribution = $2,000,000 \times 0.8 = \$1,600,000$

Sensitivity = NPV/PV of project variable = $200,000/1,600,000 \times 100 = 12.5\%$

Syllabus area D3(d)

CBE style OTQ bank – Specific investment decisions

125 **The third statement is correct**

The first statement is incorrect. With buying an asset, the company receives tax allowances (tax-allowable depreciation) which results in cash savings on tax. It is the tax saving that is the relevant cash flow as opposed to the tax allowable depreciation. With leasing, the lessor does not receive these allowances. However, the lease rental is allowable for tax purposes which results in cash savings on tax.

The second statement is incorrect. They need to be discounted at the cost of capital, not just the cost of debt.

The third statement is correct. Ranking using the profitability index can be used if projects are divisible.

The final statement is incorrect. Soft capital rationing is brought about by internal factors and decisions by management, not external government decisions.

Syllabus area D4(c)

126 **The 2-year cycle should be chosen with an equivalent annual cost of $10,093.**

Net present cost of 1-year cycle = $20,000 - (10,000 \times 0.909) = \$10,910$ cost
Net present cost of 2-year cycle = $20,000 - [(8,000 - 5,000) \times 0.826] = \$17,522$ cost
EAC 1-year cycle = $10,910/0.909 = 12,002$
EAC 2-year cycle = $17,522/1.736 = 10,093$
The 2-year cycle should be chosen with an equivalent annual cost of $10,093.

Syllabus area D4(b)

127   **The correct answer is: Lease is better than buy.**

The saved outlay is a benefit of the lease so if it outweighs the present value of the costs relevant to the lease then the lease is financially worthwhile.

Syllabus area D4(a)

128   **'No – After-tax cost of the loan if they borrow and buy'**

Interest should not be included as a cash flow as it is part of the discount rate.

As a financing decision the alternatives should be assessed at the after-tax cost of borrowing – the risk associated with each is the risk of borrowing (or not), and not related to what is done with the asset.

Syllabus area D4(a)

129   **Both are false.**

The profitability index is only suitable for handling single-period capital rationing problems if projects are divisible.

Whether a project may be considered divisible or not depends on the project – for example investing in a machine is unlikely to be divisible (half a machine will not generate half the return); however, buying a chain of shops could be divisible; it might be possible to buy half the chain for half the cost and expect half the net present value.

Syllabus area D4(c)

130   **$13m**

Project	Initial cost $m	NPV $m	Profitability index*	Ranking
1	40	4	1.10	3
2	30	5	1.167	1
3	50	6	1.12	2
4	60	5	1.08	4

*(NPV + initial cost)/initial cost

Investment plan:

	Investment $m	NPV $m
100% of Project 2	30	5
100% of Project 3	50	6
50% of Project 1	20	2
	100	13

Syllabus area D4(c)

131   **$11m**

Projects 2 and 3 give the highest NPV without breaking the $100m constraint.

Syllabus area D4(c)

132   **Avoiding tax exhaustion**

'Avoiding tax exhaustion' is potentially a benefit. Tax exhaustion is when a business has negative taxable income so it cannot benefit from tax relief such as tax-allowable depreciation. In this case, it may be beneficial to lease the asset from a business that **can** benefit from the tax-allowable depreciation and share in that benefit via lower lease payments.

'Attracting lease customers that may not have been otherwise possible' is a potential benefit to a lessor, not a lessee.

'Exploiting a low cost of capital' is a potential benefit for the purchaser, not the lessee.

'Potential future scrap proceeds' is a potential benefit for the purchaser, not the lessee, as the lessee is not entitled to scrap proceeds.

Syllabus area D4(a)

133 **'Electric because its equivalent annual benefit is higher'**

The NPVs cannot be directly compared as they relate to different time periods. Equivalent annual benefits (EAB) should be compared. This is similar in principle to equivalent annual cost.

EAB gas = $50,000/AF$_{1-5}$ = 50,000/3.993 = $12,522 pa

EAB electric = $68,000/AF$_{1-7}$ = 68,000/5.206 = $13,062 pa

Therefore electric should be chosen as its EAB is higher.

Syllabus area D4(b)

134 **Higher scrap value**

Better company image and efficiency

Statement 1 is a benefit. Scrapped assets will be newer hence worth more.

Statement 2 is a benefit. Newer assets look better, motivate employees and are more efficient.

Statement 3 is not true hence not a benefit. Typically depreciation is higher in earlier years, meaning annual depreciation charges will be higher with a shorter replacement cycle.

Statement 4 is inaccurate hence not a benefit. Although owned for a shorter period, the asset will be replaced so ownership of that type of asset will be indefinite.

Syllabus area D4(b)

Sensitivity analysis

135 **C** 11.9%

Year	Contribution $'000	Discount factor 9%	PV $'000
1–2	7,100 (10,300 – 3,200)	1.759	12,489

Sensitivity of project to sales volume = $\dfrac{1,490}{12,489} \times 100\% = 11.9\%$

136 **D** 1.75 years

Year	Net cash flow $'000	Discount factor 9%	PV $'000	Cumulative PV $'000
0	(11,000)	1	(11,000.00)	(11,000.00)
1	7,100	0.917	6,510.70	(4,489.30)
2	7,100	0.842	5,978.20	

4,489.30/5,978.20 = 0.75

Therefore the discounted payback = 1.75 years

137 A   18.9%

Using discount rates of 15% and 20% per the question we have:

Year	Net cash flow $'000	Discount factor 15%	PV $'000	Discount factor 20%	PV $'000
0	(11,000)	1	(11,000)	1	(11,000)
1	7,100	0.870	6,177	0.833	5,914
2	7,100	0.756	5,368	0.694	4,927
			NPV = 545		NPV = (159)

$$IRR = 15 + \left[\frac{545}{545 + 159} \times (20 - 15) \right] = 18.9\%$$

138 C   The statement concerning simulation models is true. They use probabilities to carry out a statistical analysis of possible project outcomes.

A   Incorrect sensitivity definition

Selecting this answer indicates a lack of understanding of sensitivity analysis. The sensitivity of NPV to a change in sales volume can be calculated as NPV divided by the present value of contribution. Comparing NPV to the present value of future sales income would be estimating the sensitivity of NPV to a change in selling price.

B   The certainty equivalent approach

This approach to investment appraisal requires that the riskless equivalent amounts are discounted by a riskless discount rate; that is, the risk-free rate of return. A CAPM-derived project-specific cost of capital is not the risk-free rate of return, but rather a rate of return that reflects the systematic risk of a particular investment project.

D   Risk and uncertainty

A common way to distinguish between risk and uncertainty is to say that risk can be quantified whereas uncertainty cannot be quantified, so stating that neither can be measured or quantified is not true.

139 B   1 and 3

The IRR ignores the relative sizes of investments. It therefore does not measure the absolute increase in company value, and therefore shareholder wealth, which can be created by an investment.

Where cash flows change from negative to positive more than once there may be as many IRRs as there are changes in the direction of cash flows. So IRR is not easy to use in this situation.

NPV is widely used in practice.

NPV is technically superior to IRR.

Guilder Co

140   1. Utrec, 2. Tilbur, 3. Eind, 4. Amster

PI = PV of future cash flows/PV of capital investment

Project	Outlay in Year 0 $	PV $	NPV $	Ratio (PV/ outlay)	Ranking
Amster	100,000	111,400	11,400	1.114	4th
Eind	56,000	62,580	6,580	1.118	3rd
Utrec	60,000	68,760	8,760	1.146	1st
Tilbur	90,000	102,400	12,400	1.138	2nd

141 **PI can only be used if projects are divisible.**

The weaknesses of the PI method are:

It does not take into account the absolute size of the individual projects. A project with a high index might be very small and therefore only generate a small NPV.

It does not highlight the projects which are slowest in generating returns. It is possible that the project with the highest PI is the slowest in generating returns.

It does not allow for uncertainty about the outcome of each project. In fact it assumes that there is complete certainty about each outcome.

142 **$105,406**

Present value of cash flows = (250,000 + 17,860 + 23,113 + 22,784 + 6,360) = ($320,117)
Cumulative present value factor = 3.037
Equivalent annual cost = $320,117/3.037 = $105,406

143 **Statement 1 is false and statement 2 is true.**

The equivalent annual cost method is the most convenient method of analysis to use in a period of **no** inflation, because it is converting the NPV of the cost of buying and using the asset into an equivalent annual cost. In times of high inflation, this cost would keep increasing (so statement 1 is false).

The EAC method assumes that the machine can be replaced by exactly the same machine in perpetuity and this is one of the weaknesses of the EAC method. It is not usually possible to replace something with exactly the same thing as assets are constantly developing. Computers, in particular, are developing very quickly and so it can make sense to replace certain assets more often than the EAC method dictates.

144 **$17,654**

EV of Year 2 cash flow = (19,000 × 0.55) + (26,000 × 0.45) = 22,150
PV discounted at 12% = 22,150 × 0.797 = $17,654

Trecor Co

145 **56%**

Depreciation = $250,000 − $5,000 = $245,000
Accounting profit = total cash inflows − depreciation = $530,000 − $245,000 = $285,000
Average profit per year = $285,000/4 = $71,250
Average investment = (250,000 + 5,000)/2 = $127,500
ROCE = 71,250/127,500 × 100 = 56%

146 **The first statement is false.**

ROCE needs to be higher than the target ROCE for the machine purchase to be recommended. The second statement is true. Two (or more) mutually exclusive projects can be compared using ROCE. The project with the highest ROCE should be selected.

147 **$10,547**

	Tax-allowable depreciation			Tax benefits	
		$			$
1	250,000 × 0.25 =	62,500	2	62,500 × 0.3 =	18,750
2	62,500 × 0.75 =	46,875	3	46,875 × 0.3 =	14,063
3	46,875 × 0.75 =	35,156	4	35,156 × 0.3 =	10,547

148 **1 year 11 months**

Year 1 cumulative balance = −250,000 + 122,000 = −128,000

(128,000/143,000) × 12 months = 11 months ∴ payback is 1 year 11 months

149 **IRR ignores the relative sizes of investments.**

IRR and NPV sometimes give conflicting rankings over which project should be prioritised.

Statement 1 is true. The IRR ignores the relative sizes of investments. It therefore does not measure the absolute increase in company value, and therefore shareholder wealth, which can be created by an investment.

Statement 2 is therefore false. When discount rates are expected to differ over the life of the project, such variations can be incorporated easily into NPV calculations, but not into IRR calculations. Therefore statement 3 is also false.

Statement 4 is true. NPV and IRR methods can give conflicting rankings as to which project should be given priority.

BRT Co

150   **$8,487 (or $8,488)**

$1,600,000 \times \$5 \times 1.03^2 = \$8,487,200$ or

$1,600,000 \times 5.305 = \$8,488,000$ (if you have rounded the inflated price)

151   **$6,884**

$2,100,000 \times \$3 \times 1.03^3 = \$6,884,180$

152   **$84**

Tax-allowable depreciation		Tax benefits	
Year		Year	
1	$2,000,000 \times 0.25 = \$500,000$	2	$\$500,000 \times 0.3 = \$150,000$
2	$500,000 \times 0.75 = \$375,000$	3	$\$375,000 \times 0.3 = \$112,500$
3	$\$375,000 \times 0.75 = \$281,250$	4	$\$281,250 \times 0.3 = \$84,375$

153   The trainee accountant has used the wrong percentage for the cost of capital – False

As inflated sales and costs have been used, the cost of capital should be the nominal cost of capital (at 12%).

Ignoring sales after four years underestimates the value of the project – True

Cutting off cash flows after four years will underestimate the value of the project as future cash inflows will be ignored.

The working capital figure in Year 4 is wrong – True

The final year should recover the total working capital and so should be:
$750k + $23k + $23k + $24k = $820k.

154   **Both statements are true.**

When there are **unconventional** cash flow patterns there may be multiple IRRs and so the NPV and IRR decisions may not be the same.

A project is financially viable under the IRR criteria if the IRR is greater than the cost of capital (12% in this case).

155 Calvic Co

Text reference. Capital rationing is covered in Chapter 11.

Top tips. Part (b) can be answered with no reference to the rest of the question. You might choose to do it first and to get these marks before doing the calculations in part (a).

In part (a) show your workings. This will ensure you earn good marks even if you make an arithmetic error.

Marking scheme

			Marks
(a)	Servicing costs	1	
	Cleaning costs	1	
	Present values of total costs	1	
	Present values of trade-in values	2	
	Net present values of costs of each cycle	3	
	Annuity factors	1	
	Equivalent annual costs	2	
	Recommendation	1	
			12
(b)	Single-period capital rationing	2–3	
	Project divisibility	3–4	
	Investment of surplus funds	3–4	
Maximum		Maximum	8
			20

(a)

Replace every year

Year	0	1
Initial cost	(15,000)	
Trade-in value		11,250
Service cost		(1,000)
Cleaning cost		(500)
Net cost	(15,000)	9,750
Discount factor @ 10%	1	0.909
Present value	(15,000)	8,863
NPV	(6,137)	
Annuity factor	0.909	
Equivalent annual cost	**(6,751) pa**	

Replace every two years

Year	0	1	2
Initial cost	(15,000)		
Trade-in value			9,000
Service cost		(1,000)	(1,400)
Cleaning		(500)	(625)
Net cost	(15,000)	(1,500)	6,975
Discount factor 10%	1	0.909	0.826
Present value	(15,000)	(1,364)	5,761
NPV	(10,603)		
Annuity factor	1.736 for 2 years		
Equivalent annual cost	**(6,108) pa**		

Replace every three years

Year	0	1	2	3
Initial cost	(15,000)			
Trade-in value				6,200
Service cost		(1,000)	(1,400)	(1,960)
Cleaning cost		(500)	(625)	(781)
Net cost	(15,000)	(1,500)	(2,025)	3,459
Discount factor @ 10%	1	0.909	0.826	0.751
Present value	(15,000)	(1,364)	(1,673)	2,598
NPV	(15,439)			
Annuity factor	2.487 for 3 years			
Equivalent annual cost	**(6,208) pa**			

As the lowest cost option, the decision should be made to replace every two years.

(b)   The net present value decision rule is to invest in all projects that have a **positive** net present value. By following this decision rule, managers **will maximise the value of a company** and therefore maximise the **wealth of ordinary shareholders**, which is a primary objective of financial management. Even when capital is rationed, it is still essential to be able to offer advice on which capital investment projects should be selected in order to secure the **maximum return** for the investing company, ie the maximum overall net present value.

Single-period capital rationing

The approach to solving single-period capital rationing problems depends on whether projects are divisible or not. A **divisible project** is one where a partial investment can be made in order to gain a pro rata net present value. For example, investing in a forest is a divisible project, since the amount of land purchased can be varied according to the funds available for investment (providing the seller agrees to a partial sale, of course). A non-divisible project is one where it is not possible to invest less than the full amount of capital. When building an oil refinery, for example, it is not possible to build only one part of the overall facility.

Where projects are divisible, the objective of maximising the net present value arising from invested funds can be achieved by **ranking projects** according to their profitability index and investing sequentially in order of decreasing profitability index, beginning with the highest, assuming that each project can be invested in only once, ie is non-repeatable.

The **profitability index** can be defined as net present value divided by initial investment. Ranking projects by profitability index is an example of **limiting factor analysis**. When projects are divisible, there will be no investment funds left over because when investment funds are insufficient for the whole of the next ranked project, part of the project can be taken on.

When projects are non-divisible, the objective of maximising the net present value arising from invested funds can be achieved by calculating the net present value arising from different combinations of projects. With this approach, there will usually be some surplus funds remaining from the funds initially available.

The investment of surplus funds

When investigating combinations of non-divisible projects in order to find the combination giving rise to the highest net present value, any **return from investing surplus funds is ignored**. The net present value analysis has been based on the company's average cost of capital and it is unlikely that surplus funds can be invested in order to earn a return as high as this.

Investment of surplus funds in, for example, the money markets would therefore be an investment project that would be rejected as having a negative net present value, or an internal rate of return less than the company's average cost of capital if using IRR to assess investment projects. However, it is **good working capital management** to ensure that liquid funds are invested to earn the highest available return, subject to any risk constraints, in order to increase overall profitability.

156 Project E

Marking scheme

		Marks
(a)	Sales income	1
	Inflation of sales income	1
	Variable cost	1
	Inflation of variable cost	1
	Inflated fixed costs	1
	Tax liability	1
	Timing of tax liability	1
	Tax-allowable depreciation years 1–3	1
	Balancing allowance	1
	Tax-allowable depreciation tax benefits	1
	Scrap value	1
	Calculation of present values	1
	Calculation of NPV	1
	Comment on financial acceptability and that E must be undertaken	1
		14
(b)	Reasons for not raising equity	2–3
	Reasons for not raising debt	2–3
	Other relevant discussion, definitions etc	1–2
		Max 6
		20

(a) As inflation rates differ for revenue and cost, nominal cash flows (ie including inflation) need to be calculated and discounted at the nominal rate (also including inflation).

	Year 0 $'000	Year 1 $'000	Year 2 $'000	Year 3 $'000	Year 4 $'000	Year 5 $'000
Sales (W1)		5,670	6,808	5,788	6,928	
Variable cost (W2)		(3,307)	(4,090)	(3,514)	(4,040)	
Fixed costs (W3)		(776)	(803)	(832)	(861)	
Taxable cash flow		1,587	1,915	1,442	2,027	
Taxation			(444)	(536)	(404)	(568)
Capital expenditure	(5,000)					
Scrap value					400	
Tax benefit of tax depn (W4)			350	263	197	479

	Year 0	Year 1	Year 2	Year 3	Year 4	Year 5
	$'000	$'000	$'000	$'000	$'000	$'000
	(5,000)	1,587	1,821	1,169	2,220	(89)
Discount factors @ 13%	1	0.885	0.783	0.693	0.613	0.543
Present value	(5,000)	1,405	1,426	810	1,361	(48)

Net present value = –5,000 + 1,405 + 1,426 + 810 + 1,361 – 48 = (46)

The net present value is negative and the investment is not financially worthwhile. However, the board has decided that it is strategically important to undertake this project.

Workings

1   *Sales*

	Volume	Price	Inflation	Revenue
		$		$
Year 1	12,000 ×	450 ×	1.05	5,670,000
Year 2	13,000 ×	475 ×	1.05^2	6,807,938
Year 3	10,000 ×	500 ×	1.05^3	5,788,125
Year 4	10,000 ×	570 ×	1.05^4	6,928,386

2   *Variable costs*

	Volume	Price	Inflation	Revenue
		$		$
Year 1	12,000 ×	260 ×	1.06	3,307,200
Year 2	13,000 ×	280 ×	1.06^2	4,089,904
Year 3	10,000 ×	295 ×	1.06^3	3,513,497
Year 4	10,000 ×	320 ×	1.06^4	4,039,926

3   *Fixed costs*

Fixed costs $750,000 per year inflating at 3.5%

		Fixed costs
Year		$
1	750 × 1.035	776,250
2	750 × 1.035^2	803,419
3	750 × 1.035^3	831,538
4	750 × 1.035^4	860,642

4   Tax-allowable depreciation tax benefits

		Tax-allowable depn	Tax benefit @ 28%
Year		$	$
1	5,000,000 × 25%	1,250,000	350,000
2	1,250,000 × 75%	937,500	262,500
3	937,500 × 75%	703,125	196,875
4	Balancing charge	1,709,375	478,625
Scrap value		400,000	
		5,000,000	

Tax benefits and tax charges affect the following period since tax is paid in arrears.

(b)   Capital rationing means that a company is unable to invest in all projects with a positive net present value and hence it is not acting to maximise shareholder wealth. When a company restricts or limits investment funds, it is undertaking 'soft' or internal capital rationing.

There are several reasons why the board of OAP Co may decide to limit investment funds.

It may not wish to issue new equity finance in order to avoid diluting earnings per share. Issuing new equity finance may also increase the risk of a company's shares being bought by a potential acquirer, leading to a future takeover bid.

The board of OAP Co may not wish to issue new debt finance if it wishes to avoid increasing its commitment to fixed interest payments. This could be because economic prospects are seen as poor or challenging, or because existing debt obligations are high and so the board does not wish to increase them.

The board of OAP Co may wish to follow a strategy of organic growth, financing capital investment projects from retained earnings rather than seeking additional external finance.

Finally, the board of OAP Co may wish to create an internal market for capital investment funds, so that capital investment proposals must compete for the limited funds made available in the budget set by the board. This competition would mean that only robust capital investment projects would be funded, while marginal capital investment projects would be rejected.

157 AGD Co

Text references. Leasing is covered in Chapter 11.

Top tips. This question is in three parts and each part of the question could be answered separately.

Easy marks. Parts (b) and (c) are straightforward regurgitation of textbook knowledge.

ACCA examining team's comments. While many candidates made errors in this question, answers were usually of a satisfactory overall standard. Common errors included timing the investment when borrowing to buy as occurring at the end of the first year, omitting the tax savings on the maintenance costs incurred by buying the asset, and omitting the tax savings on the lease rental payments.

Marking scheme

			Marks
(a)	Purchase price	1	
	Sale proceeds	1	
	Tax-allowable depreciation and balancing allowance	2	
	Tax-allowable depreciation tax benefits	1	
	Maintenance costs after tax	2	
	PV of borrowing to buy	1	
	Lease rentals	1	
	Lease rental tax benefits	1	
	PV of leasing	1	
	Selection of cheapest option	1	
			12
(b)	Explanation and discussion		
	Risk reduction (technological obsolescence, avoid risk of lower residual value, insurance)	2–3	
	Source of finance (speed, availability, lack of loan covenants)	2–3	
		Maximum	5
(c)	Risk and uncertainty		3
			20

(a) (i) **Present value of purchase costs**

	Year 0 $'000	Year 1 $'000	Year 2 $'000	Year 3 $'000	Year 4 $'000
Cash outflows					
Capital costs	(320)				
Annual maintenance costs		(25)	(25)	(25)	
	(320)	(25)	(25)	(25)	0

	Year 0 $'000	Year 1 $'000	Year 2 $'000	Year 3 $'000	Year 4 $'000
Cash inflows					
Disposal proceeds				50	
Taxation (at 30% in following year)			8	8	8
Tax-allowable depn (W)			24	18	39
			32	76	47
Net cash flows	(320)	(25)	7	51	47
Discount at 7%	1.000	0.935	0.873	0.816	0.763
PV of cash flow	(320)	(23)	6	42	36
NPV of cash flow	**($259k)**				

Working: Tax-allowable depreciation

	$'000	Tax-allowable depn $'000	Tax benefit $'000	Year of cash flow
Initial investment	320			
Allowances at 25% pa on a reducing balance basis over 3 years				
Year 1	(80)	(80)	24	Y2
	240			
Year 2	(60)	(60)	18	Y3
	180			
Year 3				
Proceeds on sale	(50)			
Balancing allowance	130		39	Y4

(ii) **Present value of leasing costs**

	Year 0 $'000	Year 1 $'000	Year 2 $'000	Year 3 $'000	Year 4 $'000
Cash outflows					
Annual lease rentals	(120)	(120)	(120)		
	(120)	(120)	(120)		
Cash inflows					
Taxation (at 30% in following year) – tax deduction for lease rentals			36	36	36
Net cash flows	(120)	(120)	(84)	36	36
Discount at 7%	1.000	0.935	0.873	0.816	0. 763
PV of cash flow	(120)	(112)	(73)	29	27
NPV of cash flow	**($249k)**				

Therefore the machine should be **leased** rather than purchased as the NPV of the cost is lower.

(b) **Risk reduction**

The lease is for a three-year term but contains an annual break clause. This will have the impact of reducing risk because if the machinery is no longer needed (perhaps because the project is failing) or if there is a change in technology so better technology is available in future years then it will be easier to exit from the lease agreement than to sell the machinery (if owned).

Also when the machinery needs to be sold (either at the end of the three years or earlier) there is the risk that the residual value is lower than expected. This risk is not faced if lease finance is used.

Finally the inclusion of insurance and maintenance could also be argued to reduce risk.

Source of finance

Lease finance can also be easier and quicker to obtain because the lessor remains the legal owner of the machinery. In addition, if a loan is used then covenants may be imposed (for example on dividend payments, or the use of other debt finance) and this can restrict the flexibility of the firm in future years; the use of lease finance avoids this.

(c) **Risk and uncertainty**

Risk can be applied to a situation where there are several possible outcomes and, on the basis of past relevant experience, probabilities can be assigned to the various outcomes that could prevail. The risk of a project increases as the **variability of returns** increases.

Uncertainty can be applied to a situation where there are several possible outcomes but there is little past relevant experience to enable the probability of the possible outcomes to be predicted. Uncertainty increases as the **project life** increases.

158 Basril Co

Text references. Capital rationing is covered in Chapter 11.

Top tips. Calculate the NPVs for each project first and then look at the best combination of divisible or indivisible projects.

Easy marks. These can be achieved by setting out the correct format for calculating NPVs.

ACCA examining team's comments. This question asked for optimal selection under capital rationing. Good answers calculated the NPV and profitability index, and gave the optimum investment schedule and total NPV for the cases of divisible and non-divisible projects. Errors included: failing to calculate profitability indexes, not calculating the total NPV (even though required by the question), failing to account correctly for inflation in the case of the project where real cash flows were provided (inflating real cash flows to money terms or deflating the nominal rate were both acceptable), and using annuity factors rather than discount factors in calculations. Part (c) asked for an explanation, with examples, of 'relevant cost' in the context of investment appraisal. Weaker answers showed a lack of understanding of cost classification.

(ai)

	Project 1	12% discount factor	
	$		$
Initial investment	(300,000)	1	(300,000)
Year 1	85,000	0.893	75,905
Year 2	90,000	0.797	71,730
Year 3	95,000	0.712	67,640
Year 4	100,000	0.636	63,600
Year 5	95,000	0.567	53,865
			32,740
Profitability index	332,740/300,000		1.11

	Project 2	12% discount factor	
	$		$
Initial investment	(450,000)	1	(450,000)
Year 1	140,800	0.893	125,734
Year 2	140,800	0.797	112,218
Year 3	140,800	0.712	100,250
Year 4	140,800	0.636	89,549
Year 5	140,800	0.567	79,834
			57,585
Profitability index	507,585/450,000		1.13

	Project 3	12% discount factor	
	$		$
Initial investment	(400,000)	1	(400,000)
Year 1 (120,000 × 1.036)	124,320	0.893	111,018
Year 2 (120,000 × 1.036²)	128,796	0.797	102,650
Year 3	133,432	0.712	95,004
Year 4	138,236	0.636	87,918
Year 5	143,212	0.567	81,201
			77,791
Profitability index	477,791/400,000		1.19

The most profitable projects are Projects 3 and 2, so if they are **divisible** it is suggested that Basril Co invests $400k in Project 3 for an NPV of $77,791, and the remaining $400k in Project 2 for an NPV of 400/450 × $57,585 = $51,187.

(aii) If the projects are **indivisible**, then Basril Co can either invest in Project 1 and Project 2 at a cost of $750,000, or Project 1 and Project 3 at a cost of $700,000 (Project 2 and Project 3 would cost too much). The NPV of

1 + 2 = $32,740 + $57,584 = $90,324. The NPV of 1 + 3 = $32,740 + $77,791 = $110,531. Therefore the best combination is Projects 1 and 3.

(b) **Cash shortages**

A period of capital rationing is often associated with more general problems of cash shortage. Possible reasons for this include the following.

(i) The business has become **loss making** and is unable to cover the depreciation charge. Since one purpose of the depreciation charge is to allow for the cost of the assets used in the statement of profit or loss, the implication is that there will be insufficient cash with which to replace these assets when necessary.

(ii) High inflation may mean that even though the business is profitable in historical cost terms, it is still failing to **generate sufficient funds** to replace assets.

(iii) If the business is growing it may face a **shortage of working capital** with which to finance expansion, and this may result in a period of capital rationing.

(iv) If the business is seasonal or cyclical it may **face times of cash shortage** despite being fundamentally sound. In this situation, there may be a periodic need for capital rationing.

(v) A **large one-off item** of **expenditure** such as a property purchase may mean that the company faces a temporary shortage of cash for further investment.

Investment opportunities

A further reason for capital rationing arises in the situation where the company has **more investment opportunities** available than the **funds allocated** to the capital budget permit. This means that projects must be ranked for investment, taking into account both financial and strategic factors.

(c) When appraising an investment project, it is essential that only those cash flows relevant to the project be taken into account, otherwise an incorrect investment decision could be made. A 'relevant cash flow' is an incremental cash flow that arises or changes as a direct result of the investment being made. Some costs will be sunk before an investment decision is made. An example would be research and development or market research costs into the viability of a new product. Once incurred, such costs become irrelevant to the decision as to whether or not to proceed, and so should be excluded from the analysis. Cash flows that would be relevant include an increase in production overheads or labour costs, new purchases that are necessary, and any incremental tax effects. It is important to note that any interest payments on the finance for a new project are relevant to the project decision, but are not taken into account in any NPV calculation. The interest payments will already be 'built in' to the calculation in the discount factor that is being applied.

159 Degnis Co

Marking scheme

			Marks
(a)	Sales income	1	
	Conversion cost	1	
	Before-tax cash flow	1	
	Tax paid	1	
	Tax-allowable depreciation benefits	1	
	After-tax cash flow	1	
	NPV calculations	1	7
(b)	PV of future cash flows ignoring tax-allowable depreciation	1	
	PV of tax-allowable depreciation benefits	1	
	Comment on financial acceptability	1	
			3
(c)	Risk and uncertainty	1	
	Explanation of probability analysis	2–3	
	Problems – repeatability assumption, difficulty in determining probabilities	2–4	
	Maximum		5
(d)	Reason for hard rationing	1–4	
	Reasons for soft rationing	1–4	Max 5
			20

(a) **Calculation of NPV over four years**

Year	1	2	3	4
	$'000	$'000	$'000	$'000
Sales income	12,525	15,030	22,545	22,545
Conversion cost	(7,913)	(9,495)	(14,243)	(14,243)
Contribution	4,612	5,535	8,302	8,302
Fixed costs	(4,000)	(5,000)	(5,500)	(5,500)
Before-tax cash flow	612	535	2,802	2,802
Tax liability at 28%	(171)	(150)	(785)	(785)
Tax-allowable depreciation benefits	112	112	112	112
After-tax cash flow	553	497	2,129	2,129
Discount at 11%	0.901	0.812	0.731	0.659
Present values	498	404	1,556	1,403

	$'000
Sum of present values	3,861
Initial investment	4,000
NPV	(139)

Workings

Average selling price = (30,000 × 0.20) + (42,000 × 0.45) + (72,000 × 0.35) = $50,100 per unit

Average conversion cost = (23,000 × 0.20) + (29,000 × 0.45) + (40,000 × 0.35) = $31,650 per unit

Year	1	2	3	4
Sales volume (units/year)	250	300	450	450
Average selling price ($/unit)	50,100	50,100	50,100	50,100
Sales income ($'000/year)	12,525	15,030	22,545	22,545

Year	1	2	3	4
Sales volume (units/year)	250	300	450	450
Average selling price ($/unit)	31,650	31,650	31,650	31,650
Sales income ($'000/year)	7,913	9,495	14,243	14,243

Contribution may be calculated directly, with small rounding differences. Average contribution = 50,100 – 31,650 = $18,450 per unit.

Year	1	2	3	4
Sales volume (units/year)	250	300	450	450
Average selling price ($/unit)	18,450	18,450	18,450	18,450
Sales income ($'000/year)	4,613	5,535	8,303	8,303

Tax-allowable depreciation = 4,000,000/10 = $400,000 per year

Benefit of tax-allowable depreciation = 400,000 × 0.28 = $112,000 per year

(b) Ignoring tax-allowable depreciation, after-tax cash flow from Year 5 onwards will be:

2,802,000 – 785,000 = $2,017,000 per year

Present value of this cash flow in perpetuity = (2,017,000/0.11) × 0.659 = $12,083,664

There would be a further six years of tax benefits from tax-allowable depreciation. The present value of these cash flows would be 112,000 × 4.231 × 0.659 = $312,282.

Increase in NPV of production and sales continuing beyond the first four years would be

12,083,664 + 312,282 = $12,395,946 or approximately $12.4m.

If only the first four years of operation are considered, the NPV of the planned investment is negative and so it would not be financially acceptable. If production and sales beyond the first four years are considered, the NPV is strongly positive and so the planned investment is financially acceptable. In fact, the NPV of the planned investment becomes positive if only one further year of operation is considered:

NPV = (2,129,000 × 0.593) – 139,000 = 1,262,497 – 139,000 = $1,123,497

(c) Risk in investment appraisal refers to a range of outcomes whose probability of occurrence can be quantified. Risk can therefore be distinguished from uncertainty in investment appraisal, where the likelihood of particular outcomes occurring cannot be quantified.

As regards incorporating risk into investment appraisal, probability analysis can be used to calculate the values of possible outcomes and their probability distribution, the value of the worst possible outcome and its probability, the probability that an investment will generate a positive NPV, the standard deviation of the possible outcomes and the expected value (mean value) of the NPV. Standard deviation is a measure of risk in financial management.

One difficulty with probability analysis is its assumption that an investment can be repeated a large number of times. The expected value of the NPV, for example, is a mean or average value of a number of possible NPVs, while standard deviation is a measure of dispersal of possible NPVs about the expected (mean) NPV. In reality, many investment projects cannot be repeated and so only one of the possible outcomes will actually occur. The expected (mean) value will not actually occur, causing difficulties in applying and interpreting the NPV decision rule when using probability analysis.

Another difficulty with probability analysis is the question of how the probabilities of possible outcomes are assessed and calculated. One method of determining probabilities is by considering and analysing the outcomes of similar investment projects from the past. However, this approach relies on the weak assumption that the past is an acceptable guide to the future. Assessing probabilities this way is also likely to be a very subjective process.

(d)   Theoretically, a company should invest in all projects with a positive net present value in order to maximise shareholder wealth. If a company has attractive investment opportunities available to it, with positive net present values, it will not be able to maximise shareholder wealth if it does not invest in them, for example, because investment finance is limited or rationed.

If investment finance is limited for reasons outside a company, it is called 'hard capital rationing'. This may arise because a company is seen as too risky by potential investors, for example, because its level of gearing is so high that it is believed it may struggle to deliver adequate returns on invested funds.

Hard capital rationing could also arise if a company wants to raise debt finance for investment purposes, but lacks sufficient assets to offer as security, leading again to a risk-related problem. During a time of financial crisis, investors may seek to reduce risk by limiting the amount of funds they are prepared to invest and by choosing to invest only in low-risk projects. It is also true to say that companies could struggle to secure investment when the capital markets are depressed, or when economic prospects are poor, for example, during a recession.

If investment funds are limited for reasons within a company, the term 'soft capital rationing' is used. Investing in all projects with a positive net present value could mean that a company increases in size quite dramatically, which incumbent managers and directors may wish to avoid in favour of a strategy of controlled growth, limiting the investment finance available as a consequence. Managers and directors may limit investment finance in order to avoid some consequences of external financing, such as an increased commitment to fixed interest payments if new debt finance were raised, or potential dilution of earnings per share if new equity finance were raised, whether from existing or new shareholders.

Investment finance may also be limited internally in order to require investment projects to compete with each other for funds. Only robust investment projects will gain access to funds, it is argued, while marginal projects with low net present values will be rejected. In this way, companies can increase the likelihood of taking on investment projects which will actually produce positive net present values when they are undertaken, reducing the uncertainty associated with making investment decisions based on financial forecasts.

160 Warden Co

Text references. NPV and IRR are covered in Chapter 8. Sensitivity analysis is covered in Chapter 10.

Top tips. Part (a) is a fairly straightforward NPV calculation without many of the difficulties that can be present. Ensure that you recover the working capital at the end of the five years and that the tax on profits is paid one year in arrears.

Easy marks. There are easy marks available in the calculations in parts (a) and (b) and for the explanation of sensitivity analysis in part (c).

		Marks
(a)	Sales revenue	0.5
	Variable costs	0.5
	Fixed costs	0.5
	Tax liabilities	1
	Working capital recovered	1
	Scrap value	0.5
	Initial working capital	1
	Initial investment	0.5
	Discount factors	0.5
	NPV calculation	1
	Decision as to financial acceptability	1
		__
		8
(b)	Calculation of revised NPV	1
	Calculation of IRR	2
	Comment on financial acceptability	1
		__
		4
(c)	(i) Explanation of sensitivity analysis	2
	(ii) After-tax present value of sales revenue	2
	Selling price sensitivity	2
	Discount rate sensitivity	1
	Comment on findings	1
		__
		6
		==
		20

(a) **Calculation of net present value (NPV)**

Year	0	1	2	3	4	5	6
	$'000	$'000	$'000	$'000	$'000	$'000	$'000
Sales revenue		1,600	1,600	1,600	1,600	1,600	
Variable costs		(1,100)	(1,100)	(1,100)	(1,100)	(1,100)	
Fixed costs		(160)	(160)	(160)	(160)	(160)	
Before-tax cash flows		340	340	340	340	340	
Taxation at 30%			(102)	(102)	(102)	(102)	(102)
Capital investment	(800)					40	
Working capital	(90)					90	
Project cash flows	(890)	340	238	238	238	368	(102)
Discount factor 11%	1.000	0.901	0.812	0.731	0.659	0.593	0.535
Present value	(890)	306	193	174	157	218	(55)
NPV	**103**						

The NPV is positive and therefore the project is financially acceptable.

(b) **Calculation of IRR**

Year	0	1	2	3	4	5	6
	$'000	$'000	$'000	$'000	$'000	$'000	$'000
Project cash flows	(890)	340	238	238	238	368	(102)
Discount factor 17%	1.000	0.855	0.731	0.624	0.534	0.456	0.390
Present value	(890)	291	174	149	127	168	(40)
NPV	**(21)**						

$$IRR \approx a + \left(\left(\frac{NPV_a}{NPV_a - NPV_b}\right)(b-a)\right)\%$$

$$IRR \approx 11 + \left[\frac{103}{103 + 21} \times (17 - 11)\right]$$

$$\approx 15.98\%, \text{ say } 16\%$$

As the IRR is greater than the cost of capital, the project is financially acceptable to Warden Co.

Note. Other discount rates may give a slightly different IRR, but it should still be around 16%.

(c) (i) The sensitivity of an investment project to a change in a variable can be calculated as the ratio of the NPV to the present value (PV) of the variable. This shows the relative change in the variable which will make the NPV of the project zero. Sensitivity analysis can be used to calculate the key variable for a project and show the area on which management should focus in order to make the project successful.

(ii) **Selling price sensitivity**

As sales revenue is a five-year annuity the present value can be calculated as follows:

100,000 units × $16 × 5-year annuity factor at 11%

100,000 × $16 × 3.696 = $5,913,600

The tax liability from this revenue also needs to be considered as the NPV includes the tax paid.

Tax liability (before taking account of paying in arrears) = $5,913,600 × 30% = $1,774,080

Discounting by one year to give PV of tax liability = $1,774,080 × 0.901 = $1,598,446

Total PV relating to sales revenue = $5,913,600 − $1,598,446 = $4,315,154

Sensitivity of project to sales revenue = (103,000/4,315,154) × 100% = 2.4%

Discount rate sensitivity

Change in discount rate required for NPV to be zero = 16 − 11 = 5%

Sensitivity of project to the discount rate = (5/11) × 100% = 45.5%

As can be seen from the analysis above the critical variable is the selling price as the investment is significantly more sensitive to changes in the sales price than the discount rate.

161 BQK Co

Text references. NPV is covered in Chapters 8 and 9 and ARR (ROCE) in Chapter 7. The impact of high interest rates is covered in Chapters 2 and 8.

Top tips. Part (a) is a fairly straightforward NPV calculation without many of the difficulties that can be present. Ensure that you inflate each item of cost and revenue at the correct rates and the tax on profits is paid one year in arrears. For part (b), you may not have studied the answer to this question, but apply your common sense and you should be able to obtain good marks.

Easy marks. There are plenty of easy marks for calculations in this question.

ACCA examining team's comments. Many candidates gained high marks in part (a) of this question. Some answers mistakenly used the real after-tax cost of capital of 9%, or tried to calculate another discount rate altogether using the Fisher equation, but all that was needed was to use the 12% rate provided. Some answers chose not to comment on the financial acceptability of the investment project and so lost a relatively straightforward mark.

		Marks	
(a)	Sales income without inflation	1	
	Inflation of sales income	1	
	Variable costs without inflation	1	
	Inflation of variable costs	1	
	Inflated fixed costs	1	
	Calculation of tax-allowable depreciation	1	
	Correct use of tax-allowable depreciation	1	
	Calculation of tax liabilities	1	
	Correct timing of tax liabilities	1	
	Selection of correct discount rate	1	
	Selection of discount factors	1	
	Calculation of net present value	1	
	Comment on financial acceptability	1	
			13
(b)	Customer financing costs	2–3	
	Company financing costs	2–3	
	Effect on investment appraisal process	2–3	
		Maximum	7
			20

(a) Present value of cash flows

Year	0	1	2	3	4	5
	$'000	$'000	$'000	$'000	$'000	$'000
Capital cost	(4,000)					
Sales revenue (W1)		5,614	7,214	9,015	7,034	
Variable costs (W2)		(3,031)	(3,931)	(5,135)	(4,174)	
Fixed costs*		(1,530)	(1,561)	(1,592)	(1,624)	
Taxable cash flow		1,053	1,722	2,288	1,236	
Tax liabilities			(316)	(517)	(686)	(371)
TAD tax benefits**			300	300	300	300
After-tax cash flow		1,053	1,706	2,071	850	(71)
Discount at 12%	1	0.893	0.797	0.712	0.636	0.567
Present values	(4,000)	940	1,360	1,475	541	(40)
NPV	**276**					

This project has a positive NPV which indicates it should be undertaken.

*Fixed costs are inflated by 2% year on year.

**TAD tax benefits = Purchase cost $4,000k/4 years × 30%

Workings

1   *Sales revenue*

Year	1	2	3	4
Small houses selling price ($'000/house)	200	200	200	200
Small houses sales quantity	15	20	15	5
Large houses selling price ($'000/house)	350	350	350	350
Large houses sales quantity	7	8	15	15
Total sales revenue (nearest $'000)	5,450	6,800	8,250	6,250
Inflated sales revenue ($'000/year) – sales revenue × 1.03^n	5,614	7,214	9,015	7,034

2   Variable costs

Year	1	2	3	4
Small houses selling price ($'000/house)	100	100	100	100
Small houses sales quantity	15	20	15	5
Large houses selling price ($'000/house)	200	200	200	200
Large houses sales quantity	7	8	15	15
Total sales revenue (nearest $'000)	2,900	3,600	4,500	3,500
Inflated sales revenue ($'000/year) – sales revenue $\times 1.045^n$	3,031	3,931	5,135	4,174

(b)   Impact of a substantial rise in interest rates on BQK Co's financing costs

A substantial increase in interest rates will cause BQK Co's borrowing costs to rise. The company's cost of debt will increase as loans require higher interest payments. This will in turn cause the company's weighted average cost of capital (WACC) to increase – the more the company's capital structure consists of debt, the more the WACC will be affected.

Ultimately, the increase in interest rates will also cause the cost of equity to rise. This is shown in the CAPM formula: the cost of equity is linked to the risk-free rate of return at any given time, and the risk-free rate of return (the rate of return on government securities, for example) varies in accordance with the prevailing interest rate. This should have an even greater impact on the company than the increase in the cost of debt.

Impact of a substantial rise in interest rates on customers' financing costs

BQK Co's customers would be financing the purchase of their houses through long-term mortgages. As the rate of interest rises, existing and potential customers' borrowing costs will increase, making the house purchase more expensive.

Impact on the capital investment appraisal process:

(i)   BQK Co is likely to use the WACC as the discount rate to be applied in evaluating investment decisions. As the WACC increases in response to the rise in interest rates, the present value of investment projects will decrease. As a result, BQK Co is likely to invest in fewer projects – projects which, at times of lower interest rates, would have been attractive and may now be deemed unsuitable.

(ii)   BQK Co will find it more difficult to sell houses, as the higher mortgage costs put off potential house buyers.

(iii)   To make certain investment projects attractive, BQK Co may raise house prices. However, this is likely to further reduce its volume of potential sales.

(iv)   Construction and infrastructure costs may also increase, as suppliers look to pass on their higher borrowing costs.

In summary, a substantial rise in interest rates is likely to reduce BQK Co's annual profits. BQK Co will need to consider a longer time period when appraising investments.

162 Uftin Co

Text references. Net present value (NPV) is covered in Chapters 8 and 9 and incorporating risk into investment appraisal is covered in Chapter 10.

Top tips. As usual, you need to lay out a proforma for the NPV calculation and show your workings underneath. The main task is to deal with the inflation and the tax-allowable depreciation.

Easy marks. Part (a) is full of easy calculation marks! Part (b) is also a gift as you can pick any two of the revisions to discuss so you can pick the two that you feel most confident about.

		Marks
(a)	Sales revenue	1
	Inflated sales revenue	1
	Inflated variable costs	1
	Inflated fixed costs	1
	Excluding interest payments	1
	Tax-allowable depreciation	1
	Balancing allowance	1
	Tax liabilities	1
	Timing of tax liabilities	1
	Net present value	1
	Comment on financial acceptability	1
		11
(b)	Explanation of first revision	1–3
	Explanation of second revision	1–3
	Maximum	4
(c)	Discussion of two methods, 2–3 marks per method	Maximum	5
		20

(a) As inflation rates differ for revenue and cost, nominal cash flows (ie including inflation) need to be calculated and discounted at the nominal rate (also including inflation).

		0	1	2	3	4	5
			$'000	$'000	$'000	$'000	$'000
Revenue	W1		2,475	2,714	4,413	4,775	
Variable cost	W2		(1,097)	(1,323)	(2,084)	(2,370)	
Fixed cost	W3		(155)	(160)	(164)	(169)	
Before-tax cash flows			1,223	1,231	2,165	2,236	
Taxation at 22%				(269)	(271)	(476)	(492)
Investment		(1,800)					
TAD	W4			99	74	56	167
Net cash flow		(1,800)	1,223	1,063	1,968	1,816	(325)
12% discount factor (tables)		1	0.893	0.797	0.712	0.636	0.567
Present value		(1,800)	1,092	847	1,401	1,154	(184)

NPV = total of the present value line = $2,510k. As this is positive, the proposal is financially acceptable and should go ahead.

Workings

1 *Revenue*

	1	2	3	4
Price (Current terms) ($)	25	25	26	27
Inflation factor	$\times (1.042)$	$\times (1.042)^2$	$\times (1.042)^3$	$\times (1.042)^4$
Inflated price ($)	= 26.05	= 27.14	= 29.42	= 31.83
$\times$ Volume (units)	95,000	100,000	150,000	150,000
= Nominal sales ($)	2,474,750	2,714,000	4,413,000	4,774,500

2 *Variable cost*

	1	2	3	4
Unit cost (current terms) ($)	11	12	12	13
Inflation factor	$\times (1.05)$	$\times (1.05)^2$	$\times (1.05)^3$	$\times (1.05)^4$
Inflated price	= 11.55	= 13.23	= 13.89	= 15.80
$\times$ Volume (units)	95,000	100,000	150,000	150,000
= Nominal variable cost ($)	1,097,250	1,323,000	2,083,500	2,370,000

3 *Fixed cost*

	1	2	3	4
Fixed cost (forecast for Year 1) ($)	155,000	155,000	155,000	155,000
$\times$ Inflation factor		$\times (1.03)$	$\times (1.03)^2$	$\times (1.03)^3$
= Nominal fixed cost ($)		159,650	164,440	169,373

4

	Tax-allowable depreciation		Tax benefits		Year
		$		$	
1	$1,800,000 \times 0.25 =$	450,000	$450,000 \times 0.22 =$	99,000	2
2	$450,000 \times 0.75 =$	337,500	$337,500 \times 0.22 =$	74,250	3
3	$337,500 \times 0.75 =$	253,125	$253,125 \times 0.22 =$	55,688	4
4	By difference	759,375	$759,375 \times 0.22 =$	167,063	5
		1,800,000		396,001	

(b) You could have chosen any **two** of the following revisions.

Inflation

Real cash flows (cash flows in current prices) should be discounted at a real discount rate and nominal cash flows should be discounted at a nominal discount rate. The junior has correctly applied one year of inflation in Year 1, but incorrectly applied one year of inflation in each of Years 2 to 4. The inflation in Year 2 should be $\times (1 + h)^2$ and in Year 3 should be $(1 + h)^3$ and so on.

Interest payments

Interest repayments on the loan should not be included as these are dealt with via the cost of capital.

Tax-allowable depreciation

Tax-allowable depreciation is calculated on a reducing balance basis and not a straight-line basis as the junior employee has done. There is also a balancing allowance in the final year.

The dates should correspond with the tax payments, so should be received a year in arrears.

Tax timing

The tax liability due in Year 5 was omitted. This is a cash flow which is relevant to the proposal and should therefore be included.

(c) **Note. Only two methods are required to be discussed.**

Risk and uncertainty

A distinction should be made between the terms risk and uncertainty. Risk can be applied to a situation where there are several possible outcomes and, on the basis of past relevant experience, probabilities can be assigned to the various outcomes that could prevail. Uncertainty can be applied to a situation where there are several possible outcomes but there is little past relevant experience to enable the probability of the possible outcomes to be predicted.

There are a wide range of techniques for incorporating risk into project appraisal.

Probability analysis

Probability analysis involves assigning probabilities to either the outcome of an investment project or different values of variables in a project. The range of NPVs and their associated joint probabilities can be used to calculate an expected NPV which would arise if the project was repeated a number of times. This analysis can also show worst and best case scenario results and their associated probabilities. It can also show the most and least likely outcomes. This would allow managers to consider the risk profile of the project before making a decision.

Risk-adjusted discount rate

In investment appraisal, a risk-adjusted discount rate can be used for particular types or risk classes of investment projects to reflect their relative risks. For example, a high discount rate can be used so that a cash flow which occurs quite some time in the future will have less effect on the decision. Alternatively, with the launch of a new product, a higher initial risk premium may be used with a decrease in the discount rate as the product becomes established.

Sensitivity analysis

The basic approach of sensitivity analysis is to calculate the project's NPV under alternative assumptions to determine how sensitive it is to changing conditions. One variable is considered at a time. An indication is thus provided of those variables to which the NPV is most sensitive (critical variables) and the extent to which those variables may change before the investment results in a negative NPV. Sensitivity analysis therefore provides an indication of why a project might fail.

Management should review critical variables to assess whether or not there is a strong possibility of events occurring which will lead to a negative NPV. As sensitivity analysis does not incorporate probabilities it should not be described as a way of incorporating risk into investment appraisal, although it often is.

163 Hraxin Co

Text references. Net present value (NPV) is covered in Chapters 8 and 9. Risk and sensitivity analysis are covered in Chapter 10.

Top tips. As usual, you need to lay out a proforma for the expected net present value (ENPV) calculation in part (a) and show your workings underneath. The main tasks are to deal with the expected selling price, the inflation and the tax-allowable depreciation. Remember that nominal values include inflation already so don't need to be inflated. In part (c) you must explain that sensitivity analysis considers the relative change required in a variable to make the NPV zero.

Easy marks. Part (a) is full of easy calculation marks!

ACCA examining team's comments. The examining team stated that most answers to (a) gained good marks. Although the question stated that tax liabilities were paid in the year they arose, some answers incorrectly deferred the tax liabilities by one year. Many answers stated that the NPV was positive and therefore the project was financially acceptable. This ignores the fact that the ENPV is an average NPV which is not expected to occur in practice. For part (c) the examining team stated that many answers were not able to gain high marks. Many answers attempted to calculate sensitivities but the question asked for a discussion.

Marks

(a)
Mean selling price per unit	0.5
Inflated selling price per unit	1
Inflated revenue	1
Inflated overhead	1
Tax liabilities	1
Timing of tax liabilities	1
Tax-allowable depreciation benefits	1
Scrap value	0.5
Present values of future cash flows	1
Comment on financial acceptability	1
	9

(b)
Discussion of risk and uncertainty distinction	3
Value of considering risk and uncertainty	2
	5

(c)
Explanation of sensitivity analysis	1–3
Explanation of risk in investment appraisal	1–2
Discussion of sensitivity analysis and risk	1–3
Maximum	**6**
	20

(a) **Calculation of expected NPV year**

Year	1	2	3	4
	$'000	$'000	$'000	$'000
Revenue	4,524	7,843	13,048	10,179
Variable cost	(2,385)	(4,200)	(7,080)	(5,730)
Contribution	2,139	3,643	5,968	4,449
Overhead	(440)	(484)	(532)	(586)
Cash flow before tax	1,699	3,159	5,436	3,863
Tax	(510)	(948)	(1,631)	(1,159)
Depreciation benefits	338	338	338	338
Cash flow after tax	1,527	2,549	4,143	3,042
Scrap value				500
Project cash flow	1,527	2,549	4,143	3,542
Discount at 11%	0.901	0.812	0.731	0.659
Present values	1,376	2,070	3,029	2,334

	$'000
PV of future cash flows	8,809
Initial investment	(5,000)
ENPV	3,809

The investment project has a positive ENPV of $3,809,000. This is a mean or average NPV which will result from the project being repeated many times. However, as the project is not being repeated, the NPVs associated with each future economic state must be calculated as it is one of these NPVs which is expected to occur. The decision by management on the financial acceptability of the project will be based on these NPVs and the risk associated with each one.

Workings

Mean or average selling price = (25 × 0.35) + (30 × 0.5) + (35 × 0.15) = $29 per unit

Year	1	2	3	4
Inflated selling price ($ per unit)	30.16	31.37	32.62	33.93
Sales volume (units/year)	150,000	250,000	400,000	300,000
Sales revenue ($'000/year)	4,524	7,843	13,048	10,179

Year	1	2	3	4
Inflated overhead ($'000/year)	440	484	532	586

Total tax-allowable depreciation = 5,000,000 – 500,000 = $4,500,000
Annual tax-allowable depreciation = 4,500,000/4 = $1,125,000 per year
Annual cash flow from tax-allowable depreciation = 1,125,000 × 0.3 = $337,500 per year

(b)   A project's potential NPV is **one** important piece of management information because it quantifies the expected **return**. However, this return is based on a forecast and is not guaranteed so before a project is accepted the potential **risk or uncertainty** of a project should be assessed.

The terms **risk** and **uncertainty** are often used interchangeably but a distinction should be made between them. With risk, there are **several possible outcomes** which, upon the basis of past relevant experience, can be **quantified**. In areas of uncertainty, again there are several possible outcomes but, with little past experience, it will be **difficult to quantify** its likely effects.

A risky situation is one where we can say that there is a 70% probability that returns from a project will be in excess of $100,000 but a 30% probability that returns will be less than $100,000. If, however, no information can be provided on the returns from the project, we are faced with an uncertain situation. Managers need to exercise caution when assessing future cash flows to ensure that they make appropriate decisions. If a project is too risky, it might need to be rejected, depending upon the prevailing **attitude to risk**.

In general, risky projects are those whose future cash flows, and hence the project returns, are likely to be **variable**. The greater the variability is, the greater the risk. The problem of risk is more acute with capital investment decisions than other decisions because estimates of cash flows might be for several years ahead, such as for major construction projects. Actual costs and revenues may vary well above or below budget as the work progresses.

(c)   Sensitivity analysis assesses the extent to which the NPV of an investment project responds to changes in project variables. Sensitivity analysis will normally involve identifying key project variables and determining the percentage change in a project variable which results in a zero NPV. The critical project variables are identified as those to which the NPV is most sensitive, for example, ie those where the smallest percentage change in the variable results in a zero NPV. Sensitivity analysis is therefore concerned with calculating relative changes in project variables.

When discussing risk in the context of investment appraisal, it is important to note that, unlike uncertainty, risk can be quantified and measured. The probabilities of the occurrence of particular future outcomes can be assessed and used to evaluate the volatility of future cash flows, for example, by calculating their standard deviation. The probabilities of the future economic states in the assessment of the investment project of Hraxin Co are an example of probability analysis and these probabilities can lead to an assessment of project risk.

Sensitivity analysis is usually studied in investment appraisal in relation to understanding how risk can be incorporated in the investment appraisal process. While sensitivity analysis can indicate the critical variables of an investment project, sensitivity analysis does not give any indication of the probability of a change in any critical variable. Selling price (or energy prices) may be a critical variable, for example, but sensitivity analysis is not able to say whether a change in selling price is likely to occur. In the appraisal of the investment project of Hraxin Co, the probabilities of different selling prices arising from the related economic states have come from probability analysis, not from sensitivity analysis.

Sensitivity analysis will not therefore directly assist Hraxin Co in assessing the risk of the investment project. However, it does provide useful information which helps management to gain a deeper understanding of the project and which focuses management attention on aspects of the investment project where problems may arise.

164 Vyxyn Co

Marking scheme

			Marks
(a)	Explain risk	1	
	Explain uncertainty	1	
	Discuss difference	1	
			3
(b)	Inflated revenue	1	
	Mean variable cost	1	
	Inflated variable cost	1	
	Tax liabilities	1	
	TAD benefits	1	
	Timing of tax flows	1	
	Calculation of PVs	1	
	Comment on variable cost	1	
	Comment on NPV	1	
			9
(c)	Sensitivity analysis	2	
	Probability analysis	2	
	Risk-adjusted rate	2	
	Adjusted payback	2	
			8
			20

(a) The terms risk and uncertainty are often used interchangeably in everyday discussion, however, there is a clear difference between them in relation to investment appraisal.

Risk refers to the situation where an investment project has several possible outcomes, all of which are known and to which probabilities can be attached, for example, on the basis of past experience. Risk can therefore be quantified and measured by the variability of returns of an investment project.

Uncertainty refers to the situation where an investment project has several possible outcomes but it is not possible to assign probabilities to their occurrence. It is therefore not possible to say which outcomes are likely to occur.

The difference between risk and uncertainty, therefore, is that risk can be quantified whereas uncertainty cannot be quantified. Risk increases with the variability of returns, while uncertainty increases with project life.

(b) NPV calculation

Year	1	2	3	4	5
	$000	$000	$000	$000	$000
Sales income	12,069	16,791	23,947	11,936	
Variable cost	(5,491)	(7,139)	(9,720)	(5,616)	
Contribution	6,578	9,652	14,227	6,320	
Fixed cost	(1,100)	(1,121)	(1,155)	(1,200)	
Taxable cash flow	5,478	8,531	13,072	5,120	
Taxation at 28%		(1,534)	(2,389)	(3,660)	(1,434)
TAD tax benefits		1,400	1,050	788	2,362
After-tax cash flow	5,478	8,397	11,733	2,248	928
Discount at 10%	0.909	0.826	0.751	0.683	0.621
Present values	4,980	6,936	8,812	1,535	576

	$000
PV of future cash flows	22,839
Initial investment	(20,000)
NPV	2,839

Comment

The probability that variable cost per unit will be $12.00 per unit or less is 80% and so the probability of a positive NPV is therefore at least 80%. However, the effect on the NPV of the variable cost per unit increasing to $14.70 per unit must be investigated, as this may result in a negative NPV.

The expected NPV is positive and so the investment project is likely to be acceptable on financial grounds.

Workings

Sales revenue

Year	1	2	3	4
Selling price ($/unit)	26.50	28.50	30.00	26.00
Inflated at 3.5% per year	27.43	30.53	33.26	29.84
Sales volume (000 units/year)	440	550	720	400
Sales income ($000/yearl	12,069	16,791	23,947	11,936

Variable cost

Mean variable cost= $(0.45 \times 10.80) + (0.35 \times 12.00) + (0.20 \times 14.70) = \$12.00/unit$

Year	1	2	3	4
Variable cost ($/unit)	12.00	12.00	12.00	12.00
Inflated at 4% per year	12.48	12.98	13.50	14.04
Sales volume (000 units/year)	440	550	720	400
Variable cost ($000/year)	5,491	7,139	9,720	5,616

Year	1	2	3	4
TAD ($000)	5,000	3,750	2,813	8,437
Tax benefits at 28% ($000)	1,400	1,050	788	2,362*

*$(20,000 \times 0.28) - 1,400 - 1,050 - 788 = \$2,362,000$

Alternative calculation of after-tax cash flow

Year	1	2	3	4	5
	$000	$000	$000	$000	$000
Taxable cash flow	5,478	8,531	13,072	5,120	
TAD ($000)	(5,000)	(3,750)	(2,813)	(8,437)	
Taxable profit	478	4,781	10,259	(3,317)	
Taxation at 28%		(134)	(1,339)	(2,873)	929
After-tax profit	478	4,647	8,920	(6,190)	929
Add back TAD	5,000	3,750	2,813	8,437	
After-tax cash flow	5,478	8,397	11,733	2,247	929

(c) There are several ways of considering risk in the investment appraisal process.

Sensitivity analysis

This technique looks at the effect on the NPV of an investment project of changes in project variables, such as selling price per unit, variable cost per unit and sales volume. There are two approaches which are used. The first approach calculates the relative (percentage) change in a given project variable which is needed to make the NPV zero. The second approach calculates the relative (percentage) change in project NPV which results from a given change in the value of a project variable (for example, 5%).

Sensitivity analysis considers each project variable individually. Once the sensitivities for each project variable have been calculated, the next step is to identify the key or critical variables. These are the project variables where the smallest relative change makes the NPV zero, or where the biggest change in NPV results from a given change in the value of a project variable. The key or critical project variables indicate where underlying assumptions may need to be checked or where managers may need to focus their attention in order to make an investment project successful. However, as sensitivity analysis does not consider risk as measured by probabilities, it can be argued that it is not really a way of considering risk in investment appraisal at all, even though it is often described as such.

Probability analysis

This technique requires that probabilities for each project outcome be assessed and assigned. Alternatively, probabilities for different values of project variables can be assessed and assigned. A range of project NPVs can then be calculated, as well as the mean NPV (the expected NPV or ENPV) associated with repeating the investment project many times. The worst and best outcomes and their probebilities, the most likely outcome and its probability and the probability of a negative NPV can also be calculated. Investment decisions could then be based on the risk profile of the investment project, rather than simply on the NPV decision rule.

Risk-adjusted discount rate

It is often said that 'the higher the risk, the higher the return'. Investment projects with higher risk should therefore be discounted with a higher discount rate than lower risk investment projects. Better still, the discount rate should reflect the risk of the investment project.

Theoretically, the capital asset pricing model (CAPM) can be used to determine a project-specific discount rate which reflects an investment project's systematic risk. This means selecting a proxy company with similar business activities to a proposed investment project, ungearing the proxy company equity beta to give an asset beta which does not reflect the proxy company financial risk, regearing the asset beta to give an equity beta which reflects the financial risk of the investing company, and using the CAPM to calculate a project-specific cost of equity for the investment project.

Adjusted payback

If uncertainty and risk are seen as being the same, payback can consider risk by shortening the payback period. Because uncertainty (risk) increases with project life, shortening the payback period will require a risky project to pay back sooner, thereby focusing on cash flows which are nearer in time (less uncertain) and so less risky.

Discounted paybeck can also be seen as considering risk because future cash flows can be converted into present values using a risk-adjusted discount rate. The target payback period normally used by a company can then be applied to the discounted cash flows. Overall, the effect is likely to be similar to shortening the payback period with undiscounted cash flows.

165 Pelta Co

Marking scheme

				Marks
(a)	(i)	Inflated sales	1	
		Inflated VC/unit	1	
		Inflated total VC	1	
		Tax liabilities	1	
		TAD benefits yrs 1–3	1	
		TAD benefits yr 4	1	
		Timing of tax flows	1	
		Terminal value	1	
		Calculate PVs	1	
				9
	(ii)	Cumulative NPV	1	
		Discounted payback	1	
				2
(b)		Acceptability – NPV	1	
		Acceptability – Payback	1	
		Correct advice	1	
				3
(c)		Evaluation period	2	
		Terminal value	2	
		Discounted payback	2	
				6
				20

(a) (i)

Year	1	2	3	4	5
	$000	$000	$000	$000	$000
Sales income	16,224	20,248	24,196	27,655	
Variable costs	(5,356)	(6,752)	(8,313)	(9,694)	
Contribution	10,868	13,495	15,883	17,962	
Fixed costs	(700)	(735)	(779)	(841)	
Cash flows before tax	10,168	12,760	15,104	17,121	
Corporation tax		(3,050)	(3,828)	(4,531)	(5,136)
TAD tax benefits		1,875	1,406	1,055	2,789
After-tax cash flow	10,168	11,585	12,682	13,644	(2,347)
Terminal value				1,250	
Project cash flow	10,168	11,585	12,682	14,894	(2,347)
Discount at 12%	0.893	0.797	0.712	0.636	0.567
Present values	9,080	9,233	9,030	9,473	(1,331)
PV of future cash flows		35,485			
($000)					
Initial investment		(25,000)			
($000)					
NPV		10,485			

Workings

Year	1	2	3	4
Sales volume (units/year)	520,000	624,000	717,000	788,000
Selling price ($/unit)	30.00	30.00	30.00	30.00
Inflated by 4% per year	31.20	32.45	33.75	35.10
Income ($000/year)	16,224	20,248	24,196	27,655

Year	1	2	3	4
Sales volume (units/year)	520,000	624,000	717,000	788,000
Variable cost ($/unit)	10.00	10.20	10.61	10.93
Inflated by 3% per year	10.30	10.82	11.59	12.30
Total ($000/year)	5,356	6,752	8,313	9,694

Year	1	2	3	4
Fixed costs ($000 per year)	700	735	779	841

Year	1	2	3	4
TAD ($000 per year)	6,250	4,688	3,516	9,297
TAD benefits ($000/year)	1,875	1,406	1,055	2,789

(ii)

Year	1	2	3	4	5
	$000	$000	$000	$000	$000
Present values	9,080	9,233	9,030	9,473	(1,331)
Cumulative net present value	(15,920)	(6,687)	2,343	11,815	10,485
Discounted payback (years)					

Discounted payback occurs approximately 74% (6,687/9,030) through the third year ie the discounted payback period is about 2.7 years.

(b)   The investment project is financially acceptable under the NPV decision rule because it has a substantial positive NPV.

The discounted payback period of 2.7 years is greater than the maximum target discounted payback period of two years and so from this perspective the investment project Is not financially acceptable.

The correct advice is given by the NPV method, however, and so the investment project is financially acceptable.

(c)   The views of the directors on investment appraisal can be discussed from several perspectives.

Evaluation period

Sales are expected to contlnue beyond year 4 and so the view of the directors that all investment projects must be evaluated over four years of operations does not seem sensible. The investment appraisal would be more accurate if the cash flows from further years of operation were considered.

Assumed terminal value

The view of the directors that a terminal value of 5% of the initial investment should be assumed has no factual or analytical basis to it. Terminal values for individual projects could be higher or lower than 5% of the initial investment and in fact may have no relationship to the initial investment at all.

A more accurate approach would be to calculate a year 4 terminal value based on the expected value of future sales.

Discounted payback method

The directors need to explain their view that an investment projects discounted payback must be no greater than two years. Perhaps they think that an earlier payback will indicate an investment project with a lower level of risk. Although the discounted payback method does overcome the failure of simple payback to take account of the time value of money, it still fails to consider cash flows outside the payback period. Theoretically, Pelta Co should rely on the NPV investment appraisal method.

MCQ bank – Sources of finance

166 B 1 Statement 2 is incorrect. Convertible bonds give the **investor**, not the borrower, the right but not the obligation to turn the bond into a predetermined number of ordinary shares.

Syllabus area E1(a)

167 A Ordinary shares are most risky from the debt holder's perspective – the company can decide whether and how much of a dividend to pay.

Preference shares are next most risky – dividends are only payable if profit is available to pay dividends from.

Trade payables are next because they have to be paid before shareholders but are typically unsecured.

Finally, banks with fixed and floating charges face least risk.

Syllabus area E1(b)

168 D $1.92

$2	×	4	=	$8.00
$1.60	×	1	=	$1.60
		5		$9.60

Theoretical ex-rights price = $9.60/5 = $1.92

Syllabus area E1(c)

169 B A describes the redemption yield and C describes the interest yield.

Syllabus area E1(b)

170 A B is mudaraba. C is murabaha. D is ijara. A key principle is that charging interest and making money from money lending alone is forbidden under Sharia law, so providers of finance are more directly involved with the risks and rewards of the businesses they finance.

Syllabus area E1(d)

MCQ bank – Dividend policy

171 A Modigliani and Miller (M&M) assume perfect capital markets so there is no information content in dividend policy. They assume no taxes or tax preferences so investors will be indifferent between income and capital gains. They also assume no transaction costs so investors can switch between income and capital gains without cost – eg if a company withholds a dividend when the investor would prefer cash, the investor can sell some of their shares (known as 'manufacturing a dividend'). M&M's theory is not contingent upon the existence or otherwise of inflation.

Syllabus area E1(e)

172 C Residual income will not give a reliable income stream, and is geared to financing investments that will give capital gains.

Syllabus area E1(e)

173 B M&M stated that income preference is irrelevant in deciding dividend policy because, if you 'assume away' taxation and transaction costs, it is costless for investors to switch from capital gain to dividends by selling some shares.

Syllabus area E1(e)

174 B Statement A is false. A bonus issue is when a company offers free additional shares to existing shareholders. Therefore, it does not raise new equity finance.

Statement B is true. By reducing the number of shares in issue, the company can increase the earnings per share. This allows debt to be substituted for equity so gearing is raised.

Statement C is false. In a zero tax world neither the dividend decision or the financing decision matters (according to Modigliani & Miller theory). Where tax does exist, both decisions are important.

Statement D is false. Shareholders are entitled to receive a share of any agreed dividends but directors decide on the amount and frequency of dividend payments (if any).

Syllabus area E1(e)

175   **A**   Company Sun Co = Constant growth. Company Moon Co = Constant payout.
Company Nite Co = Residual/random.

Company Sun Co dividends are growing at 10% per annum even though earnings are not.

Company Moon Co is paying 50% of its earnings out as a dividend consistently.

Company Nite Co's dividends are not obviously connected with reported earnings, so its policy is either residual (ie only paying dividends once investment plans are budgeted for) or random.

Syllabus area E1(e)

MCQ bank – Gearing and capital structure

176   **C**   Operational gearing = Contribution/Profit before interest and tax.

Contribution = Revenue − variable cost = 10,123 − (70% × 7,222) − (10% × 999) = 4,967.70

Operational gearing = 4,967.70/1,902 = 2.61

Syllabus area E3(d)

177   **D**   53%

Market value of equity = $5.50 × $100m = $550m
Market value of long-term debt = $500m × (125/100) = $625m
Therefore financial gearing = 625/(625 + 550) = 53%

Syllabus area E3(d)

178   **A**   Gearing = $\dfrac{\text{Prior charge capital}}{\text{Equity}}$

Market value of preference shares = 2,000 shares × 80c = $1,600.

Prior charge capital	= preference shares + bonds + loan.
∴ Prior charge capital	= $1,600 + ($4,000 × ($105/$100)) + $6,200
	= $12,000

Market value of equity:

Number of shares = $8,000 ÷ 50c = 16,000 shares

16,000 shares × $5 = $80,000

Gearing = $\dfrac{\$12,000}{\$80,000}$ × 100% = 15.0%

Syllabus area E3(d)

179   **B**   Interest cover will rise. Gearing will fall. All else being equal, less interest to pay will mean a higher interest cover.

(Interest cover = Profit before interest and tax/Interest)
Reducing debt will reduce the gearing ratio.

Syllabus area E3(d)

180   **B**   **P/E ratio will increase. Dividend yield will decrease.**

In relation to expectations, results being better than expected would boost share price. This would increase the price/earnings ratio.

By the same logic, dividend yield would reduce. Dividend yield is calculated as dividend/share price; hence a higher share price would reduce the ratio.

Syllabus area E3(d)

181   **A**   Market value of equity = $8m × ($5.00/$0.5) = $80m

Market value of bonds = $4m × ($105/$100) = $4.2m

Market value of preference shares = $2m × ($0.80/$1.00) = $1.6m

Prior charge capital = $4.2m + $6.2m (loan) + $1.6m = $12m

Market value based gearing = 100 × ($12m/$80m) = 15.0%

Syllabus area E(5)

182   **B**   Statement 1 and Statement 2 are true.

Statement 1. The main handicap that SMEs face in accessing funds is the problem of uncertainty and risk for lenders. This is because they have neither the business history nor the long trade record that larger organisations possess.

Statement 2. Larger enterprises are subject by law to more public scrutiny and their financial statements have to contain more detail and be audited, giving greater clarity to investors than less detailed financial statements of smaller companies.

Statement 3. Once small firms have become established they do not necessarily need to seek a market listing to obtain equity finance. Shares **can** be placed privately.

Syllabus area E5

183   **C**   Both statements are true.

Statement 1 is true. For long-term loans, security can be provided in the form of property (eg mortgages) but SMEs may not have suitable security for a medium-term loan due to mismatching of the maturity of assets and liabilities. This problem is known as the maturity gap.

Statement 2 is true. A funding gap is a shortfall in capital needed to fund the ongoing operations and this is a common problem for SMEs.

Syllabus area E5

184   **D**   This is known as business angel financing. Business angels are prepared to take high risks in the hope of high returns.

Syllabus area E5

185   **B**   Statement 1 is false. SCF allows a buyer to extend the time in which it settles its accounts payable. For the supplier, it is a sale of their receivables.

Statement 2 is true. The buyer is usually a large company with a good credit rating. This means that low interest rates are charged to the supplier by the intermediary fund provider, for providing the supplier with finance, ie in the form of purchasing its invoices.

Syllabus area E5

CBE style OTQ bank – The cost of capital

186 **$1.73**

20X9 to 20Y3 covers four years of growth,

so the average annual growth rate = $\sqrt[4]{(423/220)} - 1 = 0.178 = 17.8\%$

$$K_e = \frac{d_0(1+g)}{P_0} + g$$

$$K_e - g = \frac{d_0(1+g)}{P_0}$$

$$P_0 = \frac{d_0(1+g)}{K_e - g}$$

= (423,000 × 1.178)/(0.25 − 0.178) = $6,920,750 for 4 million shares = $1.73 per share

Syllabus area F2(c)

187 **31%**

Using Gordon's growth approximation, g = br

g = proportion of profits retained × rate of return on investment

Proportion of earnings retained = ($1.50 − $0.5)/$1.50 = 66.7%

Rate of return on investment = EPS/net assets per share = $1.5/$6 = 0.25 so 25%

g = 66.7% × 25% = 16.7%

$$K_e = \frac{d_0(1+g)}{P_0} + g$$

$$= \frac{(\$0.50 \times 1.167)}{(\$4.50 - \$0.50)} + 0.167 \qquad \textbf{Note.} \text{ Share price given is cum div.}$$

= 31%

Syllabus area E2(a)

188 **The residual risk associated with investing in a well-diversified portfolio**

'The chance that automated processes may fail' is incorrect. Systematic risk refers to return volatility, not automated processes.

'The risk associated with investing in equity' is incorrect. This describes **total** risk, which has both systematic and unsystematic elements.

'The diversifiable risk associated with investing in equity' is incorrect. Systematic risk cannot be diversified away.

'The residual risk associated with investing in a well-diversified portfolio' is correct. It is the risk generated by undiversifiable systemic economic risk factors.

Syllabus area E2(a)

189 **13.4%**

The equity beta relates to the cost of equity, hence gearing and the debt beta are not relevant.

$E(r_i) = R_f + \beta (E(R_m) - R_f) = 3\% + (1.3 \times 8\%) = 13.4\%$

Syllabus area E2(a)

190 Statement 1 is correct. An increase in the cost of equity will lead to a fall in share price. Think about the dividend valuation model and how P_0 will be affected if K_e increases.

Statement 2 is correct. This is known as the risk-return trade-off.

Statement 3 is correct. Preference shares are riskier than debt and therefore a more expensive form of finance.

Syllabus area E3(a/b)

191   **11.5%**

Conversion value: Future share price = current share price including growth = $2.50 \times (1.1)^5$ = $4.03. So conversion value = $20 \times 4.03 = $80.60. The cash alternative = 100×1.1 = $110 therefore investors would not convert and redemption value = $110.

K_d = IRR of the after-tax cash flows as follows:

Time	$	DF 10%	Present value 10% $	DF 15%	Present value 15% $
0	(90)	1	(90)	1	(90)
1–5	10(1 – 0.3) = 7	3.791	26.54	3.352	23.46
5	110	0.621	68.31	0.497	54.67
			4.85		(11.87)

$$IRR = a + \frac{NPV_a}{NPV_a - NPV_b}(b - a)$$

$$= 10\% + \frac{4.85}{(4.85 + 11.87)}(15\% - 10\%)$$

$$= 11.5\%$$

Syllabus area E2(b)

192   **11.7%**

$K_d = i(1 - T)/P_0 = 13(1 - 0.3)/90 = 10.11\%$

$V_d = $7m \times (90/100) = $6.3m$

$K_e = 12\%$ (given)

$V_e = $3 \times 10m$ shares = $30m$

Note. Reserves are included as part of share price.

$V_e + V_d = $6.3m + $30m = $36.3m$

$$WACC = \left[\frac{V_e}{V_e + V_d}\right]k_e + \left[\frac{V_d}{V_e + V_d}\right]k_d$$

$$= [30/36.3]12\% + [6.3/36.3]10.11\% = 11.7\%$$

Syllabus area E2(c)

193   **All statements are true**

Changes in capital structure will affect the WACC so need to stay constant. The current WACC reflects a risk premium relating to current operations, hence the new project should be of a similar risk profile to current operations. The project should be small in size; large projects are both riskier (commanding a risk premium) and likely to affect the value of equity, in turn affecting the WACC.

Syllabus area E3(e)

194   **8.8%**

Cost of equity = $4 + (1.2 \times 5) = 4 + 6 = 10\%$

WACC = $(10 \times 0.7) + (6 \times 0.3) = 7 + 1.8 = 8.8\%$

195   **15.4%**

Ex div share price = $0.30 - (8\% \times $0.50) = 0.26

$K_p = $0.50 \times 8\%/$0.26 = 15.4\%$

Note. Dividends are not tax deductible hence no adjustment for corporation tax is required.

Syllabus area E2(b)

CBE style OTQ bank – Capital structure

196   **It should take on equity finance, as their gearing is probably beyond optimal.**

'It should take on debt finance, as to do so will save tax' refers to Modigliani-Miller (MM) with tax: raising debt finance will increase interest payments and hence save tax, adding to the total returns a business generates.

'It should take on equity finance, as their gearing is probably beyond optimal' is correct: the traditional view implies that once gearing has gone beyond optimal the weighted average cost of capital (WACC) will increase if more debt is taken on. As A Co is significantly more highly geared than the industry standard, it is probably reasonable to assume its gearing is beyond optimal.

'It doesn't matter, as it won't affect the returns the projects generate' refers to MM with no tax: paying interest or paying dividends does not affect the overall returns generated by a non-tax paying business.

'More information is needed before a decision can be made' is incorrect: see earlier comments on the traditional view.

Syllabus area E4(a&b)

197   **Interest payments are tax deductible.**

'Debt is cheaper than equity': Although true, higher gearing increases the cost of equity (financial risk) therefore this doesn't in itself explain a reducing WACC.

'Interest payments are tax deductible' is correct: The only difference between MM (no tax) and MM (with tax) is the tax deductibility of interest payments. MM demonstrated that when a business does not pay tax, returns are not affected by capital structure. However, as interest is tax deductible (and dividends are not), paying relatively more interest will reduce tax payable and increase total returns to investors.

'Reduced levels of expensive equity capital will reduce the WACC' is similar to Statement A.

'Financial risk is not pronounced at moderate borrowing levels' refers to the traditional view. MM assume financial risk is consistently proportionate to gearing across all levels.

Syllabus area E4(b)

198   **Only statement 2 is correct**

Statement 1 is incorrect because the asset beta is an ungeared beta and therefore reflects **ONLY** business risk.

Statement 3 is incorrect: An asset beta will be lower than an equity beta. The difference between an asset beta and an equity beta reflects the impact of financial risk. However, this difference (reflecting financial risk) will be **higher** if a debt beta is assumed to be zero.

Syllabus area E3(e)

199   **Traditional view – director A**

         MM (no tax) – director B

The traditional view has a 'u' shaped weighted average cost of capital (WACC) curve hence there is an optimal point where WACC is minimised.

MM (with tax) assumes 100% gearing is optimal, so there is no balance with equity.

MM (no tax) assumes the WACC is unaffected by the level of gearing. As the WACC is the discount rate for the projects of the business it follows that the value of the business is unaffected by the gearing decision.

Syllabus area E4(a&b)

200   Internal funds, debt, new equity

Pecking order theory suggests that as internal funds are free to raise and immediate they should be used first. After that, debt is relatively quick and inexpensive to raise, interest is tax deductible and the cost of debt is lower than the cost of equity. New equity is relatively expensive hence is considered last.

Syllabus area E4(d)

201   0.89

B Co is being used as a proxy company and has a different level of gearing to TR Co.

Ungear B Co's equity beta:

$$\beta_a = \beta_e \times \frac{V_e}{(V_e + V_d(1-T))}$$

$$= 1.05 \times \frac{4}{(4+1(1-0.3))}$$

$$= 0.89$$

Syllabus area E3(e)

202   8.4%

Regear βa using TR Co assumption of a gearing level of 1:3 debt : equity

$$\beta_e = \beta_a \times \frac{V_e + V_d(1-T)}{V_e}$$

$$\beta_e = 0.89 \times \frac{3 + 1(1-0.3)}{3}$$

$$\beta_e = 1.10$$

Put into CAPM:

Ke   = $R_f + \beta(E(r_m) - R_f)$ $R_f = 4\%$, $E(R_m) - R_f = 4\%$ (market premium)

Ke   =   4 + 1.10(4)

      =   **8.4%**

Syllabus area E3(e)

203   An equity beta also includes an element of financial risk.

An equity beta reflects both business risk and financial risk. An asset beta only reflects the former.

Syllabus area E3(e)

204   If the project is different from current operations

A project-specific cost of capital is relevant to appraise a project with a different risk profile from current operations. In these circumstances the current weighted average cost of capital is not relevant – so proxy information is used to calculate a project-specific cost of capital for that particular appraisal.

Syllabus area E3(e)

205   11%

If Vd/(Vd + Ve) = 0.25 then Vd = 0.25 and Ve = 0.75. So Ve/(Ve + Vd) = 0.75/1 = 0.75.

Ungearing the equity beta of the new business area gives βa = 0.75 × 2 = 1.5.

As Leah Co is an all-equity financed company, the asset beta of 1.5 does not need regearing.

The project-specific cost of equity is therefore Ke = 5 + (1.5 × 4) = 11%.

Incorrect answers:

D   Using the ungeared average equity beta

If the ungeared average equity beta of the new business area of 2.0 is used instead of the asset beta of 1.5 this gives Ke = 5 + (2 × 4) = 13.0%. This means that the average equity beta for the new business area was not ungeared.

A   Ungearing the equity beta of Leah Co

ßa = 1.2 × 0.75 = 0.9

Ke = 5 + (0.9 × 4) = 8.6%

B   Using the equity beta of Leah Co

Ke = 5 + (1.2 × 4) = 9.8%

Syllabus area E3(e)

IML Co

206   **12%**

The required rate of return on equity can be found using the capital asset pricing model:

$E(r_i) = R_f + \beta_i (E(r_m) - R_f)$

AZT Co

$E(r_i) = 5\% + 0.7(15\% - 5\%)$

$= 12\%$

207   **32%**

Total shareholder return $= \dfrac{P_1 - P_0 + D}{P_0}$

$= \dfrac{(315 - 250) + 15}{250}$

$= 0.32 = 32\%$

208   **1.2**

The equity beta for IML Co can be found using the same expression:

$17\% = 5\% + \beta(15\% - 5\%)$

$\beta = \dfrac{(17\% - 5\%)}{(15\% - 5\%)}$

The equity beta factor = 1.2

209   **Statements 1 and 4 are true.**

The equity beta factor is a measure of the volatility of the return on a share relative to the stock market. If for example a share price moved at 3 times the market rate, its equity beta factor would be 3.0.

The beta factor indicates the level of systematic risk, which is the risk of making an investment that cannot be diversified away.

It is used in the capital asset pricing model to determine the level of return required by investors; the higher the level of systematic risk, the **higher** the required level of return.

It is true that companies want a return on a project to exceed the risk-free rate.

210 **Statement 1 is true.**

Statement 2 is false.

Under the CAPM, the return required from a security is related to its systematic risk rather than its total risk. Only the risks that cannot be eliminated by diversification are relevant. The assumption is that investors will hold a fully diversified portfolio and therefore deal with the unsystematic risk themselves.

A low cost of equity would discount future earnings at a low rate – leading to a high market value and a high P/E ratio.

211 Bar Co

Text references. Rights issues are covered in Chapter 12. Gearing is covered in Chapter 15.

Top tips. For part (b) it is necessary to both calculate and discuss the effect of using the issue proceeds to buy back debt. Ensure that you also address the unlikely assumption that the price/earnings ratio remains unchanged. In part (c) if you follow the direction given in the requirement this should lead you to a good answer. Part (d) needs a discussion of the two types of risk – don't forget to define them.

Easy marks. The calculation of the theoretical ex-rights price is straightforward.

			Marks
(a)	Rights issue price	1	
	Theoretical ex-rights price	2	
			3
(b)	Nominal value of bonds redeemed	1	
	Interest saved on redeemed bonds	1	
	Earnings after redemption	1	
	Current price/earnings ratio	1	
	Revised share price	1	
	Comment on acceptability to shareholders	1–2	
	Comment on constant price/earnings ratio	1–2	
		Maximum	7
(c)	Current interest coverage	0.5	
	Revised interest coverage	1	
	Current debt/equity ratio	0.5	
	Revised debt/equity ratio	1	
	Comment on financial risk	1	
			4
(d)	Explanation of business risk	1	
	Explanation of financial risk	1	
	Up to 2 marks for each danger of high gearing	4	
			6
			20

(a) The rights issue price is at a 20% discount

$7.5 × 0.8 = $6 per share

Number of shares to be issued = $90m/$6 = 15 million shares

Current number of shares in issue = 60 million

Therefore the rights issue will be a 1 for 4 issue

Theoretical ex-rights price

	$
4 shares @ $7.50	30.00
1 share @ $6.00	6.00
	36.00

Theoretical ex-rights price (TERP) = 36/5 = $7.20

(b)   The proposal to buy back the bonds will only be acceptable to shareholders if it increases shareholder wealth.

The bonds would be bought back at market price ($112.50), which is higher than the nominal value ($100). The nominal value of bonds that will be bought back is $90 million/$112.50 × $100 = $80 million.

Interest saved on these bonds = $80m × 0.08 = $6.4m per year

New annual interest charge = $10m – $6.4m = $3.6m

Revised profit before tax = $49m – $3.6m = $45.4m

Revised profit after tax (earnings) = $45.4m × 0.7 = $31.78m

Revised earnings per share = $31.78m/75m = 42.37 cents per share

Current earnings per share = $27.3m/60m = 455 cents per share

Current price/earnings ratio = 750/455 = 16.48 times

Assuming the price/earnings ratio remains constant, the revised share price will be:

Share price = 16.48 × 42.37 = 698 cents or $6.98 per share.

This revised share price is less than the TERP by $0.22 ($7.20–6.98) and therefore using the issue proceeds to buy back debt will not be acceptable to the shareholders as their wealth will have decreased (by approximately $0.22 × 75m shares = $16.5m).

This conclusion has been reached based on the assumption that the price/earnings ratio remains unchanged. However, the share price will be determined by the stock market and this will determine the price/earnings ratio, rather than the price/earnings ratio determining the share price. Buying back debt would decrease the financial risk of Bar Co and this could cause the cost of equity to fall since shareholders will be taking on less risk. This means the share price is likely to rise and therefore the price/earnings ratio will also increase. If the share price were to increase above the TERP, which would mean the price/earnings ratio would be at least 17 times, the shareholders would find the debt buy back to be an acceptable use of funds as they would experience a capital gain.

Alternative solution to the calculations:

Tutor note. There are a number of ways of dealing with the calculations here. To illustrate this, an **alternative solution** is shown below.

Current shareholder wealth

Shareholders' current wealth can be calculated as the share price × the number of shares in issue: $7.5 × 60m shares = **$450m**.

Revised shareholder wealth

After the rights issue and debt repayment shareholder wealth could be measured as:

(1)   The revised value of the company's shares less
(2)   The amount shareholders invest in the company via the rights issue

The revised value of the shares can be assessed by valuing Bar Co's revised earnings by multiplying them by the current P/E ratio, which we are assuming will be unchanged.

Earnings will change because $90m of debt is bought back. Because the market price of debt is $112.5, this is the same as $80m (ie $90 × $\frac{100}{112.5}$) in terms of book value of debt. This saves interest of

$80m × 8% = $6.4m, which is a saving after tax of $4.48m (calculated as $6.4m × 0.7). So revised earnings will be $27.3m + $4.5m = $31.8m.

The **current** EPS is \$27.3m/60m = 455 cents, so the current P/E ratio is 7.5/0.455 = 16.48.

The new value of the shares can be estimated as \$31.78m × 16.48 which is approximately \$523.7m. So, after subtracting the \$90m invested in the rights issue, shareholders' wealth has become \$433.7m.

This is a fall in shareholder wealth of \$16.3m compared to current shareholder wealth of \$450m.

(c)   Current interest coverage ratio = 49m/10m = 4.9 times
        Revised interest coverage ratio = 49m/3.6m = 13.6 times

        Current debt/equity ratio = 125m/140m = 89.3%
        Revised book value of debt = 125m − 80m = \$45m
        Revised book value of equity = 140m + 90m − 10m = \$220m

        \$10m has been deducted because \$90m was spent to redeem bonds with a nominal value of \$80m.

        Revised debt/equity ratio = 45m/220m = 20.5%

        Note. Full credit would also be given for a calculation that omitted the \$10m loss. The revised debt/equity ratio would be 45m/230m = 19.6%.

        Redeeming the bonds with a book value of \$80m would significantly reduce the financial risk of Bar Co. This is shown by the reduction in gearing from 89.3% to 20.5% and the increase in the interest coverage from 4.9 times to 13.6 times.

(d)   (i)   **Business risk**, the inherent risk of doing business for a company, refers to the risk of making only low profits, or even losses, due to the nature of the business that the company is involved in. One way of measuring business risk is by calculating a company's operating gearing or 'operational gearing'.

$$\text{Operating gearing} = \frac{\text{Contribution}}{\text{Profit before interest and tax (PBIT)}}$$

The significance of operating gearing is as follows.

(1)   **If contribution is high but PBIT is low**, fixed costs will be high, and only just covered by contribution. Business risk, as measured by operating gearing, will be high.

(2)   **If contribution is not much bigger than PBIT**, fixed costs will be low, and fairly easily covered. Business risk, as measured by operating gearing, will be low.

        (ii)   A high level of debt creates financial risk. This is the risk of a company not being able to meet other obligations as a result of the need to make interest payments. The proportion of debt finance carried by a company is therefore as significant as the level of business risk. Financial risk can be seen from different points of view.

(1)   **The company** as a whole. If a company builds up debts that it cannot pay when they fall due, it will be forced into liquidation.

(2)   **Payables**. If a company cannot pay its debts, the company will go into liquidation owing payables money that they are unlikely to recover in full.

(3)   **Ordinary shareholders**. A company will not make any distributable profits unless it is able to earn enough PBIT to pay all its interest charges, and then tax. The lower the profits or the higher the interest-bearing debts, the less there will be, if there is anything at all, for shareholders.

212 YGV Co

Marking scheme

			Marks
(a)	Calculation of after-tax interest payment	1	
	Calculation of after-tax cost of debt	3	
			4
(b)	Current interest coverage	1	
	Revised interest coverage	1	
	Current gearing	1	
	Revised gearing	1	
			4
(c)	Comment on interest coverage ratio	1–2	
	Comment on gearing	1–2	
	Comment on need for security	2–3	
	Comment on advisability of bond issue	1–2	
	Discussion of alternative sources of finance	4–5	
	Other relevant discussion	1–2	
	Maximum		12
			20

(a)   The after-tax interest charge per bond is $9 \times 0.7 = $6.30

Two discounts should be chosen, 6% and 8%

Year	0	1–10	10
	$	$	$
Cash flow	(100)	6.30	110
Discount factor @ 8%	1.000	6.710	0.463
Present value	(100.00)	42.27	50.93

Net present value = (6.80)

Year	0	1–10	10
	$	$	$
Cash flow	(100)	6.30	110
Discount factor @ 6%	1.000	7.360	0.558
Present value	(100.00)	(46.37)	61.38

Net present value = 7.75

Cost of debt = 6 + [(8 − 6) × 7.75/(7.75 + 6.8)] = 6 + 1.1 = 7.1%

(b) (i) The current level of interest charge per year is $4.5m × 5% = $225,000

        Current interest coverage ratio = PBIT/Interest

        1m/0.225m = 4.4 times

        Interest on bonds after issue = $4m × 9% = $360,000

        Interest on overdraft = $0.5m × 5% = $25,000

        Total interest per year = $385,000

        Interest coverage ratio with bond issue = 1m/0.385m = 2.6 times

(ii) The current market capitalisation is $4.10 × 10 million shares = $41 million

        Current gearing = zero (as no long-term debt)

        Gearing following bond issue (debt/equity) = 4m/41m = 9.8%

        Alternatively if the overdraft is included in the calculations

        Current gearing = 4.5m/41m = 11.0%

        Gearing following bond issue (debt/equity) = 4.5m/41m = 11.0%

(c) **Interest coverage ratio**

The current interest coverage ratio is almost half of the sector average of 8, although with the prior year profit before tax it was 22 times. Following the bond issue this would drop to 2.6 times which is a low level of cover compared to the sector average and may create operational issues for YGV Co.

Gearing

Whether the overdraft is included in the gearing calculation or not, the revised gearing level of either 9.8% or 11% is not significantly different from the sector average of 10%. As a result, there are no concerns about the level of gearing resulting from the bond issue.

Security

The reduction in profitability will increase the likelihood of the bond issue needing to be secured against the non-current assets of YGV Co. This may create issues as the tangible non-current assets of YGV Co have a net book value of $3 million, which does not cover the value of the bond issue of $4 million. It is unlikely that the intangible assets could be used as security, but their nature has not been disclosed.

Using the bond to reduce the overdraft

Considering the issues raised above, particularly the fall in the interest coverage and the lack of assets to use as security, the bond issue is not recommended as it is unlikely to succeed. As a result, alternative sources of finance should be considered in order to reduce the overdraft.

Alternative sources of finance

There is a lack of availability of additional overdraft finance, so this is not a viable option. The issue with the lack of interest coverage will also rule out any other form of debt finance.

Any provider of finance will first need to be reassured that the fall in profitability is due to short-term reasons and that YGV Co will continue to be a going concern in the long term.

The amount of finance required is the $4 million required to reduce the overdraft, but this amount could be reduced through working capital management, particularly given the amount of working capital tied up in accounts receivable.

No information is given about dividends, but if these are being paid they could be reduced to increase the amount of retained earnings available.

Equity finance is the most likely source of finance to consider. YGV Co may consider a rights issue. The offer price will be lower than the market price and given the situation a fairly large discount may need to be applied. A discount of 25% would give a price for the rights issue of $3.08. A 1 for 7 rights issue at this price would raise $4.4 million which could reduce the overdraft to $100,000 where the interest charge would only be $5,000 per year.

A new issue of shares is a possibility as $4 million is only 9% of the total shares in issue at that point ($45 million). This means that dilution of existing holdings will not be a significant issue. New shareholders may not be attracted to invest if there are no dividends on offer though. A new issue of shares would also be more expensive for YGV Co.

Sale and leaseback is not likely to raise significant levels of finance, given the tangible non-current asset level of $3 million, but could be used alongside another source of finance.

Convertible bonds could also be considered as an alternative.

213 NN Co

Text references. Cost of capital is covered in Chapter 14. Dividend policy is covered in Chapter 13.

Top tips. For part (a) it is important to remember to use the after-tax interest payment in the internal rate of return (IRR) style calculations. Although the discount rate used can vary, it is sensible to start off with the cost of debt if the debt was irredeemable and add in the annualised capital profit made between now and redemption.

In part (b) don't get confused by the fact that there are three elements to the weighted average cost of capital (WACC). For part (c), don't confuse factors in setting dividend policy with M&M's dividend irrelevance theory.

Easy marks. There are some easy marks for textbook knowledge of dividend policy.

ACCA examining team's comments. Answers that did not gain full marks to part (a) contained errors such as using the wrong tax rate (it was 25%), addition or multiplication errors, using the before-tax interest payment, or putting incorrect values to variables in the linear interpolation calculation. For part (c), the requirement was worded carefully to encourage candidates to consider the dividend policy of a company faced with the demanding business environment of the real world. Little credit was therefore given to discussions of the dividend irrelevance theory of Miller and Modigliani, which is based on the assumption of a perfect capital market, since capital markets in the real world are no more than semi-strong form efficient.

Marking scheme

			Marks
(a)	Correct use of taxation	1	
	Calculation of after-tax cost of debt	3	
			4
(b)	Cost of preference shares	1	
	Market value of equity	1	
	Market value of preference shares	1	
	Market value of debt	1	
	Weighted average cost of capital	2	
			6
(c)	Profitability	1–2	
	Liquidity	1–2	
	Legal and other restrictions	1–2	
	The need for finance	1–2	
	The level of financial risk	1–2	
	The signalling effect of dividends	1–2	
		Maximum	10
			20

(a) The cost of redeemable debt is found by an IRR style calculation using linear interpolation.

The annual after-tax interest payment is $7 \times (1 - 0.25) = \$5.25$

Year		Cash flow $	Discount factor 5%	PV $	Discount factor 4%	PV $
0	Market value	(103.50)	1.000	(103.50)	1.000	(103.50)
1–6	Interest	5.25	5.076	26.65	5.242	27.52
6	Capital repayment	100.00	0.746	74.46	0.790	79.90
				(2.25)		3.02

The approximate cost of redeemable debt capital is therefore:

$(4 + \dfrac{3.02}{(3.02 - 2.25)} \times 1) = 4.6\%$

Note. The cost of debt will vary depending on the discount rates used. Other values calculated for the cost of debt would also be acceptable.

(b) Preference dividend = 8% × 50 cents = 4c per share

Cost of preference shares

$k_p = \dfrac{d}{P_0} = 4/67 = 0.06 = 6\%$

Number of ordinary shares = $50m/0.5 = 100m

Market value of equity V_e = 100m × 8.30 = $830m

Number of preference shares = $25m/0.5 = 50m shares

Market value of preference shares V_p = 50m × 0.67 = $33.5m

Market value of long-term borrowings = V_d = 20m × 103.50/100 = $20.7m

Market value of company = $V_e + V_d + V_p$ = 830 + 33.5 + 20.7 = $884.2m

$$\text{WACC} = \left[\dfrac{V_e}{V_e + V_d + V_p}\right] k_e + \left[\dfrac{V_d}{V_e + V_d + V_p}\right] k_d (1 - T) + \left[\dfrac{V_p}{V_e + V_d + V_p}\right] k_p$$

WACC = (830/884.2) × 0.12 + (33.5/884.2) × 0.06 + (20.7/884.2) × 4.6 = 11.6%

(c) Dividend policy will depend on a number of factors:

Profits and retained earnings

The company needs to remain profitable. Dividends are paid out of profits, and an unprofitable company cannot forever go on paying dividends out of retained profits made in the past.

Law

Company legislation may make companies bound to pay dividends solely out of accumulated net realised profits, as in the UK.

Other restrictions

There may be other dividend restraints that might be imposed, such as covenants in loan agreements.

Liquidity

Since dividends are a cash payment, a company must have enough cash to pay the dividends it declares without compromising its day to day operations.

If the company has to repay any debt in the near future, then this will also need to be considered.

Gearing

If gearing is high, then low dividend payments can help to keep retained earnings high which will then reduce the level of gearing as the level of reserves will be higher.

The signalling effect

Although the market would like to value shares on the basis of underlying cash flows on the company's projects, such information is not readily available to investors in a semi-strong form efficient market. But the directors do have this information so information asymmetry exists. The dividend declared can be interpreted as a signal from directors to shareholders about the strength of underlying project cash flows.

Investors usually expect a consistent dividend policy from the company, with stable dividends each year or, even better, steady dividend growth.

The need for finance

Another factor is the ease with which the company could raise extra finance from sources other than retained earnings. Small companies which find it hard to raise finance might have to rely more heavily on retained earnings than large companies.

Inflation

The effect of inflation means that there is a need to retain some additional profit within the business just to keep its operating capability unchanged.

214 AQR Co

Text references. Weighted average cost of capital (WACC) is covered in Chapter 14. Cost of capital theories are explained in Chapter 16.

Top tips. Part (b) is a general discussion about capital structure theories.

Easy marks. Part (a) is a WACC calculation that you should be able to obtain good marks for.

ACCA examining team's comments. Some answers treated existing bonds as irredeemable and used the after-tax cost of debt provided as a before-tax interest rate. This implies learning a WACC calculation method without understanding the underlying principles, leading to an attempt to make the information provided fit the calculation method learned. There were also a significant number of errors in calculating the cost of equity using the dividend growth model. Alarm bells should sound if the calculated cost of equity is less than the cost of debt, or if the calculated cost of equity is quite large. A glance through past exams will show that a realistic approach has been used, with the cost of equity lying between, say, 5% and 15%.

Marking scheme

			Marks
(a)	Calculation of historic dividend growth rate	1	
	Calculation of cost of equity using DGM	2	
	Calculation of market weights	1	
	Calculation of pre-issue WACC	2	
	Correct use of tax as regards new debt	1	
	Setting up linear interpolation calculation	1	
	Calculating after-tax cost of debt of new debt	1	
	Calculation of post issue WACC	2	
	Comment	1	
			12
(b)	Marginal and average cost of debt	1–2	
	Traditional view of capital structure	1–2	
	Miller and Modigliani 1 and 2	1–3	
	Market imperfections view	1–2	
	Pecking order theory	1–2	
	Other relevant discussion	1–2	
	Maximum		8
			20

(a)   Cost of equity

Geometric average growth rate = $\sqrt[4]{(21.8/19.38)} - 1 = 0.0298 = 2.98\%$ or 3%

Putting this into the dividend growth model gives $k_e = ((21.8 \times 1.03)/250) + 0.03$

$= 0.09 + 0.03 = 0.12 = 12\%$

Market values of equity and debt

Market value of equity = Ve = 100m × $2.50 = $250m

Market value of bonds = Vd = 60m × (104/100) = $62.4m

Total market value = $250m + $62.4m = $312.4m

WACC calculation

The current after-tax cost of debt is 7%

$$\begin{aligned}
\text{WACC} &= ((k_e \times V_e) + (k_d(1 - T) \times V_d)/(V_e + V_d)) \\
&= ((12 \times 250m) + (7 \times 62.4m))/312.4m \\
&= 11\%
\end{aligned}$$

Cost of debt

After-tax interest payment = 100 × 8% × (1 − 30%) = 5.6%

Year		Cash flow $	5% discount factors	PV $	6% discount factors	PV $
0	Market value	(100.00)	1.000	(100.00)	1.000	(100.00)
1-10	Interest	5.60	7.722	43.24	7.360	41.22
10	Capital repayment	105.00	0.614	64.47	0.558	58.59
				7.71		(0.19)

Calculate the cost of debt using an internal rate of return (IRR) calculation.

$$\text{IRR} = a\% + \left[\frac{NPV_a}{NPV_a - NPV_b} \times (b - a) \right]\%$$

$$= 5\% + \frac{7.71}{7.71 + 0.19}(6\% - 5\%)$$

$$= 5.98\% \text{ or } 6\%$$

Note. Other discount factors and therefore costs of debt are acceptable.

Revised WACC calculation

Market value of the new issue of bonds is $40m

New total market value = $312.4m + $40m = $352.4m

Cost of debt of bonds is 6% (from above)

$$\begin{aligned}
\text{WACC} &= ((12 \times 250m) + (7 \times 62.4m) + (6 \times 40m))/352.4m \\
&= 10.4\%
\end{aligned}$$

The debt issue has reduced the WACC. This is because of the addition of relatively cheap debt. Gearing up in this manner would usually be assumed to increase financial risk. However, this hasn't been included in the above calculations.

(b)   There is a relationship between the WACC and the value of a company as the value can be expressed as the present value of the future cash flows with the WACC as the discount rate.

Marginal and average cost of debt

If the marginal cost of capital for the issue of the new capital, in this case the bond issue, is less than the current WACC then it may be expected that the WACC will decrease. However, as new debt increases gearing it will also increase financial risk. This increased risk may lead to an increase in the cost of equity which could offset the effect of the cheaper debt.

Traditional view

Under the traditional view there is an optimal capital mix at which the average cost of capital, weighted according to the different forms of capital employed, is minimised. The traditional view is that the WACC, when plotted against the level of gearing, is saucer shaped. The optimum capital structure is where the WACC is lowest.

As the level of gearing increases, the cost of debt remains unchanged up to a certain level of gearing. Beyond this level, the cost of debt will increase. The cost of equity rises as the level of gearing increases and financial risk increases. There is a non-linear relationship between the cost of equity and gearing.

The WACC does not remain constant, but rather falls initially as the proportion of debt capital increases, and then begins to increase as the rising cost of equity (and possibly of debt) becomes more significant. The optimum level of gearing is where the company's WACC is minimised. Under this theory the finance director may be correct in his view that issuing debt will decrease WACC depending on the position of AQR Co relative to the optimum capital structure.

Modigliani and Miller (MM)

In their 1958 theory, MM proposed that the total market value of a company, in the absence of tax, will be determined only by two factors: the total earnings of the company and the level of operating (business) risk attached to those earnings. The total market value would be computed by discounting the total earnings at a rate that is appropriate to the level of operating risk. This rate would represent the WACC of the company. Thus MM concluded that the capital structure of a company would have no effect on its overall value or WACC.

In 1963, MM modified their theory to admit that tax relief on interest payments does lower the WACC. The savings arising from tax relief on debt interest are the tax shield. They claimed that the WACC will continue to fall, up to gearing of 100%. Under this theory the finance director of AQR is correct in his belief that issuing bonds will decrease the WACC.

Market imperfections

MM's theory assumes perfect capital markets so a company would always be able to raise finance and avoid bankruptcy. In reality, however, at higher levels of gearing there is an increasing risk of the company being unable to meet its interest payments and being declared bankrupt. At these higher levels of gearing, the bankruptcy risk means that shareholders will require a higher rate of return as compensation.

As companies increase their gearing they may reach a point where there are not enough profits from which to obtain all available tax benefits. They will still be subject to increased bankruptcy and agency costs but will not be able to benefit from the increased tax shield.

Pecking order theory

Pecking order theory has been developed as an alternative to traditional theory. It states that firms will prefer retained earnings to any other source of finance, and then will choose debt, and last of all equity. The order of preference is: retained earnings, straight debt, convertible debt, preference shares and equity shares.

215 BKB Co

Text references. Weighted average cost of capital (WACC) is covered in Chapter 14. The advantages of issuing convertible bonds are discussed in Chapter 12.

Top tips. If you know your formulas well, the calculations in part (a) should be straightforward. You should know that overdrafts should not be considered as part of the capital structure.

You will need to apply logic in answering part (b). In part (c), briefly plan your answer before you start to answer the question.

Easy marks. Marks are available for straightforward calculations in part (a).

ACCA examining team's comments. In part (a) few answers were able to calculate correctly the cost of the preference shares and some answers chose to use the dividend percentage relative to nominal as the cost of capital, or to assume a value for the cost of capital. Some answers mistakenly calculated the after-tax cost of the preference shares. As preference shares pay a dividend, which is a distribution of after-tax profit, they are not tax efficient. A common error was to mix bond-related values (such as the $4.90 after-tax interest payment) with total debt-related values (such as the $21m market value of the bond issue), producing some very high values in the linear interpolation calculation. Some candidates were unable to calculate the future share price as part of the conversion value calculation. Most candidates were able to calculate a WACC value, although some omitted the cost of preference shares from the calculation. In part (b) many answers were not of a high standard and tried to make some general points about market efficiency or about the window-dressing of financial statements. The important point here is that the weightings used in the WACC calculation need to reflect the relative importance of the different sources of finance used by a company if the WACC is to be used in investment appraisal.

Marking scheme

			Marks
(a)	Calculation of cost of equity using CAPM	2	
	Calculation of bond market price	0.5	
	Calculation of current share price	0.5	
	Calculation of future share price	1	
	Calculation of conversion value	1	
	After-tax interest payment	1	
	Setting up interpolation calculation	1	
	Calculation of after-tax cost of debt	1	
	Calculation of cost of preference shares	1	
	Calculation of after-tax WACC	2	
	Explanation of any assumptions made	1	
			12
(b)	Market values reflect current market conditions	1–2	
	Market values and optimal investment decisions	1–2	
	Other relevant discussion or illustration	1–2	
		Maximum	4
(c)	Self-liquidating	1	
	Lower interest rate	1	
	Increase in debt capacity on conversion	1	
	Other relevant advantages of convertible debt	1–3	
		Maximum	4
			20

(a) **Equity**

The market value (MV) of equity is given as $125m.

CAPM: $E(r_i) = R_f + \beta_i(E(r_m) - R_f)$

R_f = Risk-free rate = 4%

β_i = Equity beta = 1.2

$(E(r_m) - R_f)$ = Equity risk premium = 5%

Therefore the cost of equity = 4% + 1.2 × 5% = 10%

Convertible bonds

Assume that bondholders will convert if the MV of 19 shares in 5 years' time is greater than $100.

MV per bond = $100 × $21m/$20m = $105

MV per share today = $125m/25m = $5

MV per share in 5 years' time = $5 × 1.04^5 = $6.08 per share

Conversion value = $6.08 × 19 = $115.52

The after-tax cost of the convertible bonds can be calculated by linear interpolation, assuming the bondholders will convert.

Time	Cash flow $	Discount factor 7%	Present value $	Discount factor 5%	Present value $
0	(105)	1	(105)	1	(105)
1–5	4.9*	4.100	20.09	4.329	21.21
5	115.52	0.713	82.37	0.784	90.57
			(2.54)		6.78

* After-tax interest payment = 7 × (1 − 0.3) = $4.90 per bond

Cost of convertible bonds = 5 + [(7 − 5) × 6.78/6.78 + 2.54)] = 5 + 1.45 = 6.45%

Preference shares

After-tax cost of preference shares = 5% × $10m/$6.25m = 8%

WACC

Total value = $125m + $21m + $6.25m = $152.25m

After-tax WACC = [($125m × 10%) + ($21m × 6.45%) + ($6.25m × 8%)/$152.25m]

After-tax WACC = 9.4% per year

Note. As overdraft represents a short-term source of finance, it has been assumed not to form part of the company's capital and has therefore been excluded from the WACC calculation. The overdraft is large, however, and seems to represent a fairly constant amount. The company should evaluate whether it should be taken into account.

(b) MVs are preferable to book values when calculating WACC, because they reflect the current value of the company's capital.

If book values are used instead of MVs, this will seriously understate the proportion that equity represents in the company's capital structure. This is because the MV of ordinary shares is usually significantly higher than its nominal book value.

Understating the impact of the cost of equity on the WACC will most likely cause the WACC to be understated since, as we can see in the answer above, the cost of equity is greater than the cost of debt. Underestimating the WACC will skew the company's investment appraisal process as a lower discount rate is used, and cause the company to make sub-optimal investment decisions.

Using book values instead of market values will also change the value of debt in the company's capital structure. The impact of understating or overstating the value of debt would be less significant than is the case for equity, because debt instruments are often traded at close to their nominal value.

(c)   Convertible bonds are attractive for companies for the following reasons:

(i)   **Lower rates of interest:** Investors are normally willing to accept a lower coupon rate of interest on convertible bonds, because of the additional value offered by the conversion rights. This helps to ease the burden on cash flows.

(ii)   **The possibility of not redeeming the debt at maturity:** Companies issue convertible bonds with the expectation that they will be converted. If the bonds are converted, this frees the company from a cash repayment at redemption. The cash advantage is further augmented by the greater flexibility that equity shares allow in terms of returns.

(iii) **Availability of finance:** Issuing convertible bonds may allow greater access to finance, as lenders who would otherwise not provide ordinary loan finance may be attracted by the conversion rights.

(iv)   **Impact on gearing:** On conversion, the company's gearing will be reduced not only because of the removal of debt, but also because equity replaces the debt. This can send positive signals about the company's financial position.

(v)   **Delayed equity:** The fact that convertible bonds allow the issue of shares at a predetermined point in the future permits the company to plan the impact on its earnings per share upon conversion.

216 Fence Co

Text references. Cost of debt, capital asset pricing model (CAPM), risk and weighted average cost of capital (WACC) are covered in Chapter 14.

Top tips. Be careful not to miss out the tax effect in part (b). Try not to mix up systematic risk and unsystematic risk in part (c).

Easy marks. There are easy marks for calculations in part (a). The limitations of CAPM should always present straightforward marks.

ACCA examining team's comments. For part (a) the examining team commented that students should aim to calculate a reasonably accurate after-tax cost of debt. For example, if the first cost of debt estimate produces a negative NPV, then the second estimate should be lower as the first estimate was too high.

Marking scheme

		Marks	
(a)	Calculation of equity risk premium	1	
	Calculation of cost of equity	1	
	After-tax interest payment	1	
	Setting up IRR calculation	1	
	Calculating after-tax cost of debt	1	
	Market value of equity	0.5	
	Market value of debt	0.5	
	Calculating WACC	1	
			7
(b)	Ungearing proxy company equity beta	2	
	Regearing equity beta	1	
	Calculation of cost of equity	1	
			4
(c)	Risk diversification	1	
	Systematic risk	1	
	Unsystematic risk	1	
	Portfolio theory and the CAPM	1	
			4
(d)	1–2 marks per point made		
	Maximum	5	
			20

(a) After-tax cost of debt (K_d) can be calculated by linear interpolation.

Year		Cash flow $	Discount factor 4%	PV $	Discount factor 5%	PV $
0	Market value	(107.14)	1.000	(107.14)	1.000	(107.14)
1–7	Interest (7 × (1 – 0.2))	5.60	6.002	33.61	5.786	32.40
7	Redemption	100.00	0.760	76.00	0.711	71.10
				2.47		(3.64)

After-tax cost of debt $= 4\% + \dfrac{2.47}{2.47+3.64}(5\% - 4\%) = 4.4\%$

Cost of equity (K_e) can be found using CAPM.

$E(r_i) = R_f + \beta_i(E(r_m) - R_f)$
$\quad = 4 + 0.9\,(11 - 4)$
$\quad = 10.3\%$

Market value of equity (V_e) = $10m × $7.50 = $75m

Market value of debt (V_d) = $14m $\times \dfrac{107.14}{100}$ = $15m

$$\text{WACC} = \left[\frac{V_e}{V_e + V_d}\right]k_e + \left[\frac{V_d}{V_e + V_d}\right]k_d$$

$$= \left[\frac{75}{75+15}\right]10.3 + \left[\frac{15}{75+15}\right]4.4$$

$$= 9.3\%$$

(b) Ungear to remove the financial risk

$$\beta_a = \beta_e \times \frac{V_e}{V_e + V_d(1-T)}$$

$$\beta_a = 1.2 \times \frac{54m}{54m + (12m \times 0.8)}$$

$$= 1.019$$

Convert back to a geared beta

$$\beta_e = \beta_a \times \frac{V_e + V_d(1-T)}{V_e}$$

$$\beta_e = 1.019 \times \frac{75 + 15(1-0.2)}{75}$$

$$= 1.182$$

Use CAPM to estimate cost of equity.

Equity or market risk premium = 11 – 4 = 7%

Cost of equity = 4 + (1.182 × 7) = 4 + 8.3 = 12.3%

(c) **Unsystematic** risk can be **diversified away** but even well-diversified portfolios will be exposed to **systematic risk**. This is the risk **inherent in the market as a whole**, which the shareholder cannot mitigate by holding a diversified investment portfolio.

Portfolio theory is concerned with **total risk** (systematic and unsystematic). The **CAPM** assumes that investors will hold a fully diversified portfolio and therefore ignores unsystematic risk.

(d) **Diversification**

Under the CAPM, the return required from a security is **related** to its **systematic risk** rather than its total risk. Only the risks that **cannot** be **eliminated** by diversification are **relevant**. The assumption is that investors will hold a **fully diversified portfolio** and therefore deal with the unsystematic risk themselves. However, in practice, markets are **not totally efficient** and investors do not all hold fully diversified portfolios. This means that total risk is relevant to investment decisions, and that therefore the relevance of the CAPM may be limited.

Excess return

In practice, it is difficult to determine the excess return ($R_m - R_f$). **Expected rather than historical returns** should be used, although historical returns are used in practice.

Risk-free rate

It is similarly difficult to **determine the risk-free rate**. A risk-free investment might be a government security; however, interest rates vary with the term of the debt.

Risk aversion

Shareholders are risk averse, and therefore **demand higher returns** in compensation for increased levels of risk.

Beta factors

Beta factors based on historical data may be a **poor basis** for future **decision making**, since evidence suggests that beta values fluctuate over time.

Unusual circumstances

The CAPM is unable to forecast accurately returns for companies with low price/earnings ratios, and to take account of seasonal 'month of the year' and 'day of the week' effects that appear to influence returns on shares.

217 Tinep Co

Text references. The capital asset pricing model (CAPM) and the weighted average cost of capital (WACC) is covered in Chapter 14, and rights issues are covered in Chapter 12. Scrip dividends are explained in Chapter 13.

Top tips. Part (a) is a WACC question which, with practice, is straightforward. You need to calculate the cost of equity using CAPM and the cost of debt using the internal rate of return (IRR) formula. The WACC formula is given on the exam formula sheet. Part (b) requires you to have an understanding of rights issues. Use headings in your answer to this part to help the marker.

Easy marks. Part (a) has lots of easy calculation marks, even if you make a mistake in some of your workings. Part (b) contains some easy marks if you've learned your theory. Part (c) is a textbook explanation of a scrip dividend and the advantages and disadvantages from a company's point of view.

Marks

(a) Cost of equity — 1
After-tax interest payment — 1
Setting up IRR calculation — 1
After-tax cost of debt of loan notes — 1
Market values — 1
Market value WACC — 1
Book value WACC — 1
Comment on difference — 2

9

(b) Issue price — 1–2
Relative cost — 1–2
Ownership and control — 1–2
Gearing and financial risk — 1–2

Maximum — 6

(c) Explanation of scrip dividend — 1–2
Advantages of scrip dividend to company — 2–3
Disadvantages of scrip dividend to company — 2–3

Maximum — 5

20

(a) **Cost of equity using CAPM**

$K_e = R_f + \beta(E(r_m) - R_f)$ $R_f = 4\%$, $E(R_m) - R_f = 6\%$ (market premium)

$K_e = 4 + (1.15 \times 6) = 10.9\%$

After-tax cost of debt K_d

Time		Cash flow $	Discount factor 4%	Present value $	Discount factor 5%	Present value $
0	Market value	(103.50)	1	(103.50)	1	(103.50)
1–6	Interest	(6% × 100) × 75% = 4.5	5.242	23.59	5.076	22.84
6	Redemption	106	0.790	83.74	0.746	79.08
				3.83		(1.58)

$$K_d = 4 + \frac{3.83}{3.83 + 1.58} \times 1 = 4.7\%$$

Market value of equity

Number of shares = $200m/0.5 = 400m

Market value = 400m × $5.85 = $2,340m

Market value of debt

$$200m \text{ loan notes} \times \frac{103.50}{100.00} = \$207m$$

Total market value = $2,340 + $207 = $2,547

Using the formula from the formula sheet:

$$WACC = \left[\frac{V_e}{V_e + V_d}\right]k_e + \left[\frac{V_d}{V_e + V_d}\right]k_d$$

WACC using market values

WACC = (2,340/2,547)10.9% + (207/2,547)4.7% = **10.40%**

WACC using book values

WACC = (850/1,050)10.9% + (200/1,050)4.7% = **9.72%**

The WACC using book values is lower than the WACC using market values. This is because the market values of shares are nearly always higher than the nominal values. Book values are based on historical costs and their use will understate the impact of the cost of equity finance on the average cost of capital. Market values should always be used if data is available. If the WACC is understated then unprofitable projects will be accepted.

(b) **Considerations of rights issue**

Issue price

Tinep Co must set a price which is low enough to secure the acceptance of shareholders but not too low so as to dilute earnings per share. This balance can be difficult to estimate.

Relative cost

Rights issues are cheaper than, say, initial public offerings to the general public. This is partly because no prospectus is normally required, partly because the admin is simpler and partly because the cost of underwriting will be less.

Ownership and control

Relative voting rights are unaffected if shareholders take up their rights.

Gearing and financial risk

The finance raised may be used to reduce gearing by increasing share capital. The shareholders may see this as a positive move depending on their risk preference.

(c) A scrip dividend is a dividend paid by the issue of additional company shares, rather than by cash. It is offered pro rata to existing shareholdings.

From a company point of view there are a couple of main advantages of scrip dividends. They can preserve a company's cash position if a substantial number of shareholders take up the share option and a share issue will decrease the company's gearing, and may therefore enhance its borrowing capacity.

There are two main disadvantages of scrip dividends. Assuming that dividend per share is maintained or increased, the total cash paid as a dividend will increase. Scrip dividends may be seen as a negative signal by the market ie the company is experiencing cash flow issues.

218 Grenarp Co

Text references. Rights issues and sources of finance are covered in Chapter 12. Capital structure is covered in Chapter 16.

Top tips. For part (a), start by considering the planned rights issue and calculate the rights issue price, the number of new shares offered in the rights issue, the net cash raised after issue costs and the theoretical ex-rights price (TERP). For part (b), start by defining an optimal capital structure.

Easy marks. There are easy marks for calculations in part (a) and you should score well in parts (b) and (c) if you have learnt the material on capital structure and sources of finance.

ACCA examining team's comments. For part (a) many students did not gain many marks. Some answers adopted a 5 for 1 basis for the rights instead of 1 for 5. Some students added the issue costs to the cash raised figure provided. Many answers to part (b) were unsatisfactory. Some answers incorrectly stated that an optimal capital structure was a 50/50 mix of equity and debt.

			Marks
(a)	Rights issue price	0.5	
	New shares issued	0.5	
	Net cash raised by rights issue	0.5	
	TERP per share	1	
	Buy-back price of loan notes	0.5	
	Nominal value of loan notes redeemed	1	
	Before-tax interest saving	0.5	
	After-tax interest saving	0.5	
	Revised earnings	0.5	
	Revised earnings per share	0.5	
	Revised share price using P/E ratio method	1	
	Comment on effect of redemption on shareholders' wealth	1	
			8
(b)	Traditional view of capital structure	1–3	
	M&M views of capital structure	1–3	
	Other relevant discussion	1–3	
		Maximum	7
(c)	1–2 marks per source of finance		
		Maximum	5
			20

(a) Rights issue price = 3.50 × 0.8 = $2.80 per share

Grenarp Co currently has 20 million shares in issue ($10m/0.5)
The number of new shares issued = 20m/5 = 4 million shares

Cash raised by the rights issue before issue costs = 4m × 2.80 = $11,200,000
Net cash raised by the rights issue after issue costs = 11,200,000 − 280,000 = $10,920,000

Revised number of shares = 20m + 4m = 24 million shares

Market value of Grenarp Co before the rights issue = 20,000,000 × 3.50 = $70,000,000
Market value of Grenarp Co after the rights issue = 70,000,000 + 10,920,000 = $80,920,000
TERP = 80,920,000/24,000,000 = $3.37 per share

(Alternatively, issue costs are $0.07 per share (280,000/4m) and this is a 1 for 5 rights issue, so the TERP = (5 × 3.50 + (2.80 − 0.07))/6 = 20.23/6 = $3.37 per share.)

Redemption price of loan notes = 104 × 1.05 = $109.20 per loan note
Nominal value of loan notes redeemed = 10,920,000/(109.20/100) = $10,000,000

Before-tax interest saving = 10,000,000 × 0.08 = $800,000 per year
After-tax interest saving = 800,000 × (1 − 0.3) = $560,000 per year

Earnings after redeeming loan notes = 8,400,000 + 560,000 = $8,960,000 per year

Revised earnings per share (EPS) = 100 × (8,960,000/24,000,000) = $0.373 per share

Price/earnings ratio of Grenarp Co before the rights issue = 3.50/0.42 = 8.33 times
This price/earnings ratio is not expected to be affected by the redemption of loan notes.
Share price of Grenarp Co after redeeming loan notes = 8.33 × 0.373 = $3.11 per share (total market value = $3.11 × 24m shares = $74.64m).

The wealth of shareholders of Grenarp Co has decreased as they have experienced a capital loss of $0.26 per share ($3.37 − $3.11) compared to the TERP per share. This means that shareholder wealth has fallen by $0.26 × 24m shares = $6.24m (excluding issue costs, or $6.24 + $0.28m issue costs = $6.52m after issue costs).

Alternative solution

Revised shareholder wealth

After the rights issue and debt repayment shareholder wealth could be measured as:

(1)   The revised value of the company's shares **less**

(2)   The amount shareholders invest in the company via the rights issue

The revised value of the shares can be assessed by valuing Grenarp's revised earnings by multiplying them by the current P/E ratio.

Current earnings are $0.42 × 20m shares = $8.4m. The amount raised net of issue costs is $11.2m – $0.28m = $10.92m. This will be used to buy back debt, and the interest saved will boost earnings.

$10.92m of debt is bought back. The redemption price is 5% above the market price of debt of $104; this is: 1.05 × 104 = $109.2. So $10.92m buys back $10m (ie $10.92 \times \dfrac{100}{109.4}$) in terms of book value of debt.

This saves interest of $10m × 8% = $0.8m, which is a saving after tax of $0.56m (calculated as 0.8 × 0.7). So the revised earnings will be $8.4m + $0.56m = $8.96m.

The **current** EPS is $0.42, so the current P/E ratio is 3.5/0.42 = 8.333.

The new value of the shares can be estimated as $8.96m × 8.333 which is approximately $74.66m.

So, after subtracting the $11.2m invested in the rights issue, shareholders' wealth has become $74.66m – $11.2m = $63.46m.

This is a fall in shareholder wealth of $6.54m.

(b)   The capital structure is considered to be optimal when the weighted average cost of capital (WACC) is at a minimum and the market value of a company is at a maximum. The goal of maximising shareholder wealth might be achieved if the capital structure is optimal.

The question of whether Grenarp Co might achieve its optimal capital structure following the rights issue can be discussed from a theoretical perspective by looking at the traditional view of capital structure, the views of Miller and Modigliani on capital structure, and other views such as the market imperfections approach. It is assumed that a company pays out all of its earnings as dividends, and that these earnings and the business risk of the company are constant. It is further assumed that companies can change their capital structure by replacing equity with debt, and vice versa, so that the amount of finance invested remains constant, irrespective of capital structure. The term 'gearing up' therefore refers to replacing equity with debt in the context of theoretical discussions of capital structure.

Traditional view

The traditional view of capital structure, which ignores taxation, held that an optimal capital structure did exist. It reached this conclusion by assuming that shareholders of a company financed entirely by equity would not be very concerned about the company gearing up to a small extent. As expensive equity was replaced by cheaper debt, therefore, the WACC would initially decrease. As the company continued to gear up, shareholders would demand an increasing return as financial risk continued to increase, and the WACC would reach a minimum and start to increase. At higher levels of gearing still, the cost of debt would start to increase, for example, because of bankruptcy risk, further increasing the WACC.

Views of Miller and Modigliani

Miller and Modigliani assumed a perfect capital market, where bankruptcy risk does not exist and the cost of debt is constant. In a perfect capital market, there is a linear relationship between the cost of equity and financial risk, as measured by gearing. Ignoring taxation, the increase in the cost of equity as gearing increases exactly offsets the decrease in the WACC caused by the replacement of expensive equity by cheaper debt, so that the WACC is constant. The value of a company is therefore not affected by its capital structure.

When Miller and Modigliani included the effect of corporate taxation, so that the after-tax cost of debt was used instead of the before-tax cost of debt, the decrease in the WACC caused by the replacement of expensive equity by cheaper debt was greater than the increase in the cost of equity, so that the WACC

decreased as a company geared up. The implication in terms of optimal capital structure was that a company should gear up as much as possible in order to decrease its WACC as much as it could.

Market imperfections view

When other market imperfections are considered in addition to the existence of corporate taxation, the view of Miller and Modigliani that a company should gear up as much as possible is no longer true. These other market imperfections relate to high levels of gearing, bankruptcy risk and the costs of financial distress, and they cause the cost of debt and the cost of equity to increase, so that the WACC increases at high levels of gearing.

Grenarp Co

The question of whether Grenarp Co might achieve its optimal capital structure following the rights issue can also be discussed from a practical perspective, by considering if increasing the gearing of the company would decrease its WACC. This would happen if the marginal cost of capital of the company were less than its WACC. Unfortunately, there is no information provided on the marginal cost of capital of Grenarp Co, although its gearing is not high. Before the rights issue, the debt/equity ratio of Grenarp Co was 35% on a book value basis and 45% on a market value basis, while after the redemption of loan notes the debt/equity ratio would fall to 21% on a book value basis and 28% on a market value basis.

(c)   Remember that the question only asked for three sources of long-term finance.

Bonds

Bonds are long-term debt capital raised by a company for which interest is paid, usually half yearly and at a fixed rate. Holders of bonds are therefore long-term payables for the company. Bonds issued by large companies are marketable, but bond markets are small. They can be issued in a variety of foreign currencies.

Deep discount bonds

Deep discount bonds are bonds or loan notes issued at a price which is at a large discount to the nominal value of the notes, and which will be redeemable at nominal value (or above nominal value) when they eventually mature. The coupon rate of interest will be very low compared with yields on conventional bonds with the same maturity. For a company with specific cash flow requirements, the low servicing costs during the currency of the bond may be an attraction, coupled with a high cost of redemption at maturity. The main benefit of deep discount bonds for a company is that the interest yield on the bonds is lower than on conventional bonds. However, it will have to pay a much larger amount at maturity than it borrowed when the bonds were issued. Deep discount bonds defer much of the cost of the debt.

Convertible bonds

Convertible bonds are bonds that give the holder the right to convert to other securities, normally ordinary shares, at a predetermined price/rate and time. The coupon rate of interest is normally lower than on similar conventional bonds. They give the bondholders the right (but not an obligation) to convert their bonds at a specified future date into new equity shares of the company, at a conversion rate that is also specified when the bonds are issued. If the bonds are converted there can be a reduction in the gearing of the issuing company.

Long-term bank loan

A bank loan can be obtained with interest paid annually, bi-annually or quarterly at either a fixed rate or floating rate of interest. Bank loans are often secured and a bank may charge higher interest for an unsecured loan compared with a similar secured loan. Repayments usually include a capital element and an interest element, with the proportion of interest decreasing over time and the proportion of capital increasing over time.

219 Dinla Co

Text references. Cost of capital is covered in Chapter 14. Islamic finance is covered in Chapter 12.

Easy marks. There are easy marks for calculations in part (a) and you should score well in parts (b) and (c) if you have learnt the material on capital structure.

ACCA examining team's comments. Many candidates were able to calculate correctly the after-tax cost of debt of the loan notes by using linear interpolation, based on sensible cost of debt estimates such as 4% and 5%, although some candidates used extreme values such as 1% and 20%. These extreme values give a poor estimate of the cost of debt and should be discouraged. Some candidates incorrectly included the value of reserves when calculating the market value of equity.

Marking scheme

			Marks
(a)	Cost of equity	1	
	Cost of preference shares	1	
	Cost of loan notes	3	
	Cost of bank loan	1	
	Market values	1	
	WACC	1	
			8
(b)	Explanation of creditor hierarchy	1	
	Relative risks and costs of sources of finance	2	
			3
(c)	WACC and business risk	2	
	WACC and financial risk	2	
	CAPM and project-specific risk	1	
			5
(d)	1–2 marks for sharing of risk and reward and riba	2–4	
	Other relevant discussion	1–2	
	Maximum		4
			20

(a) Cost of equity

The dividend growth model can be used to calculate the cost of equity.

$Ke = ((0.25 \times 1.04)/4.26) + 0.04 = 10.1\%$

Cost of preference shares

$Kp = (0.05 \times 1.00)/0.56 = 8.9\%$

Cost of debt of loan notes

After-tax annual interest payment = $6 \times (1 - 0.25) = 6 \times 0.75 = \$4.50$ per year

Time	Cash flow	5% discount	PV	6% discount	PV
	$		$		$
0	(95.45)	1.000	(95.45)	1.000	(95.45)
1–5	4.50	4.329	19.48	4.212	18.95
5	100.00	0.784	78.40	0.747	74.70
			2.43		(1.80)

After-tax cost of debt of loan notes:

$Kd = 5 + (1 \times 2.43)/(2.43 + 1.0) = 5 + 0.57 = 5.6\%$

Cost of debt of bank loan

The after-tax fixed interest rate of the bank loan can be used as its cost of debt. This will be 5.25% (7×0.75). Alternatively, the after-tax cost of debt of the loan notes can be used as a substitute for the after-tax cost of debt of the bank loan.

Market values

	$'000
Equity: $4.26 \times (23,000,000/0.25)$ =	391,920
Preference shares: $0.56 \times (5,000,000/1.00)$ =	2,800
Loan notes: $95.45 \times (11,000,000/100)$ =	10,500
Bank loan	3,000
	408,220

After-tax weighted average cost of capital (WACC)

Using the formula from the formula sheet:

$$WACC = \left[\frac{V_e}{V_e + V_d} \right] k_e + \left[\frac{V_d}{V_e + V_d} \right] k_d$$

WACC = (391,920/408,220)10.1% + (2,800/408,220)8.9% + (10,500/408,220)5.6% + (3,000/408,220)5.25% = **9.90%**

(b) The creditor hierarchy refers to the order in which financial claims against a company are settled when the company is liquidated.

The hierarchy, in order of decreasing priority, is secured creditors, unsecured creditors, preference shareholders and ordinary shareholders. The risk of not receiving any cash in a liquidation increases as priority decreases. Secured creditors (secured debt) therefore face the lowest risk as providers of finance and ordinary shareholders face the highest risk.

The return required by a provider of finance is related to the risk faced by that provider of finance. Secured creditors therefore have the lowest required rate of return and ordinary shareholders have the highest required rate of return. The cost of debt should be less than the cost of preference shares, which should be less than the cost of equity.

(c) The current WACC of a company reflects the required returns of existing providers of finance.

The cost of equity and the cost of debt depend on particular elements of the existing risk profile of the company, such as business risk and financial risk. Providing the business risk and financial risk of a company remain unchanged, the cost of equity and the cost of debt, and hence the WACC, should remain unchanged.

In investment appraisal, the discount rate used should reflect the risk of investment project cash flows. Therefore, using the WACC as the discount rate will only be appropriate if the investment project does not result in a change in the business risk and financial risk of the investing company.

One of the circumstances which is likely to leave business risk unchanged is if the investment project were an expansion of existing business activities. WACC could therefore be used as the discount rate in appraising an investment project which looked to expand existing business operations.

However, business risk depends on the size and scope of business operations as well as on their nature, and so an investment project which expands existing business operations should be small in relation to the size of the existing business.

Financial risk will remain unchanged if the investment project is financed in such a way that the relative weighting of existing sources of finance is unchanged, leaving the existing capital structure of the investing company unchanged. While this is unlikely in practice, a company may finance investment projects with a target capital structure in mind, about which small fluctuations are permitted.

If business risk changes as a result of an investment project, so that using the WACC of a company in investment appraisal is not appropriate, a project-specific discount rate should be calculated. The capital asset pricing model (CAPM) can be used to calculate a project-specific cost of equity and this can be used in calculating a project-specific WACC.

(d)   Wealth creation in Islamic finance requires that risk and reward, in terms of economic benefit, are shared between the provider of finance and the user of finance. Economic benefit includes wider economic goals such as increasing employment and social welfare.

Conventional finance, which refers to finance which is not based on Islamic principles and which has historically been used in the financial system, does not require the sharing of risks and rewards between the provider of finance (the investor) and the user of finance. Interest (riba) is absolutely forbidden in Islamic finance and is seen as immoral. This can be contrasted with debt in conventional finance, where interest is seen as the main form of return to the debt holder, and with the attention paid to interest rates in the conventional financial system, where interest is the reward for depositing funds and the cost of borrowing funds.

Islamic finance can only support business activities which are acceptable under Sharia law. Murubaha and sukuk are forms of Islamic finance which can be compared to conventional debt finance. Unlike conventional debt finance, however, murubaha and sukuk must have a direct link with underlying tangible assets.

220 Tufa Co

Text references. Cost of capital is covered in Chapter 14.

Top tips. This question contains a couple of areas where candidates may get stuck - for example calculating the current dividend, and the cost of the bank loan. In such a case you will have to make a reasonable assumption (eg assuming the cost of the bank loan is the same as the cost of the redeemable debt) in order to make progress. This will be more impressive to the markers than ignoring the issue (eg ignoring the bank loan entirely).

Easy marks. Easy marks are available in parts (b) and (c).

Examining team's comments. In part (b) too many responses simply said 'the WACC can be used if business and financial risk are unchanged' without further development. Whilst correct, the statement needs further discussion.

In part (c) it should be noted that if three advantages are required, then discussing a fourth or even fifth advantage is both poor examination techniques and poor time management.

Marking scheme

		Marks
(a)	Dividend for 20X7	1
	Dividend growth rate	1
	Cost of equity	1
	Cost of pref shares	1
	After-tax interest	1
	Kd calculation setup	1
	Calculating Kd	1
	Cost of bank loan	0.5
	MV ordinary shares	0.5
	MV pref shares	0.5
	MV loan notes	0.5
	WACC calculations	2
		11
(b)	Business risk	1
	Financial risk	1
	Size on investment	1
		3

(c) First advantage   2
     Second advantage   2
     Third advantage   2

                                     6
                                     20

(a)

Interest rate of loan notes (%)			7			
Nominal value of loan notes ($)			100.00			
Market price of loan notes ($)			102.34			
Time to redemption (year)			4			
Redemption premium (%)			5			
Tax rate (%)			30			

Year	Item	$	5% DF	PV ($)	6% DF	PV ($)
0	MV	(102.34)	1.000	(102.34)	1.000	(102.34)
1–4	Interest	4.90	3.546	17.38	3.465	16.98
4	Redeem	105.00	0.823	86.42	0.792	83.16
				1.45		(2.20)

IRR (%)   5 + (1.45/(1.45 + 2.20)) = 5.40

Cost of bank loan (%)   5.40 (assumed)

The total market value of the loan notes = $10m × 102.34/100 = $10.234m

Cost of preference shares = dividend/market price = (0.05 × $0.50)/$0.31 = 8.06%

The total market value of the preference shares = $5m/$0.5 nominal value × $0.31 market value = $3.1m.

Cost of ordinary shares using

$$r_e = \frac{D_0(1+g)}{P_0} + g$$

The current dividend can be calculated as the difference between the ex div and the cum div share price: $7.52 – $7.07 = $0.45.

Annual growth over 4 time periods between 20X3 and 20X7 is $\left(\dfrac{0.45}{0.37}\right)^{1/4} - 1 = 5\%$

Po = the ex div share price of $7.07

So cost of equity = $\dfrac{0.45 \times 1.05}{7.07} + 0.05 = 0.117$ or 11.7%

There are 24m ordinary shares ($12m/$0.5 nominal value), so Ve = 24m shares × $7.07 = $169.68m

Total capital employed using market values = $10.234 loan notes + $3m bank loan + $3.1m preference shares + $169.68m ordinary shares = $186.014m

Overall WACC = (11.7 × 169.68/186.014) + (8.1 × 3.1/186.014) + (5.40 × 10.234/186.014) + (5.4 × 3/186.014) = **11.19%**

(b) The current WACC of Tufa Co represents the mean return required by the company's investors, given the current levels of business risk and financial risk faced by the company.

The current WACC can be used as the discount rate in appraising an investment project of the company provided that undertaking the investment project does not change the current levels of business risk and financial risk faced by the company.

BPP
LEARNING MEDIA

The current WACC can therefore be used as the discount rate in appraising an investment project of Tufa Co in the same business area as current operations, for example, an expansion of current business, as business risk is likely to be unchanged in these circumstances.

Similarly, the current WACC can be used as the discount rate in appraising an investment project of Tufa Co if the project is financed in a way that mirrors the current capital structure of the company, as financial risk is then likely to be unchanged.

The required return of the company's investors is likely to change if the investment project is large compared to the size of the company, so the WACC is likely to be an appropriate discount rate providing the investment is small in size relative to Tufa Co.

(c) The following advantages of using convertible loan notes as source of long-term finance could be discussed.

Conversion rather than redemption

If the holders of convertible loan notes judge that conversion into ordinary shares will increase their wealth, conversion of the loan notes will occur on the conversion date and Tufa Co will not need to find the cash needed to redeem the loan notes. This is sometimes referred to as 'self-liquidation'.

Lower interest rate

The option to convert into ordinary shares has value for investors as ordinary shares normally offer a higher return than debt. Investors in convertible loan notes will therefore accept a lower interest rate than on ordinary loan notes, decreasing the finance costs for the issuing company.

Debt capacity

If Tufa Co issued convertible loan notes, its gearing and financial risk will increase and its debt capacity will decrease. When conversion occurs, its gearing and financel risk will decrease and its debt capacity will increase because of the elimination of the loan notes from its capital structure. However, there will a further increase in debt capacity due to the issue of new ordinary shares in order to facilitate conversion.

Attractive to investors

Tufa Co may be able to issue convertible loan notes to raise long-term finance even when investors might not be attracted by an issue of ordinary loan notes, because of the attraction of the option to convert into ordinary shares in the future.

Facilitates planning

It has been suggested than an issue of fixed-interest debt such as convertible loan notes can be attractive to a company as the fixed nature of future interest payments facilitates financial planning.

221 Dartig Co

Text references. Rights issues are covered in Chapter 12, estimating the growth rate and the dividend growth model are covered in Chapter 15 and the price/earnings (P/E) ratio is covered in Chapter 14.

Top tips. You need to recognise the need to calculate the growth rate of dividends in this question for both parts (b) and (d). If this is too tricky, state a suitable figure and carry on with the calculations. Make sure you write suitably detailed points in the discussion parts and don't just focus on the calculations.

Easy marks. There are easy marks available for the calculations in parts (a) and (d).

Examining team's comments. In part (a) many candidates gained full marks for their calculations. Weaker answers made errors as regards the form of the issue (it was 1 for 4, not 4 for 1), or thought the theoretical ex-rights price was the rights issue price, or calculated the value of the rights. In part (b) a number of candidates were not able to calculate the P/E ratio by dividing the current share price by the current earnings per share (EPS). Calculating the EPS after the expansion by multiplying the current EPS by the average historic EPS growth rate was also a problem for some candidates, who were unable to calculate average historic growth rate, or who applied the growth rate to the average EPS rather than the current EPS. Some students were also unfamiliar with the P/E valuation method, even though this is discussed in the Study Text.

Better answers in part (c) looked to compare the theoretical ex-rights price per share (the share price before the rights issue funds were invested) with the share price after the investment had taken place (for example the share price calculated in part (b)), or to compare the return from the investment (for example, total shareholder return, which is the sum of capital gain and dividend yield) with the cost of equity.

Many candidates gained full marks in part (d). Marks were lost where candidates used EPS rather than dividend per share in the dividend growth model, or were not able to calculate the dividend growth rate, or used incorrect values in the dividend growth model. A surprising number of candidates did not use the dividend growth model given in the formula sheet, but used the rearranged version of the formula that is used to calculate the cost of equity. Some candidates mistakenly thought that the cost of equity calculated by this formula was the same as the share price.

Marking scheme

		Marks	
(a)	Rights issue price	2	
	Theoretical ex-rights price per share	2	
			4
(b)	Existing P/E ratio	1	
	Revised EPS	1	
	Share price using P/E method	2	
			4
(c)	Discussion of share price comparisons	4	
	Calculation of capital gain and comment	2	
			6
		Marks	
(d)	Average dividend growth rate	2	
	Ex div market price per share	2	
	Discussion	2	
			6
			20

(a) Rights issue price = $2.50 × 80% = $2.00 per share

Theoretical ex-rights price

	$
4 shares @ $2.50	10.00
1 share @ $2.00	2.00
5	12.00

Theoretical ex-rights price (TERP) = 12.00/5 = **$2.40**

(b) Average growth rate of EPS:

$$1 + g = \sqrt[4]{\frac{32.4}{27.7}}$$

$1 + g = 1.03996$

$g = 4\%$

EPS following expansion = 32.4 × 1.04 = 33.7 cents per share

Current P/E ratio = 250/32.4 = 7.7 times

Share price following expansion = $0.337 × 7.7 = **$2.60**

(c) A company will only be able to raise finance if investors think the **returns** they can expect are satisfactory in view of the **risks** they are taking. The proposed business expansion will be an acceptable use of the rights issue funds if it **increases shareholder wealth**.

This can be measured by looking at the effect on the **share price**. The current share price is $2.50 and the future share price predicted by the P/E method is $2.60. This indicates that shareholder wealth would increase. However, the capital gain is actually larger than this as shareholders will obtain new shares at a discount, resulting in a TERP of $2.40. The **capital gain for shareholders** is therefore $2.60 − $2.40 = 20 cents per share.

Alternatively, we can consider the effect on **total shareholder wealth**. The rights issue involves 2.5 million shares ($5m/$2 per share). There were therefore 10 million shares (2.5 × 4) before the investment and Dartig Co was worth $25m (10m × $2.50). After the investment, Dartig Co is worth $27.5m (12.5m × $2.60 − $5m) which is a **capital gain** of $2.5m.

If investors believe that the expansion will enable the business to grow even further, the capital gain could be even greater. If, however, investors do not share the company's confidence in the future, the share price could fall.

(d)   **Dividend growth model**

$$P_0 = \frac{D_0(1+g)}{r_e - g}$$

Cost of equity (r_e) = 10%

$$g = \sqrt[4]{\frac{15.0}{12.8}} = 4\%$$

Alternative approach

Using the Gordon growth model $g = br_e$

Average payout ratio over the last 4 years has been 47%, so the average retention ratio has been 53%.

$g = 53\% \times 10\% = 5.3\%$

$D_0 = \$0.15$

$$P_0 = \frac{0.15(1+0.04)}{0.1 - 0.04}$$

= **$2.60**

This is 10 cents per share more than the current share price of Dartig Co.

Reasons for difference in share price

The dividend growth model assumes that the **historical trend** of dividend per share payments will **continue into the future**. The future dividend growth rate may however differ from the average historical dividend growth rate, and the current share price may incorporate a more conservative estimate of the future dividend growth rate.

The **cost of equity** of Dartig Co may not be 10%. It may be difficult to make a confident estimate of the cost of capital.

The dividend valuation model assumes that investors act **rationally** and **homogenously**. In reality, different shareholders will have different expectations and there may be a degree of **inefficiency** in the capital market on which the shares of Dartig Co are traded.

MCQ bank – Business valuations

222   C   A is only valid if the company is listed.

B and D are unlikely because both imply that an asset value will be used and this is unlikely for a service company where most of its assets will be intangible.

C is correct, but because of the need to value ML's shares, not X's shares.

Syllabus area F1(a)

223   A   Net asset value (NAV) = 140m – 15m – 20m = $105m

Number of ordinary shares = 25m/0·5 = 50m shares

NAV per share = 105m/50m = $2·10 per share

Syllabus area F2(a)

224   A $P_0 = \dfrac{D_0(1+g)}{(r_e - g)}$ Given on the formula sheet

Growth 'g' – Dividends grew from ($0.50 – $0.10) = $0.40 to $0.50 in 3 years. This is an average annual growth rate of:

$0.40 (1 + g)^3 = $0.50

$(1 + g) = \sqrt[3]{(0.5/0.4)}$

g = 0.077 = 7.7%

$P_0 = \dfrac{\$0.50\,(1+0.077)}{(0.10 - 0.077)} = \$23.41$

Syllabus area F2(c)

225   C   Share price = (0.826 × 0.5)/(0.1 – 0.03) + (0.25 × 0.826) = $6.11 per share

The dividend valuation model states that the ex dividend market value of an ordinary share is equal to the present value of the future dividends paid to the owner of the share. No dividends are to be paid in the current year and in Year 1, so the value of the share does not depend on dividends from these years. The first dividend to be paid is in Year 2 and this dividend is different from the dividend paid in Year 3 and in subsequent years. The present value of the Year 2 dividend, discounted at 10% per year, is (0.25 × 0.826) = $0.2065.

The dividends paid in Year 3 can subsequently be valued using the dividend growth model. By using the formula P0 = D1/(re – g) we can calculate the present value of the future dividend stream beginning with $0.50 per share paid in Year 3. This present value will be a Year 2 value and will need discounting for two years to make it a Year 0 present value.

P0 = (0.826 × 0.5)/(0.1 – 0.03) = 0.826 × 7.1429 = $5.90

$5.90 + 0.2065 = $6.11

Syllabus area F2(c)

226   D $672m

g = br.

g = 0.2 × 0.6 = 0.12

$MV = \dfrac{D_0(1+g)}{k_e - g} = \dfrac{60m \times 1.12}{0.22 - 0.12} = \$672m$

Syllabus area F2(b)

227 **C** Earnings yield is lower. P/E ratio is higher.

For DD Co, P/E = 12, Earnings yield (= 1/(P/E ratio) = 0.0833 = 8.3%.

For competitor, P/E (= 1/earnings yield) = 10, Earnings yield = 10%.

Syllabus area F2(b)

228 **A** Discounting the interest of $5 per year at a required return of 10% to perpetuity = $5 × 1/0.1 = present value $50.

In addition a payment of $5 is about to be received

So total present value = $50 + $5 = $55.

Notes on incorrect answers:

$50 is obtained if the imminent interest payment is ignored

$76 is obtained if the post-tax cost of debt is used as the discount factor (which is incorrect because we are calculating the market value of the debt to the investor)

$40 is obtained if the post-tax interest ($5 × 0.7 = $3.5) is used, again this is incorrect because we are calculating the market value of the debt to the investor.

Syllabus area F3(a)

229 **A** Discounting the future cash flows at the required return of 9% gives:

$[7 \times AF_{1-7} 9\%] + [105 \times DF_7 9\%] = 0$

$[7 \times 5.033] + [105 \times 0.547] = 0$

∴ current MV = $92.67

Syllabus area E2(b)

230 **B** Market value = (6 × 5.971) + (105 × 0.582) = 35.83 + 61.11 = $96.94

231 **A** Should NCW Co purchase CEW Co it will acquire a cash flow of ($10 + 2) = $12m per annum, assuming that CEW Co invests the $6m in new machinery. (**Note.** It should do this as its net present value = $2m/0.1 − $6m = $14m.)

Therefore the value would be: $12m/0.1 − $6m = $114m. Note the $12m is a perpetuity.

Syllabus area F2(c)

CBE style OTQ bank – Market efficiency

232 **A strong form efficient market**

As share price reaction appears to have occurred before the information concerning the new project was made public, this suggests a strong form efficient market (and quite possibly insider dealing) because in a strong form efficient market the share price reflects even privately held information.

Syllabus area F4(a)

233 **Estimates of the present value of the synergies that are likely to result from the takeover**

If PX Co pays more for the whole of JJ Co than its current value + present value of synergies then it will have paid a price at which the investment generates a negative net present value for its shareholders.

Notes on incorrect answers:

No information is incorrect because the current share price of JJ Co is the **minimum** value of JJ Co, and ignores the value of potential synergies.

An aged accounts receivables summary is unlikely given that most retailers sell for cash/credit card.

The latest statement of financial position is more relevant for calculating a minimum value than for a maximum value.

Syllabus area F1(a)

234 **Completely inefficient**

In a weak form efficient market, all investors know previous share price movements, which will stop patterns consistently and predictably repeating. Sarah must therefore believe the markets are not even weak form efficient.

Syllabus area F4(a)

235 **The majority of share price reaction to news occurs when it is announced.**

'Repeating patterns appear to exist' supports the view that markets are completely inefficient.

'Attempting to trade on consistently repeating patterns is unlikely to work' supports the view that markets are weak form efficient.

'The majority of share price reaction to news occurs when it is announced' supports the view that markets are semi-strong form efficient because in such a market share prices reflect publicly available information, but not privately held information. Share price will therefore not reflect information before it is announced.

'Share price reaction occurs before announcements are made public' supports the view that markets are strong form efficient: they reflect all available information including that which is privately held.

Syllabus area F4(a)

236 **Both statements are true**

Fundamental analysis values shares according to the future incremental cash flows associated with owning that share, discounted by the investor's required rate of return which reflects the perceived risk associated with that investment.

Technical analysis (or charting) attempts to predict share price movements by anticipating repeating patterns following detailed analysis of past share price movements.

Syllabus area F4(a)

Phobis Co

237 **D** $20m

Earnings yield = EPS/Price which is the same as $1 \div$ P/E ratio

So the P/E ratio = 10

Price/earnings ratio method of valuation

Market value = P/E ratio $\times$ EPS

EPS = 40.0c

Average sector P/E ratio = 10

Value of shares = $40.0 \times 10 = \$4.00$ per share

(Alternatively 40.0 cents divided by earnings yield of 0.1)

Number of shares = 5 million

Value of Danoca Co = $20 million

238 **A** Statement 1 is true and statement 2 is false.

The current share price of Danoca Co is $3.30 which equates to a P/E ratio of 8.25 (3.30/0.4). This is lower than the average sector P/E ratio of 10 which suggests that the market does not view the growth prospects of Danoca Co as favourably as an average company in that business sector.

If Danoca Co has a **lower** P/E ratio, this would imply that an acquisition by Phobis could result in improved financial performance of Danoca Co.

239 **A** $14.75m

Dividend growth model method of valuation

$$P_0 = \frac{D_0(1+g)}{K_e - g}.$$

Note. The formula sheet in this exam uses r_e instead of K_e.

D_0 can be found using the proposed payout ratio of 60%.

$D_0 = 60\% \times 40c = 24c$

Value of shares = $\dfrac{0.24 \times (1 + 0.045)}{0.13 - 0.045}$

= $2.95

Value of Danoca Co = $2.95 × 5 million shares = $14.75 million

240 B $16.5m

Market capitalisation of Danoca Co is $3.30 × 5m = $16.5m.

241 B 1 and 3

'Under weak form hypothesis of market efficiency, share prices reflect all available information about past changes in share price' is true.

'If a stock market displays semi-strong efficiency then individuals can beat the market' is not true. Individuals cannot beat the market because all information publicly available will already be reflected in the share price.

'Behavioural finance aims to explain the implications of psychological factors on investor decisions' is true.

'Random walk theory is based on the idea that past share price patterns will be repeated' is not true. Chartists believe that past share price patterns will be repeated.

GWW Co

242 D $160m

Market capitalisation   = number of shares × market value

= ($20m/$0.5) × $4.00 = $160m

243 B   The net realisable value of assets at liquidation = non-current assets + inventory + trade receivables – current liabilities – bonds

= $86m + $4.2m + ($4.5m × 80%) – $7.1m – $25m

= $61.7m

244 D $171.7m

Historic earnings based on 20X2 profit after tax = $10.1m

Average P/E ratio in industry = 17 times

Assuming no adjustment required to P/E ratio (GWW Co is a listed company so no need to adjust for transferability) and using historic earnings:

P/E ratio value = 17 × $10.1m = $171.7m

245 C   Technical analysis

Technical analysts work on the basis that past price patterns will be repeated, so that future price movements can be predicted from historical patterns.

246 B   For GWW Co, P/E = 15, Earnings yield (= 1/(P/E ratio) = 6.7%.

For its competitor, P/E (= 1/earnings yield) = 16, Earnings yield = 6.25%.

Corhig Co

247   **$15m**

The value of the company can be calculated using the P/E ratio valuation as:

Expected future earnings × P/E ratio

Using Corhig Co's forecast earnings for Year 1, and taking the average P/E ratio of similar listed companies, Corhig Co can be valued at $3m × 5 = $15m.

248   **Statement 1 is true and statement 2 is false.**

The valuation above does not take into consideration the fact that earnings are expected to rise by 43% over the next 3 years. Instead of using Year 1 earnings, we could use average expected earnings over the next 3 years of $3.63m. This would give us a more appropriate valuation of $18.15m.

The P/E ratio of 5 is taken from the average of similar listed companies. However, P/E ratios vary from company to company depending on each company's business operations, capital structures, gearing, and markets. The ratio used here is therefore subject to a high degree of uncertainty. An inaccurate P/E ratio would call the valuation into question, as it is so crucial to the calculation.

Corhig Co is listed, so it would be much more appropriate to use the company's own current P/E ratio instead.

249   PV of Year 2 dividend = 500,000 × 0.797 = **$398,500** (using cost of capital of 12%)

250   **10.32%**

After-tax cost of debt = 6 × (1 − 0.2) = 4.8%

Revised after-tax WACC = 14 × 60% + 4.8 × 40% = 10.32%

251   Risk linked to the extent to which the company's profits depend on fixed, rather than variable, costs is **business risk**.

Risk that shareholder cannot mitigate by holding a diversified investment portfolio is systematic risk.

Risk that shareholder return fluctuates as a result of the level of debt the company undertakes is financial risk.

Close Co

252   **$490m**

Net assets
As no additional information is available, this is based on book values.
Net assets = 720 − 70 − 160 = $490 million

253   **$693m**

Dividend growth model

Dividends are expected to grow at 4% per year and the cost of equity is 10%.

$$P_0 = \frac{40 \times 1.04}{0.10 - 0.04}$$

$$= 41.6/0.06$$

$$= \$693 \text{ million}$$

254   **$605.5 million**

Earnings yield

Earnings are the profit after tax figure of $66.6m and the earnings yield that can be used for the valuation is 11%.

ie 66.6/0.11 = $605.5m.

255 **Both statements are true.**

The DGM is very sensitive to changes in the growth rate. A 1% change in the growth rate can give a significantly different valuation.

If dividends are expected to be paid at some point in the future, the DGM can be applied at that point to create a value for the shares which can then be discounted to give the current ex dividend share price.

In a situation where dividends are not paid and are not expected to be paid the DGM has no use.

256 **The sum of the present values of the future interest payments + the present value of the bond's conversion value**

WAW Co

257   **C** $g = \left(\dfrac{\text{latest dividend}}{\text{earliest dividend}} \right)^{\frac{1}{\text{time period}}}$

$$g = \left(\frac{3}{2.4} \right)^{\frac{1}{3}} - 1 = 0.0772$$

$$P_0 \;=\; \frac{3 \times 1.0772}{0.12 - 0.0772}$$

$$= \$75.5m$$

Divided by 10 million shares this gives = \$7.55/share

Answer A is obtained if you assume that growth has taken place over four years.

Answer B is obtained if you forget to increase the dividend by the growth rate and use four years.

Answer D is obtained if you use the wrong number of shares.

258   **C**   The cost of equity can be estimated for an unlisted company (for example using CAPM).

259   **B**   Earnings \$7.5m × P/E 15 = Value of \$112.5m

There are 10 million shares in issue so this is \$112.5/10 = \$11.25 per share

Options A and D use the incorrect number of shares.

Option D uses dividends instead of earnings.

260   **D**   Assuming an efficient stock market, the high share price indicates confidence in future growth.

261   **A**   Indifference between dividend and capital growth would be indicated by a more erratic dividend policy. Also, dividend irrelevancy theory assumes no tax, which is not the case here.

CBE style OT case DFE Co

262   **Traditional view**

The traditional view assumes there is an optimal balance between debt and equity (there is a 'U' shaped weighted average cost of capital (WACC) curve) hence choosing finance to aim for the optimum suggests the traditional view is adopted.

Modigliani-Miller (no tax) concludes the WACC is unaffected by the finance decision hence the choice of debt compared to equity is irrelevant.

Modigliani-Miller (with tax) concludes that due to the tax benefits of paying interest, as much finance as possible should be in the form of debt as increasing gearing will reduce the WACC. Hence equity would never be chosen.

Residual view/theory is not directly relevant to the capital structure decision. This term more directly relates to dividend policy.

263   **Semi-strong form efficient**

Share price in a semi-strong form market reflects all publicly available information, but not privately held information. Thus the majority of share price reaction occurs to and around public announcements.

264   **$96.40**

The conversion value is $100 cash or 70 shares, whichever is worth more (as conversion is at the investor's option). The share price on conversion is predicted to be $1.25 \times (1.04)^5 = 1.52, hence if converted the shares would be worth $70 \times $1.52 = 106.40. As this is more than the cash alternative ($100) investors would choose to convert, the conversion value = $106.40.

The investor pays market price, and they receive the pre-tax interest hence the pre-tax cost of debt is used to value the loan note:

Time		Cash flow $	Discount factor 10%	Present value $
1–5	Interest	8% × $100 = $8	3.791	30.33
5	Conversion value	$106.4	0.621	66.07
				96.40

265   **Forward rate agreements are the interest rate equivalent of forward exchange contracts.**

Statement 1 is incorrect: Although futures are flexible with timing, they are for standardised amounts which may therefore not match the size of the hedge needed exactly.

Statement 2 is incorrect: Options afford the holder the right but not the obligation to exercise an option. They can be allowed to lapse. In the case of exchange traded options they can also be sold on mid-term.

Statement 3 is correct: A forward rate agreement (FRA) creates an obligation for a 'top-up' payment or receipt. In the case of a loan, when the FRA payment is added to the underlying loan interest payment, the net interest payment is fixed at the FRA rate.

Statement 4 is incorrect: The statement refers to smoothing (a mix of fixed and floating rates to make effective interest rates less variable). Matching – generally employed by banks – refers to matching interest rates on assets to the interest rate on liabilities.

266 **1 and 2 only**

Statement 1: Increased uncertainty will increase the preference for liquidity, and will increase required yields into the future.

Statement 2: If the markets feel interest rates are going to rise, the required return on longer dated bonds will increase in line with these expectations.

Statement 3 is false. This will lead to the curve flattening.

MCQ bank – Foreign currency risk

267 **D**   A   is a financial reporting implication of retranslating foreign assets/liabilities and not immediately related to cash.

           B   is the impact on business value of long-term exchange rate trends.

           C   is the risk that the customer fails to pay.

           D   is correct: transaction risk refers to the fact that the spot rate may move between point of sale (denominated in foreign exchange) and when the customer pays, such that the net domestic receipt differs from expected.

Syllabus area G1(a)

268 **A**   A strengthening euro means euros are getting more expensive: they will cost more dollars.

           The exchange rate becomes €1 : $2.40   ($2 × 1.2)

           The euro receipt will be $1,000/2.4 = €416.67

Syllabus area G1(a)

269 **B**   The spot rate for translating $ receipts to € is $2.0010/€ (the rate at which the $ can be sold and the € can be bought)

           The euro receipt will be $2,000/2.0010 = €999.50.

Syllabus area G3(a)

270 **A**   Derivative hedging instruments that are traded on an exchange or market are standardised in nature. Futures contracts, whether interest rate futures or currency futures, relate to a standard quantity of an underlying asset. Exchange-traded options, by definition, are traded on an exchange and are therefore standardised in nature, whether interest rate options or currency options. A forward rate agreement (FRA) is the interest rate equivalent of a forward exchange contract (FEC). It is an agreement between a bank and a customer to fix an interest rate on an agreed amount of funds for an agreed future period. The FRA is tailored to the customer's needs and so is a bespoke contract rather than a standardised contract. Answers B and C were therefore not correct.

           Both currency swaps and interest rate swaps are derivatives that are available to organisations to manage or hedge long-term foreign currency risk and interest rate risk. They are essentially an agreement between two counterparties to exchange interest rate obligations on an agreed amount of funds, whether in the domestic currency or in a foreign currency. A bank will usually act as an intermediary in arranging a swap in exchange for a fee and can even arrange a swap where no counterparty is immediately available. Swaps are therefore tailored to customers' needs and are not standardised in nature. Answers C and D were therefore not correct.

Syllabus area G3(c) & G4(b)

271 **D**   The US company should borrow US$ immediately and send it to Europe. It should be left on deposit in € for three months then used to pay the supplier.

           The amount to put on deposit today = €3.5m × 1/(1 + (0.01/4)) = €3,491,272.

           This will cost €3,491,272 × $2 = $6,982,544 today (note $2 is the worst rate for buying €).

           Assuming this to be borrowed in US$, the liability in 3 months will be:

           $6,982,544 × [1 + (0.08/4)] = $7,122,195.

Syllabus area G3(a)

272 **B**   They are only available in a small amount of currencies. They are probably an imprecise match for the underlying transaction.

           Statement 1: False. Futures contracts are subject to a brokerage fee only (for example there is no spread on the rate) so are relatively cheap.

Statement 2: True. It is not possible to purchase futures contracts from every currency to every other currency – there are only limited combinations available.

Statement 3: False. Futures contracts can be 'closed out' so if, for example, customers pay early or late, the timing of the futures hedge can accommodate this.

Statement 4: True. Futures contracts are for standardised amounts so may not match the size of the transaction being hedged precisely.

Syllabus area G3(a)

273   A   The borrowing interest rate for 6 months is 8%/2 = 4%.

The company should borrow 500,000 pesos/1.04 = 480,769 today. After 6 months, 500,000 pesos will be repayable, including interest.

These pesos will be converted to $ at 480,769/15 = $32,051. The company must deposit this amount for 6 months, when it will have increased in value with interest.

$32,051 × (1 + (0.03/2)) = $32,532 or $32,500 to the nearest $100.

Syllabus area G3(a)

274   B   Using interest rate parity:

$$F_0 = S_0 \times \frac{(1+i_c)}{(1+i_b)}$$

The quarterly rates are: US: 8%/4 = 2%; Europe 4%/4 = 1%

Forward rate = 2 × 1.02/1.01 = $2.0198 : €1

Syllabus area G2(b)

275   B

The stronger forward value of the $ implies that interest rates are lower in Wengry than in Handria. This will be due to lower inflation in Wengry according to the International Fisher Effect.

Notes on incorrect answers:

The International Fisher Effect assumes that real interest rates are the same.

D is incorrect according to expectations theory (linked to the International Fisher Effect according to four-way equivalence).

Syllabus area G2(a)

276   C   Twelve-month forward rate = 1.415 × (1.02/1.018) = €1.418 per $1

Syllabus area G2(b)

MCQ bank – Interest rate risk

277   B   'A' describes gap exposure. C and D is interest rate risk but not specifically basis risk.

Syllabus area G1(b)

278   D

Statement 1 – correct: interest rates will be influenced by the desire of investors to receive a return that is above the rate of inflation.

Statement 2 – correct: market segmentation theory argues that the interest rate will be affected by demand for assets in different segments of the market (short/medium/long-term).

Statement 3 – correct, interest rate expectations will affect the slope of the yield curve.

Syllabus area G2(c)

279 C An inverted yield curve can arise if government policy is to keep short-term interest rates high in order to bring down inflation.

The term structure of interest rates suggests that the yield curve normally slopes upwards, so that debt with a longer term to maturity has a higher yield than short-term debt. Occasionally, the yield curve can be inverted, indicating that the yield on short-term debt is higher than the yield on longer-term debt. One of the reasons why this can happen is because government policy has increased short-term interest rates with the objective of reducing inflation, an action which falls in the area of monetary policy.

The incorrect responses are now considered.

A   Liquidity preference theory suggests that investors want more compensation for short-term lending than for long-term lending.

Liquidity preference theory seeks to explain the shape of the yield curve. It suggests that investors prefer to have cash now, rather than lending cash to borrowers, and that they prefer to have their cash returned to them sooner rather than later. The compensation that investors require for lending their cash increases therefore with the maturity of the debt finance provided. Liquidity preference theory does not therefore suggest that investors want more compensation for short-term lending than for long-term lending, in fact the opposite.

B   According to expectations theory, the shape of the yield curve gives information on how inflation rates are expected to influence interest rates in the future.

Expectations theory suggests that the shape of the yield curve depends upon the expectations of investors regarding future interest rates. An upward-sloping yield curve indicates an expectation that interest rates will rise in the future, while a downward-sloping yield curve indicates that interest rates are expected to fall in the future. Expectations theory does not therefore provide information on how inflation rates are expected to influence interest rates in the future.

D   Market segmentation theory suggests long-term interest rates depend on how easily investors can switch between market segments of different maturity.

Market segmentation theory suggests that the borrowing market can be divided into segments, for example the short-term end and the long-term end of the market. Investors in each segment remain in that segment and do not switch segments because of changes in factors influencing particular segments. The shape of the yield curve relating to each segment depends on the balance between the forces of supply and demand in that segment. Market segmentation theory does not therefore suggest that long-term interest rates depend on how easily investors can switch between market segments, since it states that investors do not switch between segments.

Syllabus area G2(c)

280 B The FRA guarantees a net interest payment of 8%.

As the loan has been signed for 7%, ADB Co will need to pay the bank
$1\% \times \$4$ million $\times (6/12) = \$20,000$.

Syllabus area G4(a)

281 A

Statement 3 is incorrect. A rise in interest rates (which is what borrowers are hedging against) will cause a fall in futures prices. So, borrowers hedging against an interest rate increase will **sell** interest rate futures now (at a high price) and buy them at a future date (at a lower price) in order to make a profit which will offset the impact of higher interest rate costs on their actual borrowings. So the third statement is incorrect.

Syllabus area G4(a,b)

Rose Co

282 **C** Rose Co should enter into a forward contract to sell €750,000 in 6 months. Statement 1 is incorrect. Rose Co could use a money market hedge but €750,000 would have to be borrowed, then converted into dollars and then placed on deposit. Statement 2 is incorrect. An interest rate swap swaps one type of interest payment (such as fixed interest) for another (such as floating rate interest). Therefore it would not be suitable. Statement 4 is not suitable as Rose Co does not have any euro payments to make.

283 **A** $310,945

Future value = €750,000/2.412 = $310,945.

284 **C** 4%

Rose Co is expecting a euro receipt in six months' time and it can hedge this receipt in the money markets by borrowing euros to create a euro liability. Euro borrowing rate for six months = 8.0%/2 = 4%.

285 **B** Statement A is incorrect. Currency futures have a fixed settlement date, although they can be exercised at any point before then.

Statement B is correct.

Statement C is incorrect. The bank will make the customer fulfil the contract.

Statement D is incorrect. Buying a currency option involves paying a premium to the option seller. This is a non-refundable fee which is paid when the option is acquired.

Syllabus area G3(c)

286 **B** Statement A is incorrect. This reduces the money supply and could put upward pressure on interest rates.

Statement B is correct. The longer the term to maturity, the higher the rate of interest.

Statement C is incorrect. Longer term is considered less certain and more risky. It therefore requires a higher yield.

Statement D is incorrect. Expectations theory states that future interest rates reflect expectations of future interest rate (not inflation rate) movements.

Syllabus area G2(c)

Edwen Co

287 **A** $56,079

Forward market

Net receipt in one month = (240,000 – 140,000) = 100,000 euros

Edwen Co needs to sell euros at an exchange rate of 1.7832 euros = $1

Dollar value of net receipt = 100,000/1.7832 = $56,079

288 **A** $167,999

Money market hedge

Expected receipt after 3 months = 300,000 euros

Borrowing cost in Europe for 3 months is not given in annual terms and so does not need to be adjusted = 1.35%

Euros to borrow now in order to have 300,000 liability after 3 months = 300,000/1.0135 = 296,004 euros.

Spot rate for selling euros = 1.7822 per $1

Dollar deposit from borrowed euros at spot = 296,004/1.7822 = $166,089

Country C interest rate over 3 months = 1.15%

Value in 3 months of deposit = $166,089 × 1.0115 = $167,999

289 **C** With a fall in a country's exchange rate Edwen Co's exports will be cheaper (and so be more competitive) and imports will become more expensive. Given imports may include raw materials, this pushes local prices up.

290 **C** 'The contracts can be tailored to the user's exact requirements' is false. Futures contracts are standard contracts.

'The exact date of receipt or payment of the currency does not have to be known' is true. The futures contract does not have to be closed out until the actual cash receipt or payment is made.

'Transaction costs are generally higher than other hedging methods' is false. Transaction costs are usually lower than other hedging methods.

291 **A** 'Contract price is in any currency offered by the bank' relates to forward contracts. 'Traded over the counter' also relates to forward contracts.

Zigto Co

292 **$251,256**

Forward exchange contract

500,000/1.990 = $251,256

Using the 6-month forward rate under the forward exchange contract, Zigto Co will receive $251,256.

293 **$248,781**

Money market hedge

Expected receipt after 6 months = Euro 500,000

Euro interest rate over 6 months = 5%/2 = 2.5%

Euros to borrow now in order to have Euro 500,000 liability after 6 months = Euro 500,000/1.025 = Euro 487,805

Spot rate for selling euros today = 2 euro/$

Dollar deposit from borrowed euros at spot rate = 487,805/2 = $243,903

Dollar deposit rate over 6 months = 4%/2 = 2%

Value of the dollar deposit in 6 months' time = $243,903 × 1.02 = $248,781

294 **Euro 1.971/$**

Using purchasing power parity:

$F_0 = S_0 \times (1 + i_c)/(1 + i_b)$

Where:

F_0 = expected spot rate

S_0 = current spot rate

i_c = expected inflation in country c

i_b = expected inflation in country b

$F_0 = 2.00 \times 1.03/1.045 = $ Euro 1.971/$

295 **Statement 1 is false. Statements 2 and 3 are true.**

The expected future spot rate is calculated based on the relative inflation rates between two countries. The current forward exchange rates are set based on the relative interest rates between them.

Expectations theory states that there is an equilibrium between relative inflation rates and relative interest rates, so the expected spot rate and the current forward rate would be the same. Realistically, purchasing power parity tends to hold true in the longer term, so is used to forecast exchange rates a number of years into the future. Short-term differences are not unusual.

296 **Statement 1 is true. Transaction risk affects cash flows. Statement 2 is false. Translation risk does not affect cash flows so does not directly affect shareholder wealth.**

However, **investors** may be influenced by the changing values of assets and liabilities so a company may choose to hedge translation risk through, for example, **matching the currency of assets and liabilities**. Statement 3 is true. Economic exposure can be difficult to avoid, although **diversification of the supplier and customer base** across different countries will reduce this kind of exposure to risk.

PGT Co

297 **$324,149**

Transactions to be hedged:

Three months €1,000,000 − €400,000 = €600,000 net receipt

Forward market

Three months €600,000/1.8510 = $324,149

298 **$169,134**

Transactions to be hedged:

Six months = €300,000 payments (the receipt of $500,000 does not need to be hedged).

Money market

Six months

Step 1 – Invest PV of €300,000
€300,000/1.02 (4% × 6/12) = €294,118

Step 2 – Convert to $ at spot rate (buy €)
€294,118/1.7694 = $166,225

Step 3 – Borrow $
$166,225 × 1.0175 (3.5% × 6/12) = $169,134

299 **The second statement is true, the others are false**

FRAs can also be used to manage interest rate risk on investments because they protect against the risk of interest rates falling as well as rising.

The user of an FRA does not have the option to let the contract lapse if the rate is unfavourable – this is only true of an interest rate option.

300 **The value of the dollar will be forecast to rise compared to the spot rate – leading to a fall in the cost of the transaction.**

The three-month forward shows the trend for the dollar to strengthen on the forward market. The interest rate parity formula will predict a stronger exchange rate if the interest rate is lower domestically than it is abroad – and this is the case here. If the $ gets stronger the expected payment in six months' time in euros would be lower.

301 **Statements 1 and 2 (only) are true**

The third statement is incorrect, and PPP theory relates to inflation rates anyway.

CBE style OT case TGA Co

302 **2 only**

TGA Co should enter into a forward contract to sell €500,000 in 3 months. Statement 1 is incorrect. TGA Co could use a money market hedge but €500,000 would have to be borrowed, then converted into dollars and then placed on deposit. Statement 3 is incorrect. An interest rate swap swaps one type of interest payment (such as fixed interest) for another (such as floating rate interest). Therefore it would not be suitable.

303   **$296,384**

Forward market hedge

Receipt from forward contract = €500,000/1.687 = $296,384

304   **$294,858**

Money market hedge

3-month euro borrowing rate = 9% × 3/12 = 2.25%
3-month dollar deposit rate = 4% × 3/12 = 1%
Borrow euros now   500,000/1.0225 = €488,998
Convert to $ now   488,998/1.675 = $291,939
$ after investing $291,939 × 1.01 = $294,858

305   **Statement 1 is true and statement 2 is false.**

One of the advantages of futures contracts is that the transaction costs are lower than other hedging methods. One of the disadvantages is that they cannot be tailored to the user's requirements. So statement 1 is true and statement 2 is false.

306   **Statement 1 refers to translation risk. Statement 2 relates to economic risk.**

ACCA

FM

Financial Management

Mock Examination 1

September 2016 CBE exam

Questions
Time allowed: 3 hours
ALL questions are compulsory and MUST be attempted

DO NOT OPEN THIS EXAM UNTIL YOU ARE READY TO START UNDER EXAMINATION CONDITIONS

Section A

ALL 15 questions are compulsory and MUST be attempted

Each question is worth 2 marks.

1   The owners of a private company wish to dispose of their entire investment in the company. The company has an issued share capital of $1m of $0.50 nominal value ordinary shares. The owners have made the following valuations of the company's assets and liabilities.

Non-current assets (book value)	$30m
Current assets	$18m
Non-current liabilities	$12m
Current liabilities	$10m

The net realisable value of the non-current assets exceeds their book value by $4m. The current assets include $2m of accounts receivable which are thought to be irrecoverable.

What is the minimum price per share which the owners should accept for the company (to the nearest $)?

$ [   ]

2   **Which of the following financial instruments will NOT be traded on a money market?**

- [ ] Commercial paper
- [ ] Convertible loan notes
- [ ] Treasury bills
- [ ] Certificates of deposit

3   Andrew Co is a large listed company financed by both equity and debt.

In which of the following areas of financial management will the impact of working capital management be smallest?

- [ ] Liquidity management
- [ ] Interest rate management
- [ ] Management of relationship with the bank
- [ ] Dividend policy

4   **Which TWO of the following are descriptions of basis risk?**

- [ ] It is the difference between the spot exchange rate and currency futures exchange rate.
- [ ] It is the possibility that the movements in the currency futures price and spot price will be different.
- [ ] It is the difference between fixed and floating interest rates.
- [ ] It is one of the reasons for an imperfect currency futures hedge.

5   Crag Co has sales of $200m per year and the gross profit margin is 40%. Finished goods inventory days vary throughout the year within the following range:

	Maximum	Minimum
Inventory (days)	120	90

All purchases and sales are made on a cash basis and no inventory of raw materials or work in progress is carried.

Crag Co intends to finance permanent current assets with equity and fluctuating current assets with its overdraft.

In relation to finished goods inventory and assuming a 360-day year, how much finance will be needed from the overdraft?

$\boxed{}$m

6   **In relation to an irredeemable security paying a fixed rate of interest, which of the following statements is correct?**

☐ As risk rises, the market value of the security will fall to ensure that investors receive an increased yield.

☐ As risk rises, the market value of the security will fall to ensure that investors receive a reduced yield.

☐ As risk rises, the market value of the security will rise to ensure that investors receive an increased yield.

☐ As risk rises, the market value of the security will rise to ensure that investors receive a reduced yield.

7   Pop Co is switching from using mainly long-term fixed rate finance to fund its working capital to using mainly short-term variable rate finance.

Which of the following statements about the change in Pop Co's working capital financing policy is true?

☐ Finance costs will increase
☐ Refinancing risk will increase
☐ Interest rate risk will decrease
☐ Overcapitalisation risk will decrease

8   **Which of the following is NOT an advantage of withholding a dividend as a source of finance?**

☐ Retained profits are a free source of finance.
☐ Investment plans need less justification.
☐ Issue costs are lower.
☐ It is quick.

9   A company has annual after-tax operating cash flows of $2m per year which are expected to continue in perpetuity. The company has a cost of equity of 10%, a before-tax cost of debt of 5% and an after-tax weighted average cost of capital of 8% per year. Corporation tax is 20%.

What is the theoretical value of the company?

☐ $20m
☐ $40m
☐ $50m
☐ $25m

10 **Which of the following would you expect to be the responsibility of financial management?**

- [ ] Producing annual accounts
- [ ] Producing monthly management accounts
- [ ] Advising on investment in non-current assets
- [ ] Deciding pay rates for staff

11 Lane Co has in issue 3% convertible loan notes which are redeemable in 5 years' time at their nominal value of $100 per loan note. Alternatively, each loan note can be converted in 5 years' time into 25 Lane Co ordinary shares.

The current share price of Lane Co is $3.60 per share and future share price growth is expected to be 5% per year.

The before-tax cost of debt of these loan notes is 10% and corporation tax is 30%.

What is the current market value of a Lane Co convertible loan note?

- [ ] $82.71
- [ ] $73.47
- [ ] $67.26
- [ ] $94.20

12 Country X uses the dollar as its currency and country Y uses the dinar.

Country X's expected inflation rate is 5% per year, compared to 2% per year in country Y. Country Y's nominal interest rate is 4% per year and the current spot exchange rate between the two countries is 1.5000 dinar per $1.

According to the four-way equivalence model, which of the following statements is/are true or false?

	True	False
Country X's nominal interest rate should be 7.06% per year	[ ]	[ ]
The future (expected) spot rate after one year should be 1.4571 dinar per $1	[ ]	[ ]
Country X's real interest rate should be higher than that of country Y	[ ]	[ ]

13 **Which TWO of the following government actions would lead to an increase in aggregate demand?**

- [ ] Increasing taxation and keeping government expenditure the same
- [ ] Decreasing taxation and increasing government expenditure
- [ ] Decreasing money supply
- [ ] Decreasing interest rates

14 Peach Co's latest results are as follows:

	$'000
Profit before interest and taxation	2,500
Profit before taxation	2,250
Profit after tax	1,400

In addition, extracts from its latest statement of financial position are as follows:

	$'000
Equity	10,000
Non-current liabilities	2,500

What is Peach Co's return on capital employed (ROCE)?

- [ ] 14%
- [ ] 18%
- [ ] 20%
- [ ] 25%

15   Drumlin Co has $5m of $0.50 nominal value ordinary shares in issue. It recently announced a 1 for 4 rights issue at $6 per share. Its share price on the announcement of the rights issue was $8 per share.

What is the theoretical value of a right per existing share (to 2 decimal places)?

$ [   ]

(Total = 30 marks)

Section B

ALL 15 questions are compulsory and MUST be attempted

Each question is worth 2 marks.

The following scenario relates to questions 16–20.

Herd Co is based in a country whose currency is the dollar ($). The company expects to receive €1,500,000 in 6 months' time from Find Co, a foreign customer. The finance director of Herd Co is concerned that the euro (€) may depreciate against the dollar before the foreign customer makes payment and she is looking at hedging the receipt.

Herd Co has in issue loan notes with a total nominal value of $4m which can be redeemed in 10 years' time. The interest paid on the loan notes is at a variable rate linked to LIBOR. The finance director of Herd Co believes that interest rates may increase in the near future.

The spot exchange rate is €1.543 per $1. The domestic short-term interest rate is 2% per year, while the foreign short-term interest rate is 5% per year.

16   **What is the six-month forward exchange rate predicted by interest rate parity (to 3 decimal places)?**

$ [   ]

17   **As regards the euro receipt, what is the primary nature of the risk faced by Herd Co?**

- [ ] Transaction risk
- [ ] Economic risk
- [ ] Translation risk
- [ ] Business risk

18   **Which of the following hedging methods will NOT be suitable for hedging the euro receipt?**

- [ ] Forward exchange contract
- [ ] Money market hedge
- [ ] Currency futures
- [ ] Currency swap

19   **Which of the following statements support the finance director's belief that the euro will depreciate against the dollar?**

	Supports the director's belief	Does not support the director's belief
The dollar inflation rate is greater than the euro inflation rate	[ ]	[ ]
The dollar nominal interest rate is less than the euro nominal interest rate	[ ]	[ ]

20   **As regards the interest rate risk faced by Herd Co, which of the following statements is correct?**

- [ ] In exchange for a premium, Herd Co could hedge its interest rate risk by buying interest rate options.
- [ ] Buying a floor will give Herd Co a hedge against interest rate increases.
- [ ] Herd Co can hedge its interest rate risk by buying interest rate futures now in order to sell them at a future date.
- [ ] Taking out a variable rate overdraft will allow Herd Co to hedge the interest rate risk through matching.

The following scenario relates to questions 21 to 25.

Ring Co has in issue ordinary shares with a nominal value of $0.25 per share. These shares are traded on an efficient capital market. It is now 20X6 and the company has just paid a dividend of $0.450 per share. Recent dividends of the company are as follows:

Year	20X6	20X5	20X4	20X3	20X2
Dividend per share	$0.450	$0.428	$0.408	$0.389	$0.370

Ring Co also has in issue loan notes which are redeemable in 7 years' time at their nominal value of $100 per loan note and which pay interest of 6% per year.

The finance director of Ring Co wishes to determine the value of the company.

Ring Co has a cost of equity of 10% per year and a before-tax cost of debt of 4% per year. The company pays corporation tax of 25% per year.

21   **Using the dividend growth model, what is the market value of each ordinary share?**

☐ $8.59
☐ $9.00
☐ $9.45
☐ $7.77

22   **What is the market value of each $100 loan note?**

$ ☐

23   The finance director of Ring Co has been advised to calculate the net asset value (NAV) of the company.

Which of the following formulae calculates correctly the NAV of Ring Co?

☐ Total assets less current liabilities
☐ Non-current assets plus net current assets
☐ Non-current assets plus current assets less total liabilities
☐ Non-current assets less net current assets less non-current liabilities

24   **Which of the following statements about valuation methods is true?**

☐ The earnings yield method multiplies earnings by the earnings yield.
☐ The equity market value is number of shares multiplied by share price, plus the market value of debt.
☐ The dividend valuation model makes the unreasonable assumption that average dividend growth is constant.
☐ The price/earnings ratio method divides earnings by the price/earnings ratio.

25   **Which of the following statements about capital market efficiency is/are correct?**

	Correct	Incorrect
Insider information cannot be used to make abnormal gains in a strong form efficient capital market.	☐	☐
In a weak form efficient capital market, Ring Co's share price reacts to new information the day after it is announced.	☐	☐
Ring Co's share price reacts quickly and accurately to newly released information in a semi-strong form efficient capital market.	☐	☐

The following scenario relates to questions 26 to 30.

The following information relates to an investment project which is being evaluated by the directors of Fence Co, a listed company. The initial investment, payable at the start of the first year of operation, is $3.9m.

Year	1	2	3	4
Net operating cash flow ($'000)	1,200	1,500	1,600	1,580
Scrap value ($'000)				100

The directors believe that this investment project will increase shareholder wealth if it achieves a return on capital employed greater than 15%. As a matter of policy, the directors require all investment projects to be evaluated using both the payback and return on capital employed methods. Shareholders have recently criticised the directors for using these investment appraisal methods, claiming that Fence Co ought to be using the academically preferred net present value method.

The directors have a remuneration package which includes a financial reward for achieving an annual return on capital employed greater than 15%. The remuneration package does not include a share option scheme.

26   **What is the payback period of the investment project?**

   ☐ 2.75 years
   ☐ 1.50 years
   ☐ 2.65 years
   ☐ 1.55 years

27   **Based on the average investment method, what is the return on capital employed of the investment project?**

   ☐ 13.3%
   ☐ 26.0%
   ☐ 52.0%
   ☐ 73.5%

28   **Which of the following statements about investment appraisal methods is correct?**

   ☐ The return on capital employed method considers the time value of money.
   ☐ Return on capital employed must be greater than the cost of equity if a project is to be accepted.
   ☐ Riskier projects should be evaluated with longer payback periods.
   ☐ Payback period ignores the timing of cash flows within the payback period.

29   **Which of the following statements about Fence Co is/are correct?**

		True	False
(1)	Managerial reward schemes of listed companies should encourage the achievement of stakeholder objectives.	☐	☐
(2)	Requiring investment projects to be evaluated with return on capital employed is an example of dysfunctional behaviour encouraged by performance-related pay.	☐	☐
(3)	Fence Co has an agency problem as the directors are not acting to maximise the wealth of shareholders.	☐	☐

30   **Which of the following statements about Fence Co directors' remuneration package is/are correct?**

		True	False
(1)	Directors' remuneration should be determined by senior executive directors.	☐	☐
(2)	Introducing a share option scheme would help bring directors' objectives in line with shareholders' objectives.	☐	☐
(3)	Linking financial rewards to a target return on capital employed will encourage short-term profitability and discourage capital investment.	☐	☐

(Total = 30 marks)

Section C
BOTH questions are compulsory and MUST be attempted

31 Nesud Co has credit sales of $45m per year and on average settles accounts with trade payables after 60 days. One of its suppliers has offered the company an early settlement discount of 0.5% for payment within 30 days. Administration costs will be increased by $500 per year if the early settlement discount is taken. Nesud Co buys components worth $1.5m per year from this supplier.

From a different supplier, Nesud Co purchases $2.4m per year of Component K at a price of $5 per component. Consumption of Component K can be assumed to be at a constant rate throughout the year. The company orders components at the start of each month in order to meet demand and the cost of placing each order is $248.44. The holding cost for Component K is $1.06 per unit per year.

The finance director of Nesud Co is concerned that approximately 1% of credit sales turn into irrecoverable debts. In addition, she has been advised that customers of the company take an average of 65 days to settle their accounts, even though Nesud Co requires settlement within 40 days.

Nesud Co finances working capital from an overdraft costing 4% per year. Assume there are 360 days in a year.

Required

(a) Evaluate whether Nesud Co should accept the early settlement discount offered by its supplier.

(4 marks)

(b) Evaluate whether Nesud Co should adopt an economic order quantity approach to ordering Component K.   **(6 marks)**

(c) Critically discuss how Nesud Co could improve the management of its trade receivables. **(10 marks)**

(Total = 20 marks)

32   Hebac Co is preparing to launch a new product in a new market which is outside its current business operations. The company has undertaken market research and test marketing at a cost of $500,000, as a result of which it expects the new product to be successful. Hebac Co plans to charge a lower selling price initially and then increase the selling price on the assumption that the new product will establish itself in the new market. Forecast sales volumes, selling prices and variable costs are as follows:

Year	1	2	3	4
Sales volume (units/year)	200,000	800,000	900,000	400,000
Selling price ($/unit)	15	18	22	22
Variable costs ($/unit)	9	9	9	9

Selling price and variable cost are given here in current price terms before taking account of forecast selling price inflation of 4% per year and variable cost inflation of 5% per year.

Incremental fixed costs of $500,000 per year in current price terms would arise as a result of producing the new product. Fixed cost inflation of 8% per year is expected.

The initial investment cost of production equipment for the new product will be $2.5m, payable at the start of the first year of operation. Production will cease at the end of four years because the new product is expected to have become obsolete due to new technology. The production equipment would have a scrap value at the end of 4 years of $125,000 in future value terms.

Investment in working capital of $1.5m will be required at the start of the first year of operation. Working capital inflation of 6% per year is expected and working capital will be recovered in full at the end of four years.

Hebac Co pays corporation tax of 20% per year, with the tax liability being settled in the year in which it arises. The company can claim tax-allowable depreciation on a 25% reducing balance basis on the initial investment cost, adjusted in the final year of operation for a balancing allowance or charge. Hebac Co currently has a nominal after-tax weighted average cost of capital (WACC) of 12% and a real after-tax WACC of 8.5%. The company uses its current WACC as the discount rate for all investment projects.

Required

(a)   Calculate the net present value of the investment project in nominal terms and comment on its financial acceptability.   **(12 marks)**

(b)   Discuss how the capital asset pricing model can assist Hebac Co in making a better investment decision with respect to its new product launch.   **(8 marks)**

(Total = 20 marks)

Answers

**DO NOT TURN THIS PAGE UNTIL YOU HAVE
COMPLETED THE MOCK EXAM**

A PLAN OF ATTACK

Managing your nerves

As you turn the pages to start this mock exam a number of thoughts are likely to cross your mind. At best, examinations cause anxiety so it is important to stay focused on your task for the next three hours! Developing an awareness of what is going on emotionally within you may help you manage your nerves. Remember, you are unlikely to banish the flow of adrenaline, but the key is to harness it to help you work steadily and quickly through your answers.

Working through this mock exam will help you develop the exam stamina you will need to keep going for 3 hours and 15 minutes.

Managing your time

Planning and time management are two of the key skills which complement the technical knowledge you need to succeed. To keep yourself on time, do not be afraid to jot down your target completion times for each question.

Doing the exam

Actually doing the exam is a personal experience. There is not a single **right way**. As long as you submit complete answers to all questions after the three hours are up, then your approach obviously works.

Looking through the exam

Section A has 15 objective test questions. This is the section of the exam where the examining team can test knowledge across the breadth of the syllabus. Make sure you read these questions carefully. The distractors are designed to present plausible, but incorrect, answers. Don't let them mislead you. If you really have no idea – guess. You may even be right.

Section B has three questions, each with a scenario and five objective test questions.

Section C has two longer questions:

- **Question 31** is a working capital question – show all your workings and don't panic! Part (c) is straightforward.

- **Question 32** requires you to calculate NPV, with inflation. Don't get swamped by inflation – show clear workings and lay your thinking on the page like a road map for the marker. Read the detail in part (a) carefully so that you deal with tax-allowable depreciation correctly.

Allocating your time

BPP's advice is to always allocate your time **according to the marks for the question**. However, **use common sense**. If you're doing a question but haven't a clue how to do part (b), you might be better off reallocating your time and getting more marks on another question, where you can add something you didn't have time for earlier on. Make sure you leave time to recheck the MCQs and make sure you have answered them all.

Section A

1   **$14**

They should not accept less than NRV: $(30m + 18m + 4m - 2m - 12m - 10m)/2m = \$14$ per share

2   **Convertible loan notes**

Convertible loan notes are long-term finance and are not traded on a money market.

3   **Dividend policy**

Working capital management may have an impact on dividend policy, but the other areas will be more significant.

4   **Second and fourth statements are correct**

Basis risk is the possibility that movements in the currency futures price and spot price will be different. It is one of the reasons for an imperfect currency futures hedge.

5   **$10m**

$\$200m \times 30/360 \times 0.6 = \$10m$

6   **First statement is correct**

As risk rises, the market value of the security will fall to ensure that investors receive an increased yield.

7   **Second statement is correct**

Pop Co is moving to an aggressive funding strategy which will increase refinancing risk.

8   **Retained profits are a free source of finance**

Although free to raise, using retained earnings as a source of finance (by withholding a dividend) is not free to use. It is equity finance and requires the cost of equity to be generated as a return.

Incorrect answers:
Second statement is an advantage. Other forms of finance require up-front justification to be considered by potential investors before funds are made available for investment.

Third statement is an advantage. There are no issue costs.

Fourth statement is an advantage. As the funds are already on hand, availability is essentially instant.

9   **$25m**

Theoretical value = $2m/0.08 = \$25m$. Operating cash flows are **before** interest so by discounting at the WACC the total value of the company's cash flows to all investors (debt + equity) is obtained.

10   **Advising on investments in non-current assets** is a key role of financial management.

11   **$82.71**

Conversion value = $3.60 \times 1.055 \times 25 = \$114.87$

Discounting at 10%, loan note value = $(3 \times 3.791) + (114.87 \times 0.621) = \$82.71$

12   **First two statements are TRUE.**

1: $(1.04 \times 1.05/1.02) - 1 = 7.06\%$
2: 1.5 dinar $\times 1.02/1.05 = 1.4571$ dinar/$
3: Real rates should be the same

13   **Second and fourth actions would increase aggregate demand.**

Decreasing taxation and increasing government expenditure would lead to increased aggregate demand. Decreasing interest rates reduces the incentive to save and so would lead to an increase in aggregate demand.

14   **20%**

Operating profit/(D + E) = 100 × 2,500/(10,000 + 2,500) = 20%

15   **$0.40**

Value of a right = ((5m × $8 + 1.25m × $6)/6.25m − $6)/4 shares = $0.40 per share

Section B

16   **1.566**

Forward rate = 1.543 × (1.025/1.01) = €1.566 per $1

17   **Transaction risk**

The euro receipt is subject to transaction risk.

18   **Currency swap**

A currency swap is not a suitable method for hedging a one-off transaction.

19   If the dollar inflation rate is less than the euro inflation rate, purchasing power parity indicates that the euro will appreciate against the dollar: **Does not support director's belief**

If the dollar nominal interest rate is less than the euro nominal interest rate, interest rate parity indicates that the euro will depreciate against the dollar: **Supports director's belief**

20   'In exchange for a premium, Herd Co could hedge its interest rate risk by buying interest rate options' is correct. **So the first statement is correct.**

21   **$9.45**

Historical dividend growth rate = 100 × $((0.450/0.370)^{0.25} - 1)$ = 5%
Share price = (0.450 × 1.05)/(0.1 − 0.05) = $9.45

22   **$112.01**

Market value = (6 × 6.002) + (100 × 0.760) = 36.01 + 76.0 = $112.01

23   **Non-current assets plus current assets less total liabilities** is the correct formula.

24   The dividend valuation model makes the unreasonable assumption that average dividend growth is constant **is correct**.

25   **First and third statements are correct.**

'Insider information cannot be used to make abnormal gains in a strong form efficient capital market' and 'Ring Co's share price reacts quickly and accurately to newly released information in a semi-strong form efficient capital market' are correct.

26   **2.75**

Payback period = 2 + (1,200/1,600) = 2.75 years

27   **26.0%**

Average annual accounting profit = (5,880 − 3,800)/4 = $520,000 per year
Average investment = (3,900 + 100)/2 = $2,000,000
ROCE = 100 × 520/2,000 = 26%

28   **Final statement is correct**

'Payback period ignores the timing of cash flows within the payback period' is correct.

29   **All the statements are true.**

30   **The second and third statements are true.**

Directors' remuneration should be determined by **non-executive** directors.

Section C

Question 31

Marking scheme

			Marks
(a)	Change in trade payables	1	
	Increase in finance cost	1	
	Administration cost increase	0.5	
	Early settlement discount	0.5	
	Comment on financial acceptability	1	
			4
(b)	Annual demand	1	
	Current ordering cost	1	
	Current holding cost	1	
	EOQ	1	
	EOQ ordering cost	0.5	
	EOQ holding cost	0.5	
	Comment on adopting EOQ approach to ordering	1	
			6
(c)	Credit analysis	2	
	Credit control	2	
	Collection of amounts owed	2	
	Factoring of trade receivables	2	
	Other relevant discussion	2	
			10
			20

(a) Relevant trade payables before discount = 1,500,000 × 60/360 = $250,000
Relevant trade payables after discount = 1,500,000 × 30/360 = $125,000
Reduction in trade payables = 250,000 – 125,000 = $125,000

More quickly, reduction in trade payables = 1,500,000 × (60 – 30)/360 = $125,000

The finance needed to reduce the trade payables will increase the overdraft.

Increase in finance cost = 125,000 × 0.04 = $5,000

Administration cost increase = $500

Discount from supplier = $1,500,000 × 0.005 = $7,500
Net benefit of discount = 7,500 – 5,000 – 500 = $2,000 per year

On financial grounds, Nesud Co should accept the supplier's early settlement discount offer.

(b) Annual demand = 2,400,000/5 = 480,000 units per year
Each month, Nesud Co orders 480,000/12 = 40,000 units
Current ordering cost = 12 × 248.44 = $2,981 per year

Average inventory of Component K = 40,000/2 = 20,000 units
Current holding cost = 20,000 × 1.06 = $21,200 per year
Total cost of current ordering policy = 2,981 + 21,200 = $24,181

Economic order quantity = $(2 \times 248.44 \times 480,000/1.06)^{0.5}$ = 15,000 units per order
Number of orders per year = 480,000/15,000 = 32 orders per year
Ordering cost = 32 × 248.44 = $7,950 per year
Average inventory of Component K = 15,000/2 = 7,500 units
Holding cost = 7,500 × 1.06 = $7,950 per year
Total cost of EOQ ordering policy = 7,950 + 7,950 = $15,900

On financial grounds, Nesud Co should adopt an EOQ approach to ordering Component K as there is a reduction in cost of $8,281.

(c) Management of trade receivables can be improved by considering credit analysis, credit control and collection of amounts owing. Management of trade receivables can also be outsourced to a factoring company, rather than being managed in-house.

Credit analysis

Offering credit to customers exposes a company to the risk of bad debts and this should be minimised through credit analysis or assessing creditworthiness. This can be done through collecting and analysing information about potential credit customers. Relevant information includes bank references, trade references, reports from credit reference agencies, records of previous transactions with potential customers, annual reports, and so on. A company might set up its own credit scoring system in order to assess the creditworthiness of potential customers. Where the expected volume of trade justifies it, a visit to a company can be made to gain a better understanding of its business and prospects.

Credit control

The accounts of customers who have been granted credit must be monitored regularly to ensure that agreed trade terms are being followed and that accounts are not getting into arrears. An important monitoring device here is an aged trade receivables analysis, identifying accounts and amounts in arrears, and the extent to which amounts are overdue. A credit utilisation report can assist management in understanding the extent to which credit is being used, identifying customers who may benefit from increased credit, and assessing the extent and nature of a company's exposure to trade receivables.

Collection of amounts owed

A company should ensure that its trade receivables are kept informed about their accounts, amounts outstanding and amounts becoming due, and the terms of trade they have accepted. An invoice should be raised when a sale is made. Regular statements should be sent, for example, on a monthly basis. Customers should be encouraged to settle their accounts on time and not become overdue. Offering a discount for early settlement could help to achieve this.

Overdue accounts should be chased using procedures contained within a company's trade receivables management policy. Reminders of payment due should be sent, leading to a final demand if necessary. Telephone calls or personal visits could be made to a contact within the company. Taking legal action or employing a specialised debt collection agency could be considered as a last resort. A clear understanding of the costs involved is important here, as the costs incurred should never exceed the benefit of collecting the overdue amount.

Factoring of trade receivables

Some companies choose to outsource management of trade receivables to a factoring company, which can bring expertise and specialist knowledge to the tasks of credit analysis, credit control, and collection of amounts owed. In exchange, the factoring company will charge a fee, typically a percentage of annual credit sales. The factoring company can also offer an advance of up to 80% of trade receivables, in exchange for interest.

Question 32

Text references. Investment appraisal with tax and inflation is covered in Chapter 9.

Top tips. Make sure that you show your workings for this type of question (in part (a)) to minimise the risk of making careless mistakes.

Easy marks. Part (a), for 14 marks, asked for a net present value (NPV) in nominal terms. This featured all of the normal elements of an NPV calculation – tax, capital allowances, inflation, working capital etc. This question should have been an area of strength for any well-prepared candidate, and many candidates did very well on this part of the question.

Examining team's comments. Answers to part (b) of the question were often unsatisfactory. Candidates seemed unprepared to discuss the required approach. The examining team highlighted the importance of being able to discuss this syllabus area.

Marking scheme

		Marks
(a)	Inflated selling price per unit	1
	Sales revenue	1
	Inflated variable cost	1
	Inflated fixed costs	1
	Tax liabilities	1
	Tax-allowable depreciation benefits Years 1–3	1
	Tax allowable depreciation benefits Year 4	1
	Incremental working capital and recovery	2
	Calculation of present values	1
	Correct initial investment	1
	Comment on financial acceptability	1
		12
(b)	Business risk, financial risk and WACC	2
	Using a proxy company	1
	Systematic risk, business risk and financial risk	1
	Ungearing the equity beta	1
	Regearing the asset beta	1
	Project-specific cost of equity and WACC	2
		8
		20

(a)   Calculation of NPV

Year	1	2	3	4
	$'000	$'000	$'000	$'000
Sales revenue	3,120	15,576	22,275	10,296
Variable cost	(1,890)	(7,936)	(9,378)	(4,376)
Contribution	1,230	7,640	12,897	5,920
Fixed cost	(540)	(583)	(630)	(680)
Taxable cash flow	690	7,057	12,267	5,240
Taxation	(138)	(1,411)	(2,453)	(1,048)
TAD tax benefits	125	94	70	186
After-tax cash flow	677	5,740	9,884	4,378
Scrap value				125
Working capital	(90)	(95)	(102)	1,787
Net cash flows	587	5,645	9,782	6,290
Discount at 12%	0.893	0.797	0.712	0.636
Present values	524	4,499	6,965	4,000

	$'000	
PV of future cash flows	15,988	
Initial investment	4,000	(2.5m + 1.5m)
NPV	11,988	

The NPV is strongly positive and so the project is financially acceptable.

Workings

1   *Sales revenue*

Year	1	2	3	4
Selling price ($/unit)	15	18	22	22
Inflated at 4% per year	15.60	19.47	24.75	25.74
Sales volume ('000 units/year)	200	800	900	400
Sales revenue ($'000/year)	3,120	15,576	22,275	10,296

2   *Variable cost*

Year	1	2	3	4
Variable cost ($/unit)	9	9	9	9
Inflated at 5% per year	9.45	9.92	10.42	10.94
Sales volume ('000 units/year)	200	800	900	400
Variable cost ($'000/year)	1,890	7,936	9,378	4,376

3   *Tax benefits of tax-allowable depreciation*

Year	1	2	3	4
	$'000	$'000	$'000	$'000
Tax-allowable depreciation	625	469	352	929
Tax benefit	125	94	70	186*

*((2,500 – 125) × 0.2) – 125 – 94 – 70 = $186,000

4   *Working capital*

Year	0	1	2	3	4
	$'000	$'000	$'000	$'000	$'000
Working capital	1,500				
Inflated at 6%		1,590	1,685	1,787	
Incremental		90	95	102	1,787

5   *Alternative calculation of after-tax cash flow*

Year	1	2	3	4
	$'000	$'000	$'000	$'000
Taxable cash flow	690	7,057	12,267	5,240
Tax-allowable depreciation	(625)	(469)	(352)	(929)
Taxable profit	65	6,588	11,915	4,311
Taxation	(13)	(1,318)	(2,383)	(862)
After-tax profit	52	5,270	9,532	3,449
Add back TAD	625	469	352	929
After-tax cash flow	677	5,739	9,884	4,378

(b)   A company can use its weighted average cost of capital (WACC) as the discount rate in appraising an investment project as long as the project's business risk and financial risk are similar to the business and financial risk of existing business operations. Where the business risk of the investment project differs significantly from the business risk of existing business operations, a project-specific discount rate is needed.

The capital asset pricing model (CAPM) can provide a project-specific discount rate. The equity beta of a company whose business operations are similar to those of the investment project (a proxy company) will reflect the systematic business risk of the project. If the proxy company is geared, the proxy equity beta will additionally reflect the systematic financial risk of the proxy company.

The proxy equity beta is ungeared to remove the effect of the proxy company's systematic financial risk to give an asset beta which solely reflects the business risk of the investment project.

This asset beta is regeared to give an equity beta which reflects the systematic financial risk of the investing company.

The regeared equity beta can then be inserted into the CAPM formula to provide a project-specific cost of equity. If this cost of capital is used as the discount rate for the investment project, it will indicate the minimum return required to compensate shareholders for the systematic risk of the project. The project-specific cost of equity can also be included in a project-specific WACC. Using the project-specific WACC in appraising an investment project will lead to a better investment decision than using the current WACC as the discount rate, as the current WACC does not reflect the risk of the investment project.

ACCA

FM

Financial Management

Mock Examination 2
Specimen exam - CBE exam

Questions
Time allowed: 3 hours
ALL questions are compulsory and MUST be attempted

DO NOT OPEN THIS EXAM UNTIL YOU ARE READY TO START UNDER EXAMINATION CONDITIONS

Section A – ALL 15 questions are compulsory and MUST be attempted

Each question is worth 2 marks.

1 The home currency of ACB Co is the dollar ($) and it trades with a company in a foreign country whose home currency is the Dinar. The following information is available:

	Home country	Foreign country
Spot rate	20.00 Dinar per $	
Interest rate	3% per year	7% per year
Inflation rate	2% per year	5% per year

What is the six-month forward exchange rate?

☐ 20.39 Dinar per $

☐ 20.30 Dinar per $

☐ 20.59 Dinar per $

☐ 20.78 Dinar per $

2 The following financial information relates to an investment project:

	$'000
Present value of sale revenue	50,025
Present value of variable costs	25,475
Present value of contribution	24,550
Present value of fixed costs	18,250
Present value of operating income	6,300
Initial investment	5,000
Net present value	1,300

What is the sensitivity of the net present value of the investment project to a change in sales volume?

☐ 7.1%

☐ 2.6%

☐ 5.1%

☐ 5.3%

3 Gurdip plots the historic movements of share prices and uses this analysis to make her investment decisions.

Oliver believes that share prices reflect all relevant information at all times.

Match the level of capital markets efficiency that best reflects each of Gurdip and Oliver's beliefs.

Efficiency
Not efficient at all
Weak form efficient
Semi-strong form efficient
Strong form efficient

Name
Gurdip
Oliver

4 Which of the following statements concerning capital structure theory is correct?

- [ ] In the traditional view, there is a linear relationship between the cost of equity and financial risk.

- [ ] Modigliani and Miller said that, in the absence of tax, the cost of equity would remain constant.

- [ ] Pecking order theory indicates that preference shares are preferred to convertible debt as a source of finance.

- [ ] Business risk is assumed to be constant as the capital structure changes.

5 Which of the following actions is LEAST likely to increase shareholder wealth?

- [ ] The weighted average cost of capital is decreased by a recent financing decision.
- [ ] The financial rewards of directors are linked to increasing earnings per share.
- [ ] The board of directors decides to invest in a project with a positive NPV.
- [ ] The annual report declares full compliance with the corporate governance code.

6 Which TWO of the following statements are features of money market instruments?

- [ ] A negotiable security can be sold before maturity.

- [ ] The yield on commercial paper is usually lower than that on treasury bills.

- [ ] Discount instruments trade at less than face value.

- [ ] Commercial paper is often issued by companies to fund long-term expenditure

7 The following are extracts from the statement of profit or loss of CQB Co:

	$'000
Sales income	60,000
Cost of sales	50,000
Profit before interest and tax	10,000
Interest	4,000
Profit before tax	6,000
Tax	4,500
Profit after tax	1,500

60% of the cost of sales is variable cost.

What is the operational gearing of CQB Co?

- [ ] 5.0 times
- [ ] 2.0 times
- [ ] 0.5 times
- [ ] 3.0 times

8 The management of Lamara Co has annual credit sales of $20m and accounts receivable of $4m. Working capital is financed by an overdraft at 12% interest per year. Assume 365 days in a year.

What is the annual finance cost saving if the management reduces the collection period to 60 days? (to the nearest $)

$ [   ]

9 **Are the following statements concerning financial management true or false?**

		True	False
1	It is concerned with investment decisions, financing decisions and dividend decisions.	☐	☐
2	It is concerned with financial planning and financial control.	☐	☐
3	It considers the management of risk.	☐	☐
4	It is concerned with providing information on past plans and decisions.	☐	☐

10 SKV Co has paid the following dividends per share in recent years:

Year	20X4	20X3	20X2	20X1
Dividend ($ per share)	0.360	0.338	0.328	0.311

The dividend for 20X4 has just been paid and SKV Co has a cost of equity of 12%.

Using the geometric average historical dividend growth rate and the dividend growth model, what is the market price of SKV Co shares on an ex dividend basis?

☐ $4.67
☐ $5.14
☐ $5.40
☐ $6.97

11 'There is a risk that the value of our foreign currency-denominated assets and liabilities will change when we prepare our accounts.'

To which risk does the above statement refer?

☐ Translation risk
☐ Economic risk
☐ Transaction risk
☐ Interest rate risk

12 The following information has been calculated for A Co:

Trade receivables collection period:	52 days
Raw material inventory turnover period:	42 days
Work in progress inventory turnover period:	30 days
Trade payables payment period:	66 days
Finished goods inventory turnover period:	45 days

What is the length of the working capital cycle?

☐ days

13 **Which of the following is/are usually seen as benefits of financial intermediation?**

(1) Interest rate fixing
(2) Risk pooling
(3) Maturity transformation

☐ 1 only
☐ 1 and 3 only
☐ 2 and 3 only
☐ 1, 2 and 3

14   **Which TWO of the following statements concerning working capital management are correct?**

☐   The twin objectives of working capital management are profitability and liquidity.

☐   A conservative approach to working capital investment will increase profitability.

☐   Working capital management is a key factor in a company's long-term success.

☐   The current ratio is a measure of profitability

15   Governments have a number of economic targets as part of their monetary policy.

Which TWO of the following targets relate predominantly to monetary policy?

☐   Increasing tax revenue

☐   Controlling the growth in the size of the money supply

☐   Reducing public expenditure

☐   Keeping interest rates low

(Total = 30 marks)

Section B – ALL 15 questions are compulsory and MUST be attempted

Each question is worth 2 marks.

The following scenario relates to questions 16–20.

Par Co currently has the following long-term capital structure:

	$m	$m
Equity finance		
Ordinary shares	30.0	
Reserves	38.4	
		68.4
Non-current liabilities		
Bank loans	15.0	
8% convertible loan notes	40.0	
5% redeemable preference shares	15.0	
		70.0
Total equity and liabilities		138.4

The 8% loan notes are convertible into eight ordinary shares per loan note in seven years' time. If not converted, the loan notes can be redeemed on the same future date at their nominal value of $100. Par Co has a cost of debt of 9% per year.

The ordinary shares of Par Co have a nominal value of $1 per share. The current ex dividend share price of the company is $10.90 per share and share prices are expected to grow by 6% per year for the foreseeable future. The equity beta of Par Co is 1.2.

16   The loan notes are secured on non-current assets of Par Co and the bank loan is secured by a floating charge on the current assets of the company.

Arrange the following sources of finance of Par Co in order of the risk to the investor with the riskiest first.

Order of risk (1ˢᵗ, 2ⁿᵈ etc)

Redeemable preference shares ☐

Loan notes ☐

Bank loan ☐

Ordinary shares ☐

17   **What is the conversion value of the 8% loan notes of Par Co after seven years (to 2 decimal places)?**
      $ ☐

18   **Assuming the conversion value after 7 years is $126.15, what is the current market value of the 8% loan notes of Par Co?**

☐ $115.20

☐ $109.26

☐ $94.93

☐ $69.00

19   **Which of the following statements relating to the capital asset pricing model is correct?**

☐   The equity beta of Par Co considers only business risk.

☐   The capital asset pricing model considers systematic risk and unsystematic risk.

☐   The equity beta of Par Co indicates that the company is more risky than the market as a whole.

☐   The debt beta of Par Co is zero.

20   **Which TWO of the following statements are problems in using the price/earnings ratio method to value a company?**

☐   It is the reciprocal of the earnings yield.

☐   It combines stock market information and corporate information.

☐   It is difficult to select a suitable price/earnings ratio.

☐   The ratio is more suited to valuing the shares of listed companies.

The following scenario relates to questions 21–25.

Zarona Co, whose home currency is the dollar, took out a fixed-interest peso bank loan several years ago when peso interest rates were relatively cheap compared to dollar interest rates. Zarona Co does not have any income in pesos. Economic difficulties have now increased peso interest rates while dollar interest rates have remained relatively stable.

Zarona Co must pay interest on the dates set by the bank. A payment of 5,000,000 pesos is due in 6 months' time. The following information is available:

Spot rate	12.500–12.582 pesos per $
Six-month forward rate	12.805–12.889 pesos per $

Interest rates which can be used by Zarona Co:

	Borrow	Deposit
Peso interest rates	10.0% per year	7.5% per year
Dollar interest rates	4.5% per year	3.5% per year

21   **What is the dollar cost of a forward market hedge? (to the nearest $)**

$ ☐

22   **Indicate whether the following statements apply to interest rate parity theory, purchasing power parity theory, or both,**

(1)	The currency of the country with the higher inflation rate will weaken against the other currency	**Interest rate parity theory**	**Purchasing power parity theory**
(2)	The theory holds in the long-term rather than in the short-term	**Interest rate parity theory**	**Purchasing power parity theory**
(3)	The exchange rate reflects the cost of living in the two countries	**Interest rate parity theory**	**Purchasing power parity theory**

23 **What are the appropriate six-month interest rates for Zarona Co to use if the company hedges the peso payment using a money market hedge?**

	Deposit rate	Borrowing rate
☐	7.50%	4.50%
☐	1.75%	5.00%
☐	3.75%	2.25%
☐	3.50%	10.00%

24 **Which TWO of the following methods are possible ways for Zarona Co to hedge its existing foreign currency risk?**

☐ Matching receipts and payments
☐ Currency swaps
☐ Leading or lagging
☐ Currency futures

25 Zarona Co also trades with companies in Europe which use the euro as their home currency. In 3 months' time Zarona Co will receive €300,000 from a customer.

Which of the following is the correct procedure for hedging this receipt using a money market hedge?

☐ Step 1 Borrow an appropriate amount in euro now
Step 2 Convert the euro amount into dollars
Step 3 Place the dollars on deposit
Step 4 Use the customer payment to repay the loan

☐ Step 1 Borrow an appropriate amount in dollars now
Step 2 Place the dollars on deposit now
Step 3 Convert the dollars into euro in three months' time
Step 4 Use the customer payment to repay the loan

☐ Step 1 Borrow an appropriate amount in dollars now
Step 2 Convert the dollar amount into euro
Step 3 Place the euro on deposit
Step 4 Use the customer payment to repay the loan

☐ Step 1 Borrow an appropriate amount in Euro now
Step 2 Place the euro on deposit now
Step 3 Convert the euro into dollars in three months' time
Step 4 Use the customer payment to repay the loan

The following scenario relates to questions 26–30.

Ridag Co operates in an industry which has recently been deregulated as the Government seeks to increase competition in the industry.

Ridag Co plans to replace an existing machine and must choose between two machines. Machine 1 has an initial cost of $200,000 and will have a scrap value of $25,000 after 4 years. Machine 2 has an initial cost of $225,000 and will have a scrap value of $50,000 after 3 years. Annual maintenance costs of the two machines are as follows:

Year	1	2	3	4
Machine 1 ($ per year)	25,000	29,000	32,000	35,000
Machine 2 ($ per year)	15,000	20,000	25,000	

Where relevant, all information relating to this project has already been adjusted to include expected future inflation. Taxation and tax-allowable depreciation must be ignored in relation to Machine 1 and Machine 2.

Ridag Co has a nominal before-tax weighted average cost of capital of 12% and a nominal after-tax weighted average cost of capital of 7%.

26   **In relation to Ridag Co, which TWO of the following statements about competition and deregulation are true?**

☐   Increased competition should encourage Ridag Co to reduce costs.

☐   Deregulation will lead to an increase in administrative and compliance costs for Ridag Co.

☐   Deregulation should mean an increase in economies of scale for Ridag Co.

☐   Deregulation could lead to a decrease in the quality of Ridag Co's products.

27   **What is the equivalent annual cost of Machine 1?**

☐ $90,412

☐ $68,646

☐ $83,388

☐ $70,609

28   **Is each of the following statements about Ridag Co using the equivalent annual cost method true or false?**

		True	False
1	Ridag Co cannot use the equivalent annual cost method to compare Machine 1 and Machine 2 because they have different useful lives.	☐	☐
2	The machine which has the lowest total present value of costs should be selected by Ridag Co.	☐	☐

29   Doubt has been cast over the accuracy of the Year 2 and Year 3 maintenance costs for Machine 2. On further investigation it was found that the following potential cash flows are now predicted:

Year	Cash flow	Probability
	$	
2	18,000	0.3
2	25,000	0.7
3	23,000	0.2
3	24,000	0.35
3	30,000	0.45

What is the expected present value of the maintenance costs for Year 3? (to the nearest $)

$ ☐

30   Ridag Co is appraising a different project, with a positive NPV. It is concerned about the risk and uncertainty associated with this other project.

Which of the following statements about risk, uncertainty and the project is true?

☐   Sensitivity analysis takes into account the interrelationship between project variables.

☐   Probability analysis can be used to assess the uncertainty associated with the project.

☐   Uncertainty can be said to increase with project life, while risk increases with the variability of returns.

☐   A discount rate of 5% could be used to lessen the effect of later cash flows on the decision.

(Total = 30 marks)

Section C – BOTH questions are compulsory and MUST be attempted

31   Vip Co, a large stock exchange listed company, is evaluating an investment proposal to manufacture Product W33, which has performed well in test marketing trials conducted recently by the company's research and development division. Product W33 will be manufactured using a fully automated process which would significantly increase noise levels from Vip Co's factory. The following information relating to this investment proposal has now been prepared:

Initial investment	$2 million
Selling price (current price terms)	$20 per unit
Expected selling price inflation	3% per year
Variable operating costs (current price terms)	$8 per unit
Fixed operating costs (current price terms)	$170,000 per year
Expected operating cost inflation	4% per year

The research and development division has prepared the following demand forecast as a result of its test marketing trials. The forecast reflects expected technological change and its effect on the anticipated life-cycle of Product W33.

Year	1	2	3	4
Demand (units)	60,000	70,000	120,000	45,000

It is expected that all units of Product W33 produced will be sold, in line with the company's policy of keeping no inventory of finished goods. No terminal value or machinery scrap value is expected at the end of four years, when production of Product W33 is planned to end. For investment appraisal purposes, Vip Co uses a nominal (money) discount rate of 10% per year and a target return on capital employed of 30% per year. Ignore taxation.

Required

(a)   Calculate the following values for the investment proposal:

       (i)   Net present value;   **(5 marks)**

       (ii)   Internal rate of return; and   **(3 marks)**

       (iii)   Return on capital employed (accounting rate of return) based on average investment.

                                                                         (3 marks)

(b)   Briefly discuss your findings in each section of (a) above and advise whether the investment proposal is financially acceptable.   **(4 marks)**

(c)   Discuss how the objectives of Vip Co's stakeholders may be in conflict if the project is undertaken.

                                                                             (5 marks)

                                                               Total = 20 marks

32   Froste Co has a dividend payout ratio of 40% and has maintained this payout ratio for several years. The current dividend per share of the company is 50c per share and it expects that its next dividend per share, payable in one year's time, will be 52c per share.

The capital structure of the company is as follows:

	$m	$m
Equity		
Ordinary shares (nominal value $1 per share)	25	
Reserves	35	
		60
Debt		
Bond A (nominal value $100)	20	
Bond B (nominal value $100)	10	
		30
		90

Bond A will be redeemed at nominal value in 10 years' time and pays annual interest of 9%. The cost of debt of this bond is 9.83% per year. The current ex interest market price of the bond is $95.08.

Bond B will be redeemed at nominal value in 4 years' time and pays annual interest of 8%. The cost of debt of this bond is 7.82% per year. The current ex interest market price of the bond is $102.01.

Froste Co has a cost of equity of 12.4%. Ignore taxation.

Required

(a)   Calculate the following values for Froste Co:

    (i)   Ex dividend share price, using the dividend growth model;   **(3 marks)**

    (ii)   Capital gearing (debt divided by debt plus equity) using market values; and   **(2 marks)**

    (iii) Market value weighted average cost of capital.   **(2 marks)**

(b)   Discuss whether a change in dividend policy will affect the share price of Froste Co.   **(8 marks)**

(c)   Explain why Froste Co's capital instruments have different levels of risk and return.   **(5 marks)**

(Total = 20 marks)

Answers

**DO NOT TURN THIS PAGE UNTIL YOU HAVE
COMPLETED THE MOCK EXAM**

Section A

1 **20.39**

20 × (1.035/1.015) = 20.39 Dinar per $

2 **5.3%**

Sensitivity to a change in sales volume = 100 × 1,300/24,550 = 5.3%

3 **Gurdip – not efficient at all   Oliver – strong form**

Gurdip is basing her investment decisions on technical analysis, which means that she believes the stock market is not efficient at all, not even weak form efficient.

Oliver believes markets are strong form efficient

4 **The statement about business risk is correct.**

In the traditional view, there is a curvilinear relationship between the cost of equity and financial risk.

Modigliani and Miller said that, in the absence of tax, the weighted average cost of capital (not the cost of equity) would remain constant.

Pecking order theory indicates that any shares are less attractive than debt as a source of finance.

5 **The financial rewards of directors are linked to increasing earnings per share.**

Increases in shareholder wealth will depend on increases in cash flow, rather than increases in earnings per share (ie increases in profit). If the financial rewards of directors are linked to increasing earnings per share, for example, through a performance-related reward scheme, there is an incentive to increase short-term profit at the expense of longer-term growth in cash flows and hence shareholder wealth.

6 **Both statements 1 and 3 are correct.**

Commercial paper is a source of short-term finance, it is riskier than Treasury Bills and will therefore carry a higher yield.

7 **3 times**

Operational gearing = Contribution/PBIT

= [60,000 − (50,000 × 0.6)]/10m = 3 times

8 **$85,479**

Finance cost saving = 13/365 × $20m × 0.12 = $85,479

9 **The first 3 statements (only) are correct.**

The first three statements concerning financial management are correct. However, information about past plans and decisions is a function of financial reporting, not financial management.

10 **$5.40**

The geometric average dividend growth rate is $(36.0/31.1)^{1/3} - 1 = 5\%$

The ex div share price = (36.0 × 1.05)/(0.12 − 0.05) = $5.40

11 **The statement refers to translation risk.**

12 **103**

The length of the operating cycle is 52 + 42 + 30 − 66 + 45 = 103 days.

13 **2 and 3 only**

Risk pooling and maturity transformation are always included in a list of benefits of financial intermediation.

14   **Statements 1 and 3 are correct.**

A conservative approach to working capital investment will involve maintaining high levels of working capital which may well not increase profitability.

The current ratio is a measure of liquidity, not profitability.

15   **Controlling the growth in the money supply & keeping interest rates low**

The other targets relate to fiscal policy.

Section B

16 **1st Ordinary shares, 2nd Preference shares, 3rd Bank loan, 4th Secured loan notes**

The secured loan notes are safer than the bank loan, which is secured on a floating charge. The redeemable preference shares are above debt in the creditor hierarchy. Ordinary shares are higher in the creditor hierarchy than preference shares.

17 **$131.12**

Future share price after 7 years = 10.90×1.06^7 = $16.39 per share

Conversion value of each loan note = 16.39×8 = $131.12 per loan note

18 **$109.26**

Market value of each loan note = $(8 \times 5.033) + (126.15 \times 0.547)$ = 40.26 + 69.00 = $109.26

19 **The equity beta of Par Co indicates that the company is more risky than the market as a whole.**

An equity beta of greater than 1 indicates that the investment is more risky than the market as a whole.

Notes on incorrect answers:

The equity beta of Par Co considers business and financial risk.
The capital asset pricing model only considers systematic risk.
The debt beta of Par Co is zero - this is not an assumption of the CAPM.

20 **Statements 3 and 4 only**

It is correct that the price/earnings ratio is more suited to valuing the shares of listed companies, and it is also true that it is difficult to find a suitable price/earnings ratio for the valuation.

Statements 1 and 2 are true but are not problems.

21 **$390,472**

Interest payment = 5,000,000 pesos
Six-month forward rate for buying pesos = 12.805 pesos per $
Dollar cost of peso interest using forward market = 5,000,000/12.805 = $390,472

22 **All statements relate to purchasing power parity, statement 2 also applies to interest rate parity.**

Exchange rates reflecting the different cost of living between two countries is stated by the theory of purchasing power parity.

Both theories hold in the long term rather than the short term (IRP also applies in the short-term).

The currency of the country with the higher inflation rate will be forecast to weaken against the currency of the country with the lower inflation rate in purchasing power parity.

23 **Deposit rate 2.25% and Borrowing rate 3.75%**

Dollars will be borrowed now for 6 months at $4.5 \times 6/12$ = 2.25%

Pesos will be deposited now for 6 months at $7.5 \times 6/12$ = 3.75%

24 **Currency futures and swaps could both be used.**

As payment must be made on the date set by the bank, leading or lagging are not appropriate. Matching is also inappropriate as there are no peso income streams.

25 **The first option is correct**

The correct procedure is to: Borrow euro now, convert the euro into dollars and place the dollars on deposit for three months, use the customer receipt to pay back the euro loan.

26   **Statements 1 and 4**

Deregulation to increase competition should mean managers act to reduce costs in order to be competitive. The need to reduce costs may mean that quality of products declines.

27   **$90,412**

Since taxation and capital allowances are to be ignored, and where relevant all information relating to project 2 has already been adjusted to include future inflation, the correct discount rate to use here is the nominal before-tax weighted average cost of capital of 12%.

	0	*1*	*2*	*3*	*4*
Maintenance costs		(25,000)	(29,000)	(32,000)	(35,000)
Investment and scrap	(200,000)				25,000
Net cash flow	(200,000)	(25,000)	(29,000)	(32,000)	10,000
Discount at 12%	1.000	0.893	0.797	0.712	0.636
Present values	(200,000)	(22,325)	(23,113)	(22,784)	(6,360)

Present value of cash flows ($274,582)
Cumulative present value factor 3.037
Equivalent annual cost = 274,582/3.037 = $90,412

28   **Both statements are false.**

The machine with the lowest equivalent annual cost should be purchased, not the present value of future cash flows alone. The lives of the two machines are different and the equivalent annual cost method allows this to be taken into consideration.

29   **$18,868**

EV of Year 3 cash flow = (23,000 × 0.2) + (24,000 × 0.35) + (30,000 × 0.45) = 26,500

PV discounted at 12% = 26,500 × 0.712 = $18,868

30   **The statement about uncertainty increasing with project life is true.**

Notes on incorrect answers:

Simulation (not sensitivity analysis) takes into account the interrelationship between project variables.

Probability analysis can be used to assess the risk (not uncertainty) associated with the project.

A lower discount rate of 5% would increase the present value of costs incurred in later years and would therefore increase their impact.

Section C

Question 31

			Marks
(a)	Inflated income	2	
	Inflated operating costs	2	
	Net present value	1	
	Internal rate of return	3	
	Return on capital employed	3	
			11
(b)	Discussion of investment appraisal findings	3	
	Advice on acceptability of project	1	
			4
(c)	Maximisation of shareholder wealth	1–2	
	Conflict from automation of production process	1–2	
	Conflict from additional noise	1–2	
		Maximum	5
			20

(a) (i) **Calculation of NPV**

Year	0	1	2	3	4
	$	$	$	$	$
Investment	(2,000,000)				
Income		1,236,000	1,485,400	2,622,000	1,012,950
Operating costs		676,000	789,372	1,271,227	620,076
Net cash flow	(2,000,000)	560,000	696,028	1,350,773	392,874
Discount at 10%	1.000	0.909	0.826	0.751	0.683
Present values	(2,000,000)	509,040	574,919	1,014,430	268,333
Net present value:	366,722				

Workings

1 *Calculation of income*

Year	1	2	3	4
Inflated selling price ($/unit)	20.60	21.22	21.85	22.51
Demand (units/year)	60,000	70,000	120,000	45,000
Income ($/year)	1,236,000	1,485,400	2,622,000	1,012,950

2 *Calculation of operating costs*

Year	1	2	3	4
Inflated variable cost ($/unit)	8.32	8.65	9.00	9.36
Demand (units/year)	60,000	70,000	120,000	45,000
Variable costs ($/year)	499,200	605,500	1,080,000	421,200
Inflated fixed costs ($/year)	176,800	183,872	191,227	198,876
Operating costs ($/year)	676,000	789,372	1,271,227	620,076

3   *Alternative calculation of operating costs*

Year	1	2	3	4
Variables cost ($/unit)	8	8	8	8
Demand (units/year)	60,000	70,000	120,000	45,000
Variable costs ($/year)	480,000	560,000	960,000	360,000
Fixed costs ($/year)	170,000	170,000	170,000	170,000
Operating costs ($/year)	650,000	730,000	1,130,000	530,000
Inflated costs ($/year)	676,000	789,568	1,271,096	620,025

(ii)   **Calculation of internal rate of return**

Year	0	1	2	3	4
	$	$	$	$	$
Net cash flow	(2,000,000)	560,000	696,028	1,350,773	392,874
Discount at 20%	1.000	0.833	0.694	0.579	0.482
Present values	(2,000,000)	466,480	483,043	782,098	189,365

Net present value: ($79,014)

$$\text{IRR} = a + \frac{\text{NPV}_a}{(\text{NPV}_a - \text{NPV}_b)} (b - a) = 10\% + [(366,722/(366,722 + 79,014)](20 - 10) = \textbf{18.2\%}$$

(iii)   **Calculation of return on capital employed**

Total cash inflow = 560,000 + 696,028 + 1,350,773 + 392,874 = $2,999,675
Total depreciation and initial investment are the same, as there is no scrap value.
Total accounting profit = 2,999,675 – 2,000,000 = $999,675
Average annual accounting profit = 999,675/4 = $249,919
Average investment = 2,000,000/2 = $1,000,000
Return on capital employed = 100 × 249,919/1,000,000 = 25%

(b)   The investment proposal has a positive net present value (NPV) of $366,722 and is therefore financially acceptable. The results of the other investment appraisal methods do not alter this financial acceptability, as the NPV decision rule will always offer the correct investment advice.

The internal rate of return (IRR) method also recommends accepting the investment proposal, since the IRR of 18.2% is greater than the 10% return required by Vip Co. If the advice offered by the IRR method differed from that offered by the NPV method, the advice offered by the NPV method would be preferred.

The calculated return on capital employed of 25% is less than the target return of 30% but, as indicated earlier, the investment proposal is financially acceptable as it has a positive NPV. The reason why Vip Co has a target return on capital employed of 30% should be investigated. This may be an out of date hurdle rate which has not been updated for changed economic circumstances.

(c)   As a large listed company, Vip Co's primary financial objective is assumed to be the maximisation of shareholder wealth. In order to pursue this objective, Vip Co should undertake projects, such as this one, which have a positive NPV and generate additional value for shareholders.

However, not all of Vip Co's stakeholders have the same objectives and the acceptance of this project may create conflict between the different objectives.

Due to Product W33 being produced using an automated production process, it will not meet employees' objectives of continuity or security in their employment. It could also mean employees will be paid less than they currently earn. If this move is part of a longer-term move away from manual processes, it could also conflict with government objectives of having a low rate of unemployment.

The additional noise created by the production of Product W33 will affect the local community and may conflict with objectives relating to healthy living. This may also conflict with objectives from environmental pressure groups and government standards on noise levels as well.

Question 32

		Marks
(a)	Dividend growth rate	1
	Share price using dividend growth model	2
	Capital gearing	2
	Weighted average cost of capital	2
		7
(b)	Dividend irrelevance	3–4
	Dividend relevance	3–4
	Maximum	8
(c)	Discussion of equity	1–2
	Debt and recognising business risk is not relevant	1–2
	Time until maturity of bonds	1–2
	Different value of bonds	1
	Maximum	5
		20

(a)   (i)   Dividend growth rate = $100 \times ((52/50) - 1) = 100 \times (1.04 - 1) = 4\%$ per year
Share price using DGM = $(50 \times 1.04)/(0.124 - 0.04) = 52/0.084 = 619c$ or $6.19

      (ii)   Number of ordinary shares = 25 million
Market value of equity = $25m \times 6.19 = \$154.75$ million
Market value of Bond A issue = $20m \times 95.08/100 = \$19.016m$
Market value of Bond B issue = $10m \times 102.01/100 = \$10.201m$
Market value of debt = $29.217m
Market value of capital employed = $154.75m + 29.217m = \$183.967m$
Capital gearing = $100 \times 29.217/183.967 = 15.9\%$

      (iii)   WACC = $((12.4 \times 154.75) + (9.83 \times 19.016) + (7.82 \times 10.201))/183.967 = 11.9\%$

(b)   Miller and Modigliani showed that, in a perfect capital market, the value of a company depended on its investment decision alone, and not on its dividend or financing decisions. In such a market, a change in dividend policy by Froste Co would not affect its share price or its market capitalisation. They showed that the value of a company was maximised if it invested in all projects with a positive net present value (its optimal investment schedule). The company could pay any level of dividend and, if it had insufficient finance, make up the shortfall by issuing new equity. Since investors had perfect information, they were indifferent between dividends and capital gains. Shareholders who were unhappy with the level of dividend declared by a company could gain a 'home-made dividend' by selling some of their shares. This was possible since there are no transaction costs in a perfect capital market.

Against this view are several arguments for a link between dividend policy and share prices. For example, it has been argued that investors prefer certain dividends now rather than uncertain capital gains in the future (the 'bird in the hand' argument).

It has also been argued that real-world capital markets are not perfect, but semi-strong form efficient. Since perfect information is therefore not available, it is possible for information asymmetry to exist between shareholders and the managers of a company. Dividend announcements may give new information to shareholders and as a result, in a semi-strong form efficient market, share prices may change. The size and direction of the share price change will depend on the difference between the dividend announcement and the expectations of shareholders. This is referred to as the 'signalling properties of dividends'.

It has been found that shareholders are attracted to particular companies as a result of being satisfied by their dividend policies. This is referred to as the 'clientele effect'. A company with an established dividend policy is therefore likely to have an established dividend clientele. The existence of this dividend clientele implies that the share price may change if there is a change in the dividend policy of the company, as shareholders sell their shares in order to reinvest in another company with a more satisfactory dividend policy. In a perfect capital market, the existence of dividend clienteles is irrelevant, since substituting one company for another will not incur any transaction costs. Since real-world capital markets are not perfect, however, the existence of dividend clienteles suggests that if Froste Co changes its dividend policy, its share price could be affected.

(c)   There is a trade-off between risk and return on Froste Co's capital instruments. Investors in riskier assets require a higher return in compensation for this additional risk. In the case of ordinary shares, investors rank behind all other sources of finance in the event of a liquidation so are the most risky capital instrument to invest in. This is partly why Froste Co's cost of equity is more expensive than its debt financing.

Similarly for debt financing, higher-risk borrowers must pay higher rates of interest on their borrowing to compensate lenders for the greater risk involved. Froste Co has two bonds, with Bond A having the higher interest rate and therefore the higher risk. Since both bonds were issued at the same time, business risk is not a factor in the higher level of risk.

Instead, this additional risk is likely to be due to the fact that Bond A has a greater time until maturity, meaning that its cash flows are more uncertain than Bond B's. In particular where interest rates are expected to increase in the future, longer-term debt will have a higher rate of interest to compensate investors for investing for a longer period.

A further factor is that the total nominal value (book value) of Bond A is twice as large as Bond B and therefore may be perceived to be riskier.

ACCA

FM

Financial Management

Mock Examination 3

December 2016 exam – paper based

Questions
Time allowed: 3 hours 15 minutes
ALL questions are compulsory and MUST be attempted

DO NOT OPEN THIS EXAM UNTIL YOU ARE READY TO START UNDER EXAMINATION CONDITIONS

ACCA

FM

Financial Management

Mock Examination 3

December 2016 exam – paper based

Questions

Time allowed: 3 hours 15 minutes

ALL questions are compulsory and MUST be attempted

DO NOT OPEN THIS EXAM UNTIL YOU ARE READY TO START UNDER
EXAMINATION CONDITIONS

Section A – ALL 15 questions are compulsory and MUST be attempted

Each question is worth 2 marks.

1   **Which of the following is an advantage of implementing just-in-time inventory management?**

    A   Quality control costs will be eliminated.
    B   Monthly finance costs incurred in holding inventory will be kept constant.
    C   The frequency of raw materials deliveries is reduced.
    D   The amount of obsolete inventory will be minimised.

2   **Which of the following activities are carried out by a financial intermediary?**

    (1)   Transforming interest rates
    (2)   Transforming foreign exchange
    (3)   Transforming maturity
    (4)   Transforming risk

    A   2 and 4
    B   1 and 3
    C   3 and 4
    D   1 and 2

3   Frost Co is planning a 1 for 4 rights issue with an issue price at a 10% discount to the current share price.

    The EPS is currently \$0.50 and the shares of Frost Co are trading on a price/earnings ratio of 20 times. The market capitalisation of the company is \$50m.

    Which of the following is the theoretical ex-rights price per share?

    A   \$9.80
    B   \$9.75
    C   \$10.20
    D   \$9.20

4   **In relation to business valuation, which of the following statements is true?**

    A   The earnings yield method and the dividend growth model should give similar values for a company.

    B   Market capitalisation represents the maximum value for a company.

    C   The price/earnings ratio is the reciprocal of the earnings yield.

    D   The price/earnings ratio should be increased if the company being valued is riskier than the valuing company.

5   Small and medium-sized entities (SMEs) have restricted access to capital markets.

    What is the term given to the difference between the finance required to operate an SME and the amount obtained?

    A   Forecasted gap
    B   Maturity gap
    C   Funding gap
    D   Asset gap

6   Max Co is a large multinational company which expects to have a $10m cash deficit in one month's time. The deficit is expected to last no more than two months.

Max Co wishes to resolve its short-term liquidity problem by issuing an appropriate instrument on the money market.

Which of the following instruments should Max Co issue?

A   Commercial paper
B   Interest rate futures
C   Corporate loan notes
D   Treasury bills

7   **In relation to capital markets, which of the following statements is true?**

A   The return from investing in larger companies has been shown to be greater than the average return from all companies.

B   Weak form efficiency arises when investors tend not to make rational investment decisions.

C   Allocative efficiency means that transaction costs are kept to a minimum.

D   Research has shown that, over time, share prices appear to follow a random walk.

8   The following data is available:

Country Y currency	Dollar
Country X currency	Peso
Country Y interest rate	1% per year
Country X interest rate	3% per year
Country X expected inflation rate	2% per year
Spot exchange rate in Country Y	1.60 peso per $1

What is the current six-month forward exchange rate in Country Y?

A   1.63 peso per $1
B   1.62 peso per $1
C   1.57 peso per $1
D   1.58 peso per $1

9   Green Co, a listed company, had the following share prices during the year ended 31 December 20X5:

At start of 20X5	$2.50
Highest price in the year	$3.15
Lowest price in the year	$2.40
At end of 20X5	$3.00

During the year, Green Co paid a total dividend of $0.15 per share.

What is the total shareholder return for 20X5?

A   26%
B   22%
C   32%
D   36%

10   Carp Co has announced that it will pay an annual dividend equal to 55% of earnings. Its earnings per share is $0.80, and it has 10 million shares in issue. The return on equity of Carp Co is 20% and its current cum dividend share price is $4.60.

What is the cost of equity of Carp Co?

A   19.4%
B   20.5%
C   28.0%
D   22.7%

11   Mile Co is looking to change its working capital policy to match the rest of the industry. The following results are expected for the coming year:

	$'000
Revenue	20,500
Cost of sales	(12,800)
Gross profit	7,700

Revenue and cost of sales can be assumed to be spread evenly throughout the year. The working capital ratios of Mile Co, compared with the industry, are as follows:

	Mile Co	Industry
Receivable days	50	42
Inventory days	45	35
Payable days	40	35

Assume there are 365 days in each year.

If Mile Co matches its working capital cycle with the industry, what will be the decrease in its net working capital?

A $624,600
B $730,100
C $835,600
D $975,300

12   **Which of the following statements is true?**

A   A prospective merger would need to result in a company having a market share greater than 80% before it can be described as a monopoly.

B   A government may intervene to weaken its country's exchange rate in order to eliminate a balance of payments deficit.

C   A relatively high rate of domestic inflation will lead to a strengthening currency.

D   Government fiscal policy involves the management of interest rates.

13   **Which of the following statements about interest rate risk hedging is correct?**

A   An interest rate floor can be used to hedge an expected increase in interest rates.
B   The cost of an interest rate floor is higher than the cost of an interest rate collar.
C   The premium on an interest rate option is payable when it is exercised.
D   The standardised nature of interest rate futures means that over- and under-hedging can be avoided.

14   **Which of the following statements is true?**

A   Value for money is usually taken to mean economy, efficiency and engagement.
B   Cum dividend means the buyer of the share is not entitled to receive the dividend shortly to be paid.
C   The dividend payout ratio compares the dividend per share with the market price per share.
D   The agency problem means that shareholder wealth is not being maximised.

15   Swap Co is due to receive goods costing $2,500. The terms of trade state that payment must be received within three months. However, a discount of 1.5% will be given for payment within one month.

Which of the following is the annual percentage cost of ignoring the discount and paying in three months?

A   6.23%
B   9.34%
C   6.14%
D   9.49%

(Total = 30 marks)

Section B – ALL 15 questions are compulsory and MUST be attempted

Each question is worth 2 marks.

The following scenario relates to questions 16 to 20.

Park Co is based in a country whose currency is the dollar ($). The company regularly imports goods denominated in euro (€) and regularly sells goods denominated in dinars. Two of the future transactions of the company are as follows:

Three months: Paying €650,000 for imported goods
Six months: Receiving 12 million dinars for exported capital goods

Park Co has the following exchange rates and interest rates available to it:

	Bid	Offer
Spot exchange rate (dinars per $1):	57.31	57.52
Six-month forward rate (dinars per $1):	58.41	58.64
Spot exchange rate (€ per $1):	1.544	1.552
Three-month forward rate (€ per $1):	1.532	1.540

Six-month interest rates:

	Borrow	Deposit
Dinars	4.0%	2.0%
Dollars	2.0%	0.5%

The finance director of Park Co believes that the upward-sloping yield curve reported in the financial media means that the general level of interest rates will increase in the future, and therefore expects the reported six-month interest rates to increase.

16   **What is the future dollar value of the dinar receipt using a money market hedge?**

   A $197,752
   B $201,602
   C $208,623
   D $210,629

17   **In hedging the foreign currency risk of the two transactions, which of the following hedges will Park Co find to be effective?**

   (1)   Leading the euro payment on its imported goods
   (2)   Taking out a forward exchange contract on its future dinar receipt
   (3)   Buying a tailor-made currency option for its future euro payment

   A   2 only
   B   1 and 3 only
   C   2 and 3 only
   D   1, 2 and 3

18   **Which hedging methods will assist Park Co in reducing its overall foreign currency risk?**

   (1)   Taking out a long-term euro-denominated loan
   (2)   Taking out a dinar-denominated overdraft

   A   1 only
   B   2 only
   C   Both 1 and 2
   D   Neither 1 nor 2

19   Which of the following statements is/are correct?

(1)   Purchasing power parity can be used to predict the forward exchange rate.
(2)   The international Fisher effect can be used to predict the real interest rate.

A   1 only
B   2 only
C   Both 1 and 2
D   Neither 1 nor 2

20   Which of the following statements is consistent with an upward-sloping yield curve?

A   The risk of borrowers defaulting on their loans increases with the duration of the lending.

B   Liquidity preference theory implies that short-term interest rates contain a premium over long-term interest rates to compensate for lost liquidity.

C   Banks are reluctant to lend short-term, while government debt repayments have significantly increased the amount of long-term funds available.

D   The Government has increased short-term interest rates in order to combat rising inflation in the economy.

The following scenario relates to questions 21 to 25.

The finance director of Coral Co has been asked to provide values for the company's equity and loan notes. Coral Co is a listed company and has the following long-term finance:

	$m
Ordinary shares	7.8
7% convertible loan notes	8.0
	15.8

The ordinary shares of Coral Co have a nominal value of $0.25 per share and are currently trading on an ex dividend basis at $7.10 per share. An economic recovery has been forecast and so share prices are expected to grow by 8% per year for the foreseeable future.

The loan notes are redeemable after 6 years at their nominal value of $100 per loan note, or can be converted after 6 years into 10 ordinary shares of Coral Co per loan note. The loan notes are traded on the capital market.

The before-tax cost of debt of Coral Co is 5% and the company pays corporation tax of 20% per year.

21   What is the equity market value of Coral Co?

A $221.52m
B $55.38m
C $31.20m
D $229.52m

22   Assuming conversion, what is the market value of each loan note of Coral Co?

A $110.13
B $112.67
C $119.58
D $125.70

23   Which of the following statements about the equity market value of Coral Co is/are true?

(1)   The equity market value will change frequently due to capital market forces.

(2)   If the capital market is semi-strong form efficient, the equity market value will not be affected by the release to the public of insider information.

(3)   Over time, the equity market value of Coral Co will follow a random walk.

A   1 only
B   1 and 3 only
C   2 and 3 only
D   1, 2 and 3

24   **Which of the following assumptions is/are made by the dividend growth model?**

(1)   Investors make rational decisions.
(2)   Dividends show either constant growth or zero growth.
(3)   The dividend growth rate is less than the cost of equity.

A   2 only
B   1 and 3 only
C   2 and 3 only
D   1, 2 and 3

25   **Why might valuations of the equity and loan notes of Coral Co be necessary?**

(1)   The company is planning to go to the market for additional finance.
(2)   The securities need to be valued for corporate taxation purposes.
(3)   The company has received a takeover bid from a rival company.

A   1 and 2 only
B   1 and 3 only
C   3 only
D   1, 2 and 3

The following scenario relates to questions 26 to 30.

Link Co has been prevented by the competition authorities from buying a competitor, Twist Co, on the basis that this prevents a monopoly position arising. Link Co has therefore decided to expand existing business operations instead and as a result the finance director has prepared the following evaluation of a proposed investment project for the company:

	$m
Present value of sales revenue	6,657
Present value of variable costs	2,777
Present value of contribution	3,880
Present value of fixed costs	1,569
Present value of operating cash flow	2,311
Initial capital investment	1,800
Net present value	511

The project life is expected to be four years and the finance director has used a discount rate of 10% in the evaluation.

The investment project has no scrap value.

The finance director is considering financing the investment project by a new issue of debt.

26   **What is the change in sales volume which will make the NPV zero?**

A   7.7%
B   13.2%
C   18.4%
D   22.1%

27   **Which of the following statements relating to sensitivity analysis is/are correct?**

(1)   Although critical factors may be identified, the management of Link Co may have no control over them.

(2)   A weakness of sensitivity analysis is that it ignores interdependency between project variables.

(3)   Sensitivity analysis can be used by Link Co to assess the risk of an investment project.

A   1 and 2 only
B   1 only
C   2 and 3 only
D   1, 2 and 3

28   **Using the average investment method and assuming operating cash flows of $729,000 per year, what is the return on capital employed of the investment project?**

A   16%
B   28%
C   31%
D   64%

29   **Which of the following statements relating to debt finance is correct?**

A   Link Co can issue long-term debt in the euro currency markets.

B   The interest rate which Link Co pays on its new issue of debt will depend on its weighted average cost of capital.

C   A new issue of loan notes by Link Co will take place in the primary market.

D   Link Co will not be able to issue new debt without offering non-current assets as security.

30   **Which of the following statements relating to competition policy is/are correct?**

(1)   Scale economies are an advantage of monopoly and oligopoly
(2)   Social costs or externalities are an example of economic inefficiency arising from market failure
(3)   Monopoly is discouraged because it can lead to inefficiency and excessive profits

A   1 and 2 only
B   3 only
C   2 and 3 only
D   1, 2 and 3

(Total = 30 marks)

Section C – BOTH questions are compulsory and MUST be attempted

31 Gadner Co wishes to calculate its weighted average cost of capital. The company has the following sources of finance:

	$'000
Ordinary shares	8,000
10% preference shares	2,000
8% loan notes	6,000
Bank loan	2,000
	18,000

The ordinary shares have a nominal value of $0.20 per share and are currently trading at $6.35 per share. The equity beta of Gadner Co is 1.25.

The preference shares are irredeemable and have a nominal value of $0.50. They are currently trading at $0.55 per share.

The 8% loan notes have a nominal value of $100 per loan note and a market value of $108.29 per loan note. They are redeemable in six years' time at a 5% premium to nominal value.

The bank loan charges fixed interest of 7% per year.

The yield on short-dated UK treasury bills is 4% and the equity risk premium is 5.6% per year. Gadner Co pays corporation tax of 20%.

Required

(a) Calculate the market value weighted average cost of capital of Gadner Co. **(11 marks)**

(b) Explain the meaning of the terms business risk and financial risk. **(4 marks)**

(c) Discuss the key features of a rights issue as a way of raising equity finance. **(5 marks)**

(Total = 20 marks)

32   Dysxa Co is looking to expand the capacity of an existing factory in its Alpha Division by 850,000 units per year in order to meet increased demand for one of its products. The expansion will cost $3.2 million.

The selling price of the product is $3.10 per unit and variable costs of production are $1.10 per unit, both in current price terms. Selling price inflation of 3% per year and variable cost inflation of 6% per year are expected. Nominal fixed costs of production have been forecast as follows:

Year	1	2	3	4
Fixed costs ($)	110,000	205,000	330,000	330,000

Dysxa Co has a nominal after-tax weighted average cost of capital of 10% and pays corporation tax of 20% per year one year in arrears. The company can claim 25% reducing balance tax-allowable depreciation on the full cost of the expansion, which you should assume is paid at the start of the first year of operation.

Dysxa Co evaluates all investment projects as though they have a project life of four years and assumes zero scrap value at the end of four years.

Required

(a)   Calculate the net present value of the investment project and comment on its financial acceptability.

(8 marks)

(b)   Dysxa Co has limited the capital investment funds in its Delta Division to $7m. The division has identified five possible investment projects, as follows:

Project	Initial investment	Net present value
A	$3,000,000	$6,000,000
B	$2,000,000	$3,200,000
C	$1,000,000	$1,700,000
D	$1,000,000	$2,100,000
E	$2,000,000	$3,600,000

These projects are divisible and cannot be deferred or repeated. Projects C and E are mutually exclusive.

Required

Determine the net present value of the optimum investment schedule for Delta Division.   (3 marks)

(c)   Discuss the reasons why hard and soft capital rationing occur.   (5 marks)

(d)   Discuss **TWO** ways in which the risk of an investment project can be assessed.   (4 marks)

(Total = 20 marks)

Answers

DO NOT TURN THIS PAGE UNTIL YOU HAVE
COMPLETED THE MOCK EXAM

Answers

Section A

1   **D**   Obsolete inventory is minimised under just-in-time inventory management.

> Inventory should not be held in a JIT environment, and this will be made possible by frequent deliveries from suppliers. Some inspection (quality costs) will still occur.

2   **C**   Financial intermediaries transform maturity and risk.

> Maturity is transformed by allowing short-term deposits to be lent out for the long term. Risk is transformed because any losses suffered through default by borrowers or capital losses are effectively pooled and borne as costs by the intermediary allowing money to be deposited at financial institutions without incurring substantial risk.

3   **A**   Current share price = $0.5 \times 20 = \$10$ per share
Rights issue price = $10 \times 90/100 = \$9$ per share
Number of shares to be issued = $(50m/10)/4 = 1.25m$ shares
TERP = $(10 \times 5 + 9 \times 1.25)/6.25 = \$9.80$ per share

4   **C**   It is correct that the price/earnings ratio is the reciprocal of the earnings yield (ie P/E = 1 divided by E/P).

> The other statements are incorrect.

> Earnings yield and dividend growth will often give different outcomes eg if a company pays zero dividends.

> Market capitalisation is the current market value of a company's shares, a company may be worth more than this in an acquisition if synergies could result from the acquisition.

> The price/earnings ratio should be **decreased** if the company being valued is riskier than the valuing company.

5   **C**   The difference between the finance required to operate an SME and the amount obtained is the funding gap.

6   **A**   Commercial paper will be issued at a discount and then repaid at nominal value on the settlement date. It is short term and traded on the money market. Not interest payments are made.

> *Notes on incorrect answers:*

> Interest rate futures are not a type of finance.

> Loan notes are a source of long-term finance and are therefore not suitable here.

> Treasury bills are a source of finance for governments.

7   **D**   It is correct that research has shown that, over time, share prices appear to follow a random walk.

> *Notes on incorrect answers:*

> The **risk** from investing in larger companies has been shown to be **lower** than the average for all companies. The relationship between risk and return suggests that this will translate into lower returns.

> **Zero** form efficiency arises when investors tend not to make rational investment decisions.

> **Operational** efficiency means that transaction costs are kept to a minimum.

8   **B**   Forward rate = $1.60 \times (1.015/1.005) = 1.62$ pesos per $
(Strictly $1.60 \times (1.03/1.01)^{0.5}$ but same number to 2 decimal places)

9   **A**   TSR = $100 \times (3.00 - 2.50 + 0.15)/2.50 = 26\%$

10   **B**   Dividend to be paid = $0.80 \times 0.55 = \$0.44$ per share
Retention ratio = $100\% - 55\% = 45\%$
Dividend growth rate = $45\% \times 20\% = 9\%$ per year
Ke = $(0.44 \times 1.09)/(4.60 - 0.44) + 0.09 = 20.5\%$

11 **A**   Reduced receivables = 8/365 × 20,500 = $449,300
             Net inventory/payables effect = (10 – 5)/365 × 12,800 = $175,300
             Total net working capital effect = 449.3 + 175.3 = $624,600

12 **B**   It is true that a government may intervene to weaken its country's exchange rate in order to eliminate a balance of payments deficit because the effect of this is to reduce the price of exports and increase the cost of imports.

             Notes on incorrect answers:

             A prospective merger would normally need to result in a company having a market share greater than 25% before regulatory authorities would be concerned about monopoly power. Strictly a monopolist has 100% market share.

             A relatively high rate of domestic inflation will lead to a **weakening** currency according to purchasing power parity theory.

             Government fiscal policy involves the management of tax and spending policies, not interest rates.

13 **B**   It is correct that the cost of an interest rate floor is higher than the cost of an interest rate collar. This is because a floor involves buying a call option, whereas a collar involves selling a put option as well (which offsets the cost of buying a call).

             Notes on incorrect answers:

             An interest rate cap (not floor) can be used to hedge an expected increase in interest rates.
             The premium on an interest rate option is payable when it is purchased not when it is exercised.
             The standardised nature of interest rate futures means that over- and under-hedging occurs because a company is often unable to hedge exactly the amount that it requires.

14 **D**   *Notes on incorrect answers:*

             Value for money is usually taken to mean economy, efficiency and effectiveness (not engagement).
             Ex (not cum) dividend means the buyer of the share is not entitled to receive the dividend shortly to be paid.

             The dividend payout ratio compares the dividend per share with the earnings per share.

15 **D**   If the discount is accepted, the company must pay $2,462.50 at the end of one month.

             Alternatively, the company can effectively borrow the $2,462.50 for an additional 2 months at a cost of $37.50.

             The 2-month rate of interest is therefore 37.50/2,462.5 × 100 = 1.5228%

             The annual equivalent rate (AER) = $(1 + 0.015228)^6 - 1 = 0.0949$ or 9.49%

Section B

16 **B** Dollar value = (12m × 1.005)/(1.04 × 57.52) = $201,602

17 **D** All three hedges will allow Park Co to hedge its foreign currency risk.

18 **B** Only the dinar-denominated overdraft will be effective, by matching assets and liabilities. The long-term euro-denominated loan will increase payments to be made in euros and hence increase foreign currency risk.

19 **D** Purchasing power parity predicts the future spot rate, not the forward exchange rate. The international Fisher effect does not predict 'real' interest rates.

20 **A** If default risk increases with duration, compensation for default risk increases with time and hence the yield curve will slope upwards.

Notes on incorrect answers:

Liquidity preference theory implies that **long-term** interest rates contain a premium over **short-term** interest rates to compensate for lost liquidity.

If government debt repayments have significantly increased the amount of long-term funds available this will decrease the cost of borrowing in the long-term.

If the Government has increased short-term interest rates in order to combat rising inflation in the economy this may lead to a downward sloping yield curve.

21 **A** Equity market value = 7.10 × (7.8m/0.25) = $221.52m

22 **C** Conversion value = 7.10 × 1.08^6 × 10 = $112.67 per loan note
Market value = (7 × 5.076) + (112.67 × 0.746) = 35.53 + 84.05 = $119.58

23 **B** If the capital market is semi-strong form efficient, newly-released insider information will quickly and accurately be reflected in share prices. The other statements are true.

24 **D** All three are assumptions made by the dividend growth model

25 **B** A valuation for corporate taxation purposes is not necessary.

26 **B** 100 × 511/3,880 = 13.2%

27 **A** Sensitivity Analysis assesses the **uncertainty** of a project, not the risk (probability analysis does this).

28 **C** The total operating cash flow = 4 × (2,311/3.170) = $2,916,088
The average annual accounting profit = (2,916,088 − 1,800,000)/4 = $279,022
Average investment = 1,800,000/2 = $900,000
ROCE = 100 × 279,022/900,000 = 31%

29 **C** A new issue of loan notes takes place in the primary market.

Notes on incorrect answers:

Link Co can issue **short-term** debt in the euro currency markets.

The interest rate which Link Co pays on its new issue of debt will depend factors such as risk and the duration of the debt, not on its weighted average cost of capital.

Link Co will be able to issue new debt using debt covenants or floating charges on its asset base as a whole.

30 **D** All three statements are correct

Section C

Question 31

> **Text references.** Sources of finance are covered in Chapter 12 and cost of capital is covered in Chapter 14.
>
> **Top tips.** Neat workings will be important to avoid careless errors in part (a).
>
> Read the discussion parts of the question carefully to make sure that you are answering the question that has been set. For example in part (c) you are asked to discuss the features of a rights issue, not the motives for organising a rights issue.
>
> **Easy marks.** Each part of the calculations in part (a) will gain marks so, if you get stuck, make an assumption and move on.

Marking scheme

			Marks
(a)	Cost of equity	2	
	Cost of preference shares	1	
	After-tax loan note interest cost	1	
	Setting up Kd calculation	1	
	After-tax Kd of loan notes	1	
	Cost of debt of bank loan	1	
	Market value of equity	0.5	
	Market value of preference shares	0.5	
	Market value of loan notes	0.5	
	Total market value of sources of finance	0.5	
	Calculation of WACC	2	
			11
(b)	Nature of business risk	2	
	Nature of financial risk	2	
			4
(c)	One mark per relevant point	Maximum	5
			20

(a) Cost of equity

Using the CAPM, Ke = 4 + (1.25 × 5.6) = 11.0%

Cost of capital of 10% irredeemable preference shares

Preference share dividend = 0.1 × 0.5 = $0.05 per share
Cost of preference shares = 100 × 0.05/0.55 = 9.1%

Cost of debt of loan notes

After-tax interest cost = 8 × 0.8 = $6.40 per $100 loan note

Year	Cash flow		5% discount	PV	6% discount	PV
		$		$		$
0	Market value	(108.29)	1.000	(108.29)	1.000	(108.29)
1–6	Interest	6.40	5.076	32.49	4.917	31.47
6	Redemption	105.00	0.746	78.33	0.705	74.03
				2.53		(2.79)

After-tax Kd = IRR = 5 + (1 × 2.53)/(2.53 + 2.79) = 5 + 0.5 = 5.5%

Cost of debt of bank loan

The after-tax interest cost can be used as Kd, ie $7 \times 0.8 = 5.6\%$.
Alternatively, the after-tax cost of debt of the loan notes can be used as a substitute.

Appropriate values of the sources of finance

	$'000
Market value of equity = $6.35 × (8m/0.2) =	254,000
Market value of preference shares = 0.55 × (2m/0.5) =	2,200
Market value of loan notes = $108.29 × (6m/100) =	6,497
Book value of debt	2,000
Total market value of sources of finance	264,697

Calculation of WACC

WACC = [(11 × 254,000) + (9.1 × 2,200) + (5.5 × 6,497) + (5.6 × 2,000)]/264,697 = 10.8%

(b)   Business risk in financial management relates to the variability of shareholder returns which arises from business operations. It can be measured from a statement of profit or loss perspective by operational gearing, which considers the relative importance of fixed and variable operating costs in relation to operating profit (PBIT). One definition of operational gearing is contribution/profit before interest and tax or PBIT. Business risk is not influenced by the way in which a company is financed; that is, it is not influenced by the capital structure of a company.

Financial risk relates to the variability of shareholder returns which arises from the way in which a company finances itself; that is, from its capital structure. It can be measured from a balance sheet perspective by gearing (financial gearing, debt/equity ratio, debt ratio) and from a statement of profit or loss perspective by interest cover and income gearing.

The combination of business risk and financial risk is referred to as total risk.

(c)   **Pre-emptive right of shareholders**

In order to preserve the balance of ownership and control in a company, existing shareholders have a right to be offered new shares before they are offered to other buyers. This is known as the pre-emptive right and an offer of new shares to existing shareholders is consequently referred to as a rights issue.

Rights issue price and cum rights price

The price at which the new shares are offered to existing shareholders is called the rights issue price. The share price following the announcement of the rights issue is called the cum rights price and the rights issue price is at a discount to this price.

Theoretical ex-rights price

The share price after the rights issue has taken place is called the theoretical ex-rights price. This is a weighted average of the cum rights price and the rights issue price. The weighting arises from what is called the form of the rights issue, eg a 1 for 5 issue would allow an existing shareholder to buy 1 new share for every 5 shares already held.

Neutral effect on shareholder wealth

If issue costs and the use or application of the rights issue funds is ignored then, theoretically, rights issues have a neutral effect on shareholder wealth. The rights issue transfers cash from existing shareholders to the company in exchange for shares, so the shareholder will see cash wealth replaced by ordinary share wealth. The theoretical ex-rights price, rather than the cum rights price, is therefore a benchmark for assessing the effect on shareholder wealth of the use or application to which the rights issue funds are put.

Balance of ownership and control

Providing existing shareholders buy the shares to which they are entitled, there is no change in the balance of ownership and control in a company. Relative voting rights are therefore preserved.

Underwriting

In order to ensure that a company receives the funds it needs, rights issues are underwritten as a form of insurance. Shares which are not taken up by existing shareholders will be taken up, for a fee, by the underwriters.

Question 32

Marking scheme

		Marks
(a)	Inflated sales revenue	1
	Inflated variable cost	1
	Tax liabilities	1
	Tax-allowable depreciation benefits Years 1–3	1
	Tax-allowable depreciation benefit Year 4	1
	Timing of tax liabilities and depreciation benefits	1
	Calculation of present values	1
	Comment on financial acceptability	1
		8
(b)	Calculating profitability indexes	1
	Formulating optimum investment schedule	1
	NPV of optimum investment schedule	1
		3
(c)	Soft capital rationing	2
	Hard capital rationing	2
	Additional detail	1
		5
(d)	Risk assessment method 1	2
	Risk assessment method 2	2
		4
		20

(a) NPV calculation

Year	1	2	3	4	5
	$'000	$'000	$'000	$'000	$'000
Sales revenue	2,712	2,797	2,882	2,967	
Variable costs	(995)	(1,054)	(1,114)	(1,182)	
Contribution	1,717	1,743	1,768	1,785	
Fixed costs	(110)	(205)	(330)	(330)	
Taxable cash flow	1,607	1,538	1,438	1,455	
Taxation at 20%		(321)	(308)	(288)	(291)
TAD tax benefits		160	120	90	270
After-tax cash flow	1,607	1,377	1,250	1,257	(21)
Discount at 10%	0.909	0.826	0.751	0.683	0.621
Present values	1,461	1,137	939	859	(13)

	$'000
PV of future cash flows	4,383
Initial investment	3,200
NPV	1,183

Comment

The NPV is positive and so the investment project is financially acceptable.

Workings

1   *Sales revenue*

Year	1	2	3	4
Selling price ($/unit)	3.1	3.1	3.1	3.1
Inflated at 3% per year	3.19	3.29	3.39	3.49
Sales volume ('000 units/year)	850	850	850	850
Sales revenue ($'000/year)	2,712	2,797	2,882	2,967

2   *Variable cost*

Year	1	2	3	4
Variable cost ($/unit)	1.1	1.1	1.1	1.1
Inflated at 6% per year	1.17	1.24	1.31	1.39
Sales volume ('000 units/year)	850	850	850	850
Variable cost ($'000/year)	995	1,054	1,114	1,182

Year	1	2	3	4
TAD ($'000)	800	600	450	1,350
Tax benefits ($'000)	160	120	90	270*

*(3,200 × 0.2) – 160 – 120 – 90 = $270,000

Alternative calculation of after-tax cash flow

Year	1	2	3	4	5
	$'000	$'000	$'000	$'000	$'000
Taxable cash flow	1,607	1,538	1,438	1,455	
TAD	(800)	(600)	(450)	(1,350)	
Taxable profit	807	938	988	105	
Taxation at 20%		(161)	(188)	(198)	(21)
After-tax profit	807	777	800	(93)	(21)
Add back TAD	800	600	450	1,350	
After-tax cash flow	1,607	1,377	1,250	1,257	(21)

(b)   **Analysis of profitability indexes**

Project	Initial investment	Net present value	Profitability index*	Rank
A	$3,000,000	$6,000,000	2.0	2nd
B	$2,000,000	$3,200,000	1.6	4th
C	$1,000,000	$1,700,000	1.7	Excluded
D	$1,000,000	$2,100,000	2.1	1st
E	$2,000,000	$3,600,000	1.8	3rd

*NPV divided by initial investment (note that it is also acceptable to calculate the profitability index as the PV of future cash flows/initial investment).

Optimum investment schedule

Project	Initial investment	Rank	Net present value	
D	$1,000,000	1st	$2,100,000	
A	$3,000,000	2nd	$6,000,000	
E	$2,000,000	3rd	$3,600,000	
B	$1,000,000	4th	$1,600,000	($3.2m × $1m/$2m)
	$7,000,000		$13,300,000	

The NPV of the optimum investment schedule for Delta Division is $13.3 million.

(c) Capital rationing can be divided into hard capital rationing, which is externally imposed, or soft capital rationing, which is internally imposed.

Soft capital rationing

Investment capital may be limited internally because a company does not want to take on a commitment to increased fixed interest payments; for example, if it expects future profitability to be poor. A company may wish to avoid diluting existing earnings per share or changing existing patterns of ownership and control by issuing new equity. A company may limit investment funds because it wishes to pursue controlled growth rather than rapid growth. Given the uncertainty associated with forecasting future cash flows, a company may limit investment funds in order to create an internal market where investment projects compete for finance, with only the best investment projects being granted approval.

Hard capital rationing

External reasons for capital rationing can be related to risk and to availability of finance. Providers of finance may see a company as too risky to invest in, perhaps because it is highly geared or because it has a poor record or poor prospects in terms of profitability or cash flow. Long-term finance for capital investment may have limited availability because of the poor economic state of the economy, or because there is a banking crisis.

(d) The risk of an investment project could be assessed by using probability analysis or by using the capital asset pricing model (CAPM).

Probability analysis

Project risk can be assessed or quantified by attaching probabilities to expected investment project outcomes. At an overall level, this could be as simple as attaching probabilities to two or more expected scenarios, for example, associated with different economic states. Key project variables might then take different values depending on the economic state.

At the level of individual project variables, probability distributions of values could be found through expert analysis, and the probability distributions and relationships between variables then built into a simulation model. This model could then be used to generate a probability distribution of expected project outcomes in terms of net present values. Project risk could then be measured by the standard deviation of the expected net present value.

CAPM

The systematic business risk of an investment project can be assessed by identifying a proxy company in a similar line of business. The equity beta of the proxy company can then be ungeared to give the asset beta of the company, which reflects systematic business risk alone as the effect of the systematic financial risk of the proxy company is removed by the ungearing process. The asset beta can then be regeared to reflect the systematic financial risk of the investing company, giving an equity beta which reflects the systematic risk of the investment project.

Mathematical tables

Formulae Sheet

Economic order quantity

$$= \sqrt{\frac{2C_0 D}{C_h}}$$

Miller–Orr Model

Return point = Lower limit + $(\frac{1}{3} \times \text{spread})$

$$\text{Spread} = 3 \left[\frac{\frac{3}{4} \times \text{transaction cost} \times \text{variance of cash flows}}{\text{interest rate}} \right]^{\frac{1}{3}}$$

The Capital Asset Pricing Model

$$E(r_i) = R_f + \beta_i \left(E(r_m) - R_f \right)$$

The asset beta formula

$$\beta_a = \left[\frac{V_e}{\left(V_e + V_d (1-T) \right)} \beta_e \right] + \left[\frac{V_d (1-T)}{\left(V_e + V_d (1-T) \right)} \beta_d \right]$$

The Growth Model

$$P_0 = \frac{D_0(1+g)}{(r_e - g)} \qquad r_e = \frac{D_0(1+g)}{P_0} + g$$

Gordon's growth approximation

$$g = br_e$$

The weighted average cost of capital

$$\text{WACC} = \left[\frac{V_e}{V_e + V_d} \right] k_e + \left[\frac{V_d}{V_e + V_d} \right] k_d (1-T)$$

The Fisher formula

$$(1+i) = (1+r)(1+h)$$

Purchasing power parity and interest rate parity

$$S_1 = S_0 \times \frac{(1+h_c)}{(1+h_b)} \qquad F_0 = S_0 \times \frac{(1+i_c)}{(1+i_b)}$$

Present Value Table

Present value of 1 i.e. $(1 + r)^{-n}$

Where   r = discount rate
           n = number of periods until payment

Discount rate (r)

Periods (n)	1%	2%	3%	4%	5%	6%	7%	8%	9%	10%	
1	0·990	0·980	0·971	0·962	0·952	0·943	0·935	0·926	0·917	0·909	1
2	0·980	0·961	0·943	0·925	0·907	0·890	0·873	0·857	0·842	0·826	2
3	0·971	0·942	0·915	0·889	0·864	0·840	0·816	0·794	0·772	0·751	3
4	0·961	0·924	0·888	0·855	0·823	0·792	0·763	0·735	0·708	0·683	4
5	0·951	0·906	0·863	0·822	0·784	0·747	0·713	0·681	0·650	0·621	5
6	0·942	0·888	0·837	0·790	0·746	0·705	0·666	0·630	0·596	0·564	6
7	0·933	0·871	0·813	0·760	0·711	0·665	0·623	0·583	0·547	0·513	7
8	0·923	0·853	0·789	0·731	0·677	0·627	0·582	0·540	0·502	0·467	8
9	0·914	0·837	0·766	0·703	0·645	0·592	0·544	0·500	0·460	0·424	9
10	0·905	0·820	0·744	0·676	0·614	0·558	0·508	0·463	0·422	0·386	10
11	0·896	0·804	0·722	0·650	0·585	0·527	0·475	0·429	0·388	0·350	11
12	0·887	0·788	0·701	0·625	0·557	0·497	0·444	0·397	0·356	0·319	12
13	0·879	0·773	0·681	0·601	0·530	0·469	0·415	0·368	0·326	0·290	13
14	0·870	0·758	0·661	0·577	0·505	0·442	0·388	0·340	0·299	0·263	14
15	0·861	0·743	0·642	0·555	0·481	0·417	0·362	0·315	0·275	0·239	15

(n)	11%	12%	13%	14%	15%	16%	17%	18%	19%	20%	
1	0·901	0·893	0·885	0·877	0·870	0·862	0·855	0·847	0·840	0·833	1
2	0·812	0·797	0·783	0·769	0·756	0·743	0·731	0·718	0·706	0·694	2
3	0·731	0·712	0·693	0·675	0·658	0·641	0·624	0·609	0·593	0·579	3
4	0·659	0·636	0·613	0·592	0·572	0·552	0·534	0·516	0·499	0·482	4
5	0·593	0·567	0·543	0·519	0·497	0·476	0·456	0·437	0·419	0·402	5
6	0·535	0·507	0·480	0·456	0·432	0·410	0·390	0·370	0·352	0·335	6
7	0·482	0·452	0·425	0·400	0·376	0·354	0·333	0·314	0·296	0·279	7
8	0·434	0·404	0·376	0·351	0·327	0·305	0·285	0·266	0·249	0·233	8
9	0·391	0·361	0·333	0·308	0·284	0·263	0·243	0·225	0·209	0·194	9
10	0·352	0·322	0·295	0·270	0·247	0·227	0·208	0·191	0·176	0·162	10
11	0·317	0·287	0·261	0·237	0·215	0·195	0·178	0·162	0·148	0·135	11
12	0·286	0·257	0·231	0·208	0·187	0·168	0·152	0·137	0·124	0·112	12
13	0·258	0·229	0·204	0·182	0·163	0·145	0·130	0·116	0·104	0·093	13
14	0·232	0·205	0·181	0·160	0·141	0·125	0·111	0·099	0·088	0·078	14
15	0·209	0·183	0·160	0·140	0·123	0·108	0·095	0·084	0·074	0·065	15

Annuity Table

Present value of an annuity of 1 i.e. $\dfrac{1-(1+r)^{-n}}{r}$

Where   r = discount rate
               n = number of periods

Discount rate (r)

Periods (n)	1%	2%	3%	4%	5%	6%	7%	8%	9%	10%	
1	0·990	0·980	0·971	0·962	0·952	0·943	0·935	0·926	0·917	0·909	1
2	1·970	1·942	1·913	1·886	1·859	1·833	1·808	1·783	1·759	1·736	2
3	2·941	2·884	2·829	2·775	2·723	2·673	2·624	2·577	2·531	2·487	3
4	3·902	3·808	3·717	3·630	3·546	3·465	3·387	3·312	3·240	3·170	4
5	4·853	4·713	4·580	4·452	4·329	4·212	4·100	3·993	3·890	3·791	5
6	5·795	5·601	5·417	5·242	5·076	4·917	4·767	4·623	4·486	4·355	6
7	6·728	6·472	6·230	6·002	5·786	5·582	5·389	5·206	5·033	4·868	7
8	7·652	7·325	7·020	6·733	6·463	6·210	5·971	5·747	5·535	5·335	8
9	8·566	8·162	7·786	7·435	7·108	6·802	6·515	6·247	5·995	5·759	9
10	9·471	8·983	8·530	8·111	7·722	7·360	7·024	6·710	6·418	6·145	10
11	10·37	9·787	9·253	8·760	8·306	7·887	7·499	7·139	6·805	6·495	11
12	11·26	10·58	9·954	9·385	8·863	8·384	7·943	7·536	7·161	6·814	12
13	12·13	11·35	10·63	9·986	9·394	8·853	8·358	7·904	7·487	7·103	13
14	13·00	12·11	11·30	10·56	9·899	9·295	8·745	8·244	7·786	7·367	14
15	13·87	12·85	11·94	11·12	10·38	9·712	9·108	8·559	8·061	7·606	15

(n)	11%	12%	13%	14%	15%	16%	17%	18%	19%	20%	
1	0·901	0·893	0·885	0·877	0·870	0·862	0·855	0·847	0·840	0·833	1
2	1·713	1·690	1·668	1·647	1·626	1·605	1·585	1·566	1·547	1·528	2
3	2·444	2·402	2·361	2·322	2·283	2·246	2·210	2·174	2·140	2·106	3
4	3·102	3·037	2·974	2·914	2·855	2·798	2·743	2·690	2·639	2·589	4
5	3·696	3·605	3·517	3·433	3·352	3·274	3·199	3·127	3·058	2·991	5
6	4·231	4·111	3·998	3·889	3·784	3·685	3·589	3·498	3·410	3·326	6
7	4·712	4·564	4·423	4·288	4·160	4·039	3·922	3·812	3·706	3·605	7
8	5·146	4·968	4·799	4·639	4·487	4·344	4·207	4·078	3·954	3·837	8
9	5·537	5·328	5·132	4·946	4·772	4·607	4·451	4·303	4·163	4·031	9
10	5·889	5·650	5·426	5·216	5·019	4·833	4·659	4·494	4·339	4·192	10
11	6·207	5·938	5·687	5·453	5·234	5·029	4·836	4·656	4·486	4·327	11
12	6·492	6·194	5·918	5·660	5·421	5·197	4·988	4·793	4·611	4·439	12
13	6·750	6·424	6·122	5·842	5·583	5·342	5·118	4·910	4·715	4·533	13
14	6·982	6·628	6·302	6·002	5·724	5·468	5·229	5·008	4·802	4·611	14
15	7·191	6·811	6·462	6·142	5·847	5·575	5·324	5·092	4·876	4·675	15

Review Form – Financial Management (FM) (02/18)

Name: _____ **Address:** _____

_____

_____

How have you used this Kit?
(Tick one box only)

☐ On its own (book only)

☐ On a BPP in-centre course_____

☐ On a BPP online course

☐ On a course with another college

☐ Other _____

Why did you decide to purchase this Kit?
(Tick one box only)

☐ Have used the complimentary Study Text

☐ Have used other BPP products in the past

☐ Recommendation by friend/colleague

☐ Recommendation by a lecturer at college

☐ Saw advertising

☐ Other _____

During the past six months do you recall seeing/receiving any of the following?
(Tick as many boxes as are relevant)

☐ Our advertisement in *Student Accountant*

☐ Our advertisement in *Pass*

☐ Our advertisement in *PQ*

☐ Our brochure with a letter through the post

☐ Our website www.bpp.com

Which (if any) aspects of our advertising do you find useful?
(Tick as many boxes as are relevant)

☐ Prices and publication dates of new editions

☐ Information on product content

☐ Facility to order books

☐ None of the above

Which BPP products have you used?

Study Text	☐	*Passcards*	☐	*Other*	☐
Practice & Revision Kit	☑	*i-Pass*	☐		

Your ratings, comments and suggestions would be appreciated on the following areas.

	Very useful	Useful	Not useful
Passing FM			
Questions			
Top Tips etc in answers			
Content and structure of answers			
Mock exam answers			

Overall opinion of this Practice & Revision Kit	Excellent ☐	Good ☐	Adequate ☐	Poor ☐

Do you intend to continue using BPP products?   Yes ☐   No ☐

The BPP author of this edition can be emailed at: accaqueries@bpp.com

Review Form (continued)

TELL US WHAT YOU THINK

Please note any further comments and suggestions/errors below.